What I
Remember,
What I Know

Published by Inhabit Media Inc.
www.inhabitmedia.com

Inhabit Media Inc. (Iqaluit) P.O. Box 11125, Iqaluit, Nunavut, X0A 1H0
(Toronto) 191 Eglinton Avenue East, Suite 310, Toronto, Ontario, M4P 1K1

Editors: Neil Christopher and Grace Shaw
Art Director: Danny Christopher

We acknowledge the support of the Canada Council for the Arts for our publishing program.

This project was made possible in part by the government of Canada.

Printed in Canada

Library and Archives Canada Cataloguing in Publication

Title: What I remember, what I know / Larry Audlaluk.
Names: Audlaluk, Larry, 1950– author.
Identifiers: Canadiana 20200244558 | ISBN 9781772272376 (softcover)
Subjects: LCSH: Audlaluk, Larry, 1950– | LCSH: Forced migration—Québec (Province)—Nunavik—History.
 | LCSH: Inuit—Biography. | LCSH: Inuit—Social life and customs. | LCSH: Canada, Northern—Social
    conditions. | CSH: Native peoples—Canada—Government relations. | LCGFT: Autobiographies.
Classification: LCC E99.E7 A93 2020 | DDC 971.9004/971200904—dc23

Canada Council
for the Arts

Conseil des Arts
du Canada

What I Remember, What I Know

The Life of a High Arctic Exile

Larry Audlaluk

Inhabit Media Inc.

Nunavut

Resolute Bay •

Northwest
Territories

Taloyoak •

Cambridge Bay •

Kugaarul

Nunavut

• Kugluktuk

Baker Lake •

Rankin
Inlet

Arviat •

Dundas Harbour

Baffin
Bay

Pond Inlet

Clyde River

Baffin
Island

Iglulik

Sanirajak

Qikiqtarjuak

Pangnirtung

Northwestern
Passages

Naujaat

Iqaluit

Kinngait

Coral Harbour

Kimmirut

Nunavik

Resolution Island

Killiniq

Salluit

Kangiqsujuaq

Hudson Strait

Kangirsuk

Ungava Bay

Puvirnituq

Tasiujaq

Nauligarvik*

Kuujjuaq

Uugaqsiuvik*

Inujjuak

Deception Bay

Hudson Bay

Quebec

Sanikiluaq

Belcher Islands

Great Whale River

Kuujjuarapik

*approximate location

Baffin Island

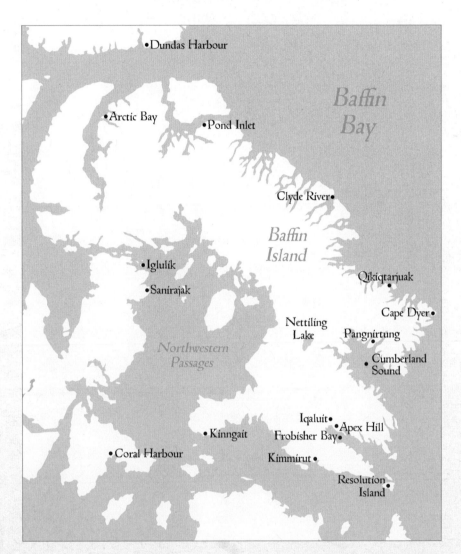

- •Dundas Harbour
- •Arctic Bay
- •Pond Inlet

Baffin
Bay

Clyde River•

Baffin
Island

- •Iglulik
- •Sanirajak

Qikiqtarjuak
•

Cape Dyer•

Nettiling
Lake

Pangnirtung
•

Northwestern
Passages

Cumberland
Sound
•

Iqaluit•
•Apex Hill
Frobisher Bay•

- •Kinngait

Kimmirut•

- •Coral Harbour

Resolution
Island•

Ellesmere and Devon Islands

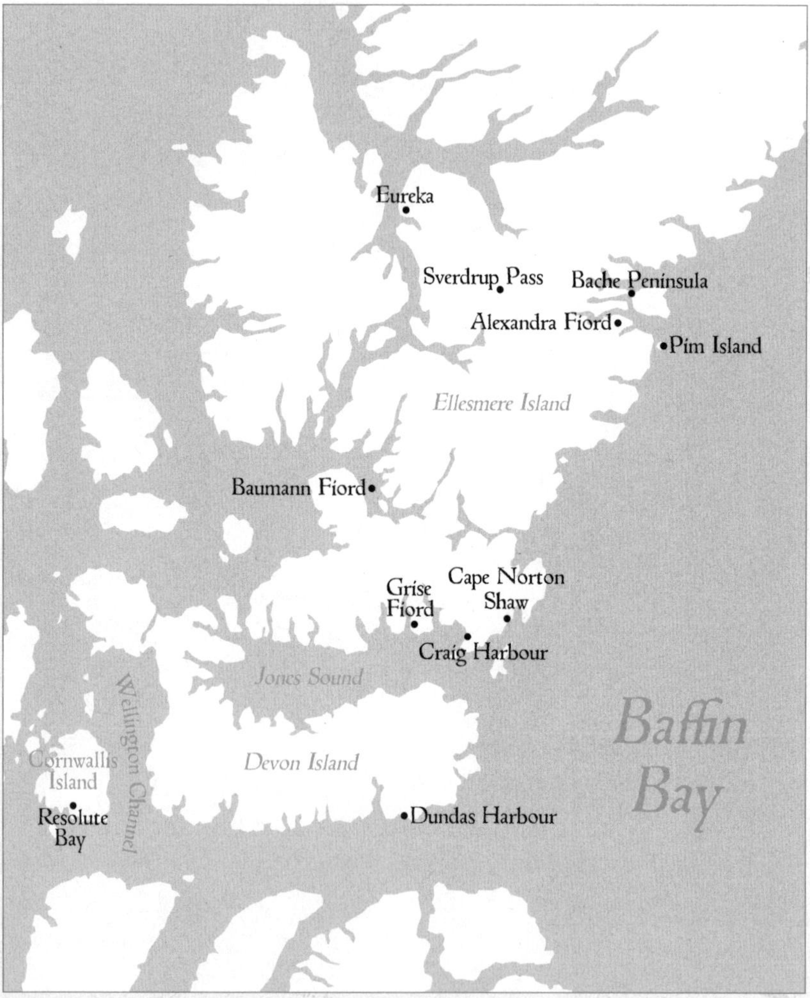

Eureka

Sverdrup Pass   Bache Peninsula

Alexandra Fiord

•Pim Island

Ellesmere Island

Baumann Fiord•

Cape Norton
Shaw

Grise
Fiord

Craig Harbour

Jones Sound

*Baffin
Bay*

*Cornwallis
Island*

Devon Island

Resolute
Bay

•Dundas Harbour

Wellington Channel

Baumann
Fiord

Makinson
Inlet

Pirlirarvirjuaq
Lake

Ellesmere Island

Lindstrom
Peninsula

Starnes
Fiord

Fram
Fiord

Harbour
Fiord

Grise
Fiord

South Cape
Fiord

Lee
Point

Anstead
Point

Goose Fiord

Cape Storm

Landslip
Island

Skerries

Brume
Point

Naqsakuluk

Jakeman
Glacier

Craig
Harbour

Viks
Fiord

Jones Sound

Cape Hardy

Coburg
Island

Cape Svarten

Truelove
Inlet

Cape Sparbo

Nookap
Island

Cape Newman
Smith

Devon Island

For my mother,
who could not forget the broken promises.
For my uncle Philipoosie,
who taught me how to survive in a harsh, unforgiving world.
For my brothers Elijah and Samwillie and my sister Anna,
who gave me a sense of belonging and protection when it was
scary during the early years.
For my sister Minnie and cousin Elisapee,
who kept me company when I had nobody else.
And for my wife and children,
who have supported me throughout this healing process.

— *Larry Audlaluk*

Publisher's Note

In 1953, seven Inuit families from Inujjuak in Nunavik, or Northern Quebec, were relocated by the Canadian government to Ellesmere Island. Larry Audaluk was almost three years old at the time. The experience had an irreversible impact on his young life, but neither he nor his family knew much about what had motivated their displacement. Over the course of his adult life, Larry began to discover the reasons behind their exile to the High Arctic. Through dedicated research, interviews, and lobbying efforts, Larry has acquired knowledge that has given clarity to not only his own personal memories but to the collective memory of the *Inujjuarmiut*, the people of Inujjuak. Much of this knowledge was gleaned by combing through old RCMP and Eastern Arctic Patrol reports, memos, telegrams, minutes of meetings held by the Special Committee on Eskimo Affairs, and delving into related materials by other researchers.

Larry has included excerpts and quotations from many of these documents, often to highlight the discrepancies between the "official" version of the story and what the Inujjuarmiut really lived through. As this is a memoir, not a history book, we have opted to forego the use of footnotes or endnotes to prevent disrupting the flow of Larry's narrative. There is, however, a comprehensive bibliography included in the back that lists all sources that the text pulls from, whether in the form of direct quotations or reference materials.

It should also be noted that the knowledge aspect of this memoir includes traditional Inuit knowledge that has been passed down over the course of generations, as well as family history.

Introduction

Many stories have been written about how Inuit families were relocated to the High Arctic. Two explanations are often given when the story is told. The one written most about is economic opportunity. The other is sovereignty. The writers are always careful to use the word "claims" when they're talking about sovereignty, as if to suggest what we say is not true. The story is long, complicated, and documented by various groups, besides the official records. The history behind our relocation dates back over one hundred years. It is too complex to cover in its entirety, but there are some things you should know.

* * *

Inughuit from the Thule region of Greenland hunted on Ellesmere Island and the rest of the Queen Elizabeth Islands for many years without issue. When concern arose that the muskox was facing extinction, the Canadian government requested that the Danish government prevent Inughuit from hunting them on Ellesmere Island. In 1919, the Danish government deferred to Knud Rasmussen, a Danish–Greenlandic anthropologist and explorer who had established a trading post at Thule in 1910. Rasmussen's reply included this: "As everyone knows, the land of the Polar Eskimo falls under what is called 'No Man's Land', there is, therefore, no authority in this country except that which I myself am able to exert through the Trading Station."

Prior to this, our own government hadn't been interested in what was going on north of seventy-five degrees latitude. It was unclear whether Indigenous hunting rights were affected by Canada's sovereignty claims, but in 1919, following Rasmussen's response, the Canadian government suddenly took notice and started to assert sovereignty in the area.

Whether on purpose or not, Rasmussen's letter had started wheels in motion. In 1922, RCMP detachments were opened at Pond Inlet and Craig Harbour. Further posts were established between 1923 and 1927 at Pangnirtung, Dundas Harbour, Bache Peninsula, and Lake Harbour (now known as Kimmirut). With the buildings up, the Canadian government was able to, for the very first time in the history of the High Arctic, truly lay claim to Ellesmere Island and the surrounding area.

This didn't affect Inuit in Inujjuak at first, but changes were coming. In 1946, it was learned that the United States was planning the construction of weather stations in the High Arctic, with the intention of using the information collected in defence against a possible Soviet attack. The detachment at Craig Harbour, which had closed in the mid-1930s, was reopened in 1951 after the start of the Cold War. However, Inughuit hunters were still active in the area, and with American presence expected to increase, there was concern that further action was needed. That further action, as it turned out, did affect us. A 1952 Eastern Arctic Patrol report suggested that "The occupation of the island by Canadian Eskimos will remove any excuse Greenlanders may presently have for crossing over and hunting there." This idea, supported by RCMP Inspector Henry Larsen, would come to be a reality.

Inuk Special Constable Lazarus Kayak was transferred to Craig Harbour at the reopening of the post. His wife, Lydia, said that she and her husband were told Inuit from Northern Quebec were being moved to Craig Harbour, which was part of the reason they were there. But it wasn't until October 1952, less than a year before we were relocated, that the first meeting of the Special Committee on Eskimo Affairs was held in Ottawa. This meeting included members of the Department of Resources and Development, the Department of National Health and Welfare, the RCMP, the Hudson's Bay Company, and even clergy members, including Reverend Marsh, Bishop of the Arctic. According to the minutes of this meeting, "consideration was given to the possibility of assisting natives to move from over-populated areas to places where they could more readily obtain a living," including Craig Harbour on Ellesmere Island.

The 1952 Eastern Arctic Patrol report claimed that game in the Craig Harbour area was "plentiful." Inujjuak, on the other hand, had been identified as one of the areas with the highest government relief payments issued annually and had been deemed "overpopulated." Officials were concerned with Inuit dependency on "handouts" in Inujjuak, and a 1952 RCMP report states that "The subsidization is not excessive when the benefits are considered but the dependency of the native on government handouts is an undesirable feature which should be considered." Seeking to "rehabilitate" Inuit, moving them from Inujjuak to a less populated area, meant that, as one constable put it, "the Eskimo could follow the native way of life and become less dependent on the white man."

I should note that those of us who were relocated were not made aware of any of this information. In fact, the architects of the plan were very careful to keep everything vague and difficult to figure out. We did not even know anything about it until two months before the move. The reasons we were given for the relocation—that we were to be given a better opportunity, that it would be a "land of plenty"—were based on nothing but speculation. The Department of Resources and Development even admitted that no wildlife resource studies had been conducted before we were moved. The Department has been criticized for the poor planning of the relocation, but I believe the execution of the move went exactly according to plan. They did not intend for us to be given any help whatsoever.

The Director of Northern Administration described the relocation as "A pioneer experiment to determine if Eskimos can be induced to live on the northern islands." A member of the Department of Resources and Development stated that the Canadian government was "anxious to have Canadians occupying as much of the north as possible and it appeared that in many cases the Eskimo were the only people capable of doing this." I have come to conclude that the relocation was a Canadian sovereignty mission that used us as human flagpoles.

The story of our relocation has been told from so many angles, from social perspectives and political perspectives. I will tell you the story of my family's relocation from personal experience.

1

Inujjuak

As long as I can remember, I have always known we were from Inujjuak. My mother, brothers, sisters, uncle, and other relatives talked about it all the time when I was growing up in the High Arctic. Inujjuak this, Inujjuak that; you name it, it was Inujjuak. It was the same way with the relocation. I heard that story so many times, I cannot forget even the most minute details.

My first memories are like pieces of a puzzle that don't quite fit together. I'm sitting on the lap of Isa Naqtai, riding in a kayak with him. I'm the only person awake inside a very bright tent while my parents are asleep, playing with my father's closed eyes as he sleeps deeply. I'm looking at a very high mountain above me and walking through a flat meadow. I'm happy in all of these scenes.

I'm running on the sea ice near our home on Lindstrom Peninsula on a beautiful clear day. I'm the smallest boy of my two friends, Allie and Salluviniq. We come to a crack in the ice and the two bigger boys jump across. I jump too, knowing very well that I cannot make it. I fall into the crack. I don't remember landing at the bottom or feeling cold, but I remember looking up from the bottom to see a dog team cut across the crack above my head. The next thing I know, I'm cold and inside our tent in a sleeping bag, though it is not yet time to sleep.

I was born in Uugaqsiuvik, which is probably where the memories of the kayak trip come from. After the relocation, I lived on Lindstrom Peninsula. I have been all over the Arctic. To understand my journey, you have to know

7

about my family. My roots are deep in Northern Quebec, called Nunavik. This is my story.

* * *

I did not know my father. He died when I was three years old. I know about my father's childhood from stories I've heard. My uncle Philipoosie Novalinga tells about his early childhood with my father, his older brother. My father, Isakallak Aqiatushuk (also known as Paddy or "Fatty"), was born on May 7, 1898, to Sandee and Lucy somewhere on the east coast of Hudson Bay. He had three younger brothers, and my uncle Philipoosie seems to have been the closest to him. I remember Philipoosie frequently referring to my father as "my dear older brother" with fondness. As boys, the two of them had their own trapline that they would walk out on foot to check. One story Uncle Philipoosie often told was from when they were young, nine or ten years old. It's an adventure story. It started on a beautiful sunny morning. The sky was clear and the air was crisp when Philipoosie, their younger sister Annie, and their friend Josie Nowra went out to check the traps. The two boys were carrying homemade knives made of steel trap springs. They played as they walked, throwing their knives on top of the hard snow the way you would skim a flat rock on water, until one of the knives got lost.

They checked their traps and were heading home when a sudden storm hit them. The snow began to blow. Being the middle of winter, it was cold—too cold for Josie Nowra, whose parka had no outer cover for protection and was made out of a thin, grey blanket material. The cold wind blew easily through it. Annie was getting cold, too. Young Philipoosie was in a dilemma, since the two smaller kids were in danger of freezing. So, he began to make an *iglu*. As soon as he had the first blocks of snow set in a circle, he put his two companions inside and finished the iglu from the outside. Throughout the night, Philipoosie made sure Josie and Annie did not give up hope. Sure enough, the next day, his father and some others found them. The dogs had smelled out the iglu with the children inside.

My father was born at a time when Inuit lived the way they'd always lived since they could remember, hunting animals for food and clothing. He first learned how to catch a seal through its *aglu*, its breathing hole, using only a harpoon. In fact, it was his preference over a rifle. Uncle Philipoosie said that when his older brother picked up a rifle to wait for an *ujjuk*, a bearded seal, he knew his brother was going to miss. As a boy, he used a bow and arrow to hunt small game. My uncle said that using an arrow fitted with a sharpened nail, bent at a perpendicular angle at the tip, my father could cut a ptarmigan's head clean off. He also made toy sailboats that could travel against the wind.

My father and his brothers were very husky in stature and very strong. They grew up at a time when boys were expected to be very self-reliant. I've heard they were very rough. My uncle could be a bit cruel to me in some situations I don't care to remember. My sister Anna once told me that he was sometimes insensitive to his wife, being too critical of her seamstress skills. But later in their lives, my father, when he was head of their traditional home in Uugaqsiuvik, made sure nobody went hungry—not only in their own village, but in any of the others near them.

I don't know much else about my father's history, except that he was a widower when he married my mother. His first wife's name was Lizzie, and they only had one son, Joatamie. As for my mother, it was a long time before I could put chronological order to any of her stories. She would make a reference to leaving Kangirsuk in one story, and leaving her sisters behind in Inujjuak in another. What makes it even more difficult is that accurate birth records, if there were any at all, did not exist back then. Governments of the day did not record birth and death statistics right away. In fact, the only people who did were missionaries, who kept records of their congregations. Many years after my mother passed away, friends and relatives started to help me piece things together and put the dates of my mother's incredible life story in order. My sister Anna Nungaq, brother Samwillie Elijasialuk, cousin Zebedee Nungak, cousin Akearok Ningiuq, and many others helped.

My mother was born Mary Aupaluk in Kangirsuk, Nunavik, on the Ungava Strait. Her birth record said she was born in 1906, but her family left Kangirsuk in 1912, and my mother always said she was in her adolescence when they left, so I believe she may have been born closer to 1901. She would have a life journey that spanned two thousand kilometres, starting when she left Kangirsuk as a young girl and ending in Grise Fiord sixty-five years later.

Inujjuak

My mother's father, Inukpuk, chose where he wanted to be and when. Like his father Qumaguaq before him, he was one of the last true nomads of the Inuit world. Because of his wandering ways, *Qallunaat*, white people, gave him the nickname "The Wandering Inukpuk." In 1912, he moved the family from Kangirsuk to the east coast of Hudson Bay, back to his birthplace, Nauligarvik, between Puvirnituq and Inujjuak. It would have been early spring, because they travelled with a large group of many dog teams. It is best for a large group with many families, children, and possessions to travel after March, once the cold winter has passed. When my wife and I were invited to Kangirsuk for their annual Arctic Char Music Festival in August 2010, my cousin Zebedee and his family took me to my grandfather's last camping spot before the move, about forty kilometres from Kangirsuk. We saw the tent rings on a hill at the edge of the river and noticed they had camped on a rather rough place. It must have been the only spot where there was no snow, which means they must have left in March or early April when the snow was just starting to melt on the hills, travelling during the warmer weather to make the most of the trip. Their journey went inland from Tasiujaq, coming out at the mouth of the Great Whale River on the west coast of Hudson Bay, near Kuujjuarapik.

Kuujjuarapik is one of the earliest mission church headquarters of the Anglican Church of Canada. I'm not sure when exactly, but sometime after they moved from Kangirsuk, Inukpuk became an Anglican catechist there. At the Anglican mission, he learned the basic principles of Christianity. I've listened to my grandfather's sermons on reel-to-reel recording tapes, and it is obvious he was very well taught. He was a dynamic preacher, and his teachings parallel the gospel. I can never forget my mother's Bible teachings on creation and the Holy days. She learned a lot from her father.

My mother's brother, my uncle Johnny Inukpuk, was born in 1911. He was just a toddler in the back of my grandmother Leetia's *amauti* when they left Kangirsuk. I don't know much about his earlier life, but the Inukpuk family was always well off in terms of food and clothing. They were a well-organized family with skilled trappers, good dog teams, and hunting equipment like wooden boats and kayaks. It was likely that they also had excellent credit at the Hudson's Bay Company in Inujjuak, or Port Harrison, as it was formerly called. The Inukpuk family owned a large Peterhead boat with a two-cylinder Acadia engine, and my uncle was responsible for that boat. He led a voyage to Kinngait when the famous *Nascopie* sank in 1947, an event that is well known throughout the Arctic. The *Nascopie* was like the *Titanic* of the North. Communities from all over the Eastern Arctic congregated at Kinngait to take advantage of the salvage after the insurance company was through. The voyage across Hudson Strait is no easy journey, and I am certain that trip would've earned Uncle Johnny captain status if he hadn't already been my grandfather's first mate. When they arrived, it was already late summer and most of the "good stuff" was gone, but my mother said the canned goods they brought back were wondrous to behold. One particular can she loved had a yellow substance inside. She finished perhaps two or three cans of it. The price she paid for eating this yellow stuff was a horrible stomach ache. She found out later she had eaten two or three cans of butter! She could never have bread, bannock, biscuits, or crackers with butter the rest of her life after that.

Uncle Johnny never stopped practicing his skill as a captain, even in old age. After the Northern Quebec Inuit Association signed their land claim agreement in 1975, Nunavik communities received boats for hunting. My uncle was the natural choice to be the captain when Inujjuak received its boat. He held the position well into his eighties, when he was an Elder with a cane. I suppose after all those years as a Peterhead captain, he had salt in his veins by that time.

My mother was the oldest of my grandfather Inukpuk's children. She had two younger siblings besides Johnny: Dalasia and Annie. She would tell me of her time living in Kangirsuk as a young girl, a time of play with Annie and Dalasia and their cousins. She would laugh when she told the story about a big boulder they used to climb—they'd get to the top, squat at the edge, and see who could pee the farthest.

Being the only son, my uncle Johnny received his father's full attention. Inukpuk passed on his skills as a hunter, trapper, and family provider. Uncle Johnny and Moses, Annie's husband, acted as mentors to my own brothers, Joanasie, Elijah, and Samwillie. They taught them about hunting, and much of what Elijah knew about dog-team driving came from Johnny. Inukpuk had a lifetime of living off the land according to the cycles of the animals, and most Inuit lived pretty much the same way when I was growing up. Elijah's life is a good example of this. He led the way of life he preferred right up to his dying day. Elijah was an exceptional trapper and an excellent dog-team driver in the High Arctic; our uncle obviously taught him well. I learned to understand why he enjoyed trapping, and hunting seal and polar bear. He told me the skills were passed down through the family from generation to generation. When I started my own dog team, I started from scratch, working with untrained dogs from the very beginning. Uncle Philipoosie started giving me a few pointers later on, which I am grateful for, but it was what Elijah taught me that I never forgot.

My mother also passed on important information to me and to my brothers and sisters. Her first husband was a man named Elijasialuk, and together, they had Anna, Joanasie, Elijah, Adamie, and Samwillie. Elijasialuk died when the children were very young. After that, when she was in her early thirties, and before she met my father, she had my sister Minnie Killiktee with a man she simply called "Saali." She taught all of us how to cope with the changing of the seasons. She would tell her sons to be ready for the coming winter by putting away extra food from their summer catch. She would tell her daughters to prepare their husbands' winter clothes before it got cold. "Now that winter is coming, we have to prepare to make new winter clothes for our men," she would say. She told us the importance of teaching children proper discipline while they were young, taking care not to spoil them. She told us that spoiled children will not know how to deal with difficulties later in life. She admonished her children to teach their children to know the difference between what is right and what is wrong. She told us stories about living in Kuujjuarapik, including her life among Cree who lived there. Her Cree neighbours made tanned caribou skins, smoked dry meat, and homemade soap. She even knew how to count in Cree.

Like most mothers are to their sons, my mother was special to me. Even when I was still a youngster and she was careful about some of the descriptions in her stories, she used to talk to me about just about anything. For example, she'd say my father could not walk on New Year's Eve. He'd crawl home after the festivities. For a long time, I could not figure out why this was. I used to think his legs stopped functioning each New Year's Eve. When I got older and learned to drink, I finally figured out what happened! She said my father quit drinking a few years before we were relocated and became involved in running Sunday services.

I remember her specifically telling me he had finished reading the gospels from cover to cover just before he died.

Her storytelling was her way of "uploading" information to my head, knowing I was at an impressionable age. And there was nobody else around she could talk to—even though I had siblings, they were not always at home. My brothers would be out hunting, and in my early years, my brothers and my sister would be out all day, leaving just my mother and me.

I think a lot of what my mother taught us was learned from trials and errors in her own experiences. She had found it necessary to survive as a young widow, and it was obvious she was not going to let what happened to her repeat itself through her children. As we struggled to survive in the High Arctic, her skills as a survivor were the backbone of our family in times of hardship, especially after my father died. She forged a life for us without any help or advice. She was determined to build for us a strong home that survived, and she succeeded.

2

The Ends of the Earth

In 1953, when I was almost three years old, my parents were living in Uugaqsiuvik, my father's traditional village, thirty-five kilometres west of Inujjuak. Living with him in Uugaqsiuvik were his son Joatamie Aqiatushuk, Joatamie's wife Ikumak, and their daughter Lizzie; Philipoosie, his wife Annie Pudjow, their son Paulassie Nungaq, and daughter Elisapee; my half-sister, Minnie; and of course my mother and me. Ikumak's sister Alicie and Alicie's husband's family, the Naqati family, also lived with us. My mother's children from her first marriage, Elijah, Anna, and Samwillie, were living with our grandfather Inukpuk in Nauligarvik, about 160 kilometres from Inujjuak (Joanasie had died by this time; I don't know much about Adamie). They were also living with Uncle Johnny, Aunt Annie and Uncle Moses and their daughters, Mina and Annie, and and a few other families.

An RCMP constable came to Uugaqsiuvik in the spring. The first time he came, nobody was interested in what he had to say about "relocating," moving away from where we lived. He came back again, trying to convince us to move to this great new place. Even upon his second arrival, we did not say yes. But he kept coming back, and each time he came, he seemed more desperate in his attempts to make us agree. He came back again and again until people didn't know what to do other than agree. We found out later that the same constable was going to other places in and around Inujjuak trying to entice our village leaders to agree to his proposals to move, and in some villages, he had become angry when he was refused. Simeonie Amagoalik, one relocatee, recalled, "When the policeman arrived, he's wearing a uniform, with a pistol strapped to his side; we felt intimidated, it was hard to ignore them."

John Amagoalik, a distant cousin of Simeonie's who was five years old at the time, recalled this as well: "[My parents'] first reaction was, 'No, we cannot leave our home, we cannot leave our families. We just cannot agree to this.' The RCMP went away but they came back, they came back two or three times as I remember, and they were very, very persistent…in 1953 the white man was viewed as almost a God by our people. They were feared. I mean we were afraid of them. We were afraid to say no to anything they wanted."

When the constable told my family that our relatives in other villages had agreed to go, we started to think about his proposals. Edith Patsauq, a relocatee from one of the villages just west of Inujjuak, remembers, "My late husband and I were visited by a police officer and his interpreter. They sat themselves in front of us and for the first time we heard about the relocation issue. They said they had come to ask us if we will want to be relocated as well since our relatives had already agreed to go. Not being able to do without our relatives, we said we would go too, for he was also saying that we could return home after two years."

After we moved, we compared stories. It turned out that he had said the same thing in each place, and told all of us that our relatives in other villages had already agreed to go.

* * *

My father, once he had agreed, specifically requested that all his stepchildren move to the High Arctic with him. My sister Anna recalls being at Nauligarvik when she learned that she, Elijah, and Samwillie were to be included in the relocation. Anna had been struck with polio when she was eight years old, leaving her unable to walk, although she told me she could stand on her one good leg. Paulassie would carry her on his back or use a homemade wooden platform to help her get around. Uncle Philipoosie and his family were also to be part of the experiment. From the way Philipoosie used to remember his big brother, I think he would've followed him anywhere he went, even to the ends of the earth.

Everyone moved to Inujjuak weeks before the ship arrived at the end of July. The CGS *C.D. Howe* was on its annual summer rounds, conducting medical checkups and testing for tuberculosis in Northern communities, as well as transporting goods and supplies. There were also government officials onboard conducting annual inspections, an RCMP inspector, and the Bishop of the Diocese of the Arctic, the head of the Anglican church in the Eastern Arctic.

"It was the very first time I was ever away from home and from my grand-father," Anna, who was twenty at the time, remembers. When they were all wait-ing for the ship to arrive in Inujjuak, he arrived by kayak to say goodbye, saying he could not stay away from his family.

Forty years later, my brother Samwillie recounted the departure at a hearing in Ottawa: "I remember, there were waves—they were waving each other good-bye, with tears streaming down their faces. 'Cousin, I am going to see you again. I will return.' And there were many people saying that as the ship was departing."

But many of us never came back.

* * *

Anna told me how it got noticeably colder as they neared the High Arctic. Near Pond Inlet, looking out at the mountains that seemed to be getting higher all the time, she thought she was seeing huge rivers coming down between them. She later learned that what she thought were white, gushing rivers was in fact frozen ice: glaciers! The ship stopped at Pond Inlet on Baffin Island to pick up more "volun-teers." There were three families from Pond Inlet who made the journey farther north with us. They were the families of Simon Akpaliapik, Samuel Arnakallak, and Zebedee Amagoalik, and they were chosen to help the *Inujjuarmiut*, those of us from Inujjuak, adjust to the unfamiliar High Arctic conditions.

The Inujjuarmiut thought they would be settled close to their relatives, the people they had lived with all their lives. It was only once the *C.D. Howe* was half-way to Craig Harbour from Pond Inlet that the families discovered they would be sent to three different places. Officials started to dictate who was going to Craig Harbour, who was going to Resolute Bay, and who was going to Alexandra Fiord.

John Amagoalik described it well: "[We] just went into a panic because they had promised us that they would not separate us…I remember we were all on the deck of the ship, the *C.D. Howe,* and all the women started to cry. And when women start to cry, the dogs join in. It was eerie."

Anna said it was like a shock wave of fear had swept over them. "We thought everyone was going to be all together, not be separated," she remembers. "I was good friends with Sarah Salluviniq. When we were being told we were going to different places and Sarah was not among us, I was struck with deep fear!"

Whenever I hear the story about what happened on the boat, I have visions of Philipoosie arguing loudly in defence of young Samwillie, only seventeen years old at that time, who was to be sent with Thamoosie Amagoalik's family to Alexandra Fiord. Even though he was a year away from being of legal age in the Qallunaat's world, in the eyes of the Inujjuarmiut, he was still a boy. Philipoosie told me, "When I realized my brother, your dad, was not going to speak up in protest, I spoke up to say Samwillie Elijasialuk was just a boy. You can't take him away from his mother. What is she going to do without him?"

Philipoosie's intervention on behalf of young Samwillie worked, but unfortunately Simeonie's protests against being sent to Resolute Bay did no good. Simeonie told me that "Simon Akpaliapik and his family was one family chosen for Alexandra Fiord. My step-brother Thamoosie Amagoalik, who had been the only reason why I agreed to leave Inujjuak in the first place, was chosen as the second family to go. My protests fell on deaf ears and didn't mean anything to the authorities. I felt helpless." Simeonie had left Inujjuak with his young wife, Sarah, who was eight months pregnant with their first child, and his eighty-five-year-old grandmother. Paul Amagoalik was born on the *C.D. Howe* and was named after the ship's captain, Paul Fournier.

None of the witnesses onboard the *C.D. Howe* that day ever forgot what happened for the rest of their lives.

* * *

When we were taken ashore at Craig Harbour, Philipoosie noticed our personal stuff being unloaded, but he saw no large boats for our use. "After we were in Craig Harbour, we were told we'd be taken to another place by the RCMP's 'big boat,'" Anna said. "So I would be looking for that 'big boat' but only saw a sturdy looking short boat anchored in the water in front of Craig Harbour." She was expecting a boat the same size as our grandfather's 45-foot Peterhead back in Inujjuak.

"Where's the big boat for our use?" Philipoosie asked the ship official. He was told they would have to use canoes for walrus hunting. He said, "No, that is not acceptable! Do you realize how dangerous walrus hunting is with just canoes?" A large male walrus is about ten feet long, four feet wide, and weighs two thousand pounds. We had only brought 20-foot lake canoes with us, fitted with 7.5-horsepower outboard motors. After this, the officials told him the RCMP at the detachment would loan them RCMP boats—32-foot, 65-horsepower utility boats—for walrus hunts, but it was just one of many oversights.

The day we arrived in Craig Harbour, Simon Akpaliapik and Thamoosie Amagoalik and their families were transferred from the *C.D. Howe* to a new icebreaker, the *D'Iberville*. Samuel Arnakallak was told he was also going to Alexandra Fiord. He never forgot moving his belongings by himself from the *C.D. Howe* to the *D'Iberville*, the ship's crew watching as he struggled with the heavy things, including his large dogsled, his tent, and all his family's personal stuff. He was halfway done when one of the officials from above shouted down to say he was not going to Alexandra Fiord after all. The official told him to take his things back to the *C.D. Howe*. He returned all of it by himself, with no help from the ship's crew. It turned out the authorities had mistaken him for Akpaliapik. It's one example of how disorganized and insensitive the government was during the relocation. Luckily for those of us taken to Lindstrom Peninsula, they could not reach Alexandra Fiord due to the ice, so the relocatees bound for that location ended up being with us.

We had to wait in Craig Harbour for a week while the RCMP carried out a promise they had made to my uncle and hosted a walrus hunt. Arnakallak said it was the only time the RCMP helped to hunt walrus. After the hunt, they did not even take the walrus meat back to the camp at Lindstrom Peninsula, just unloaded the meat at the little islands three kilometres away.

Uncle Philipoosie recalled the journey from Craig Harbour to Lindstrom Peninsula: "We passed some areas that seemed okay to land in and we just kept going past good areas towards just mountains. Later I noticed we were heading straight for a huge mountain that seemed to be just a rock cliff. I thought the pilot of the boat was lost." The driver, as it turned out, was not lost. He was right on course for Lindstrom.

Lindstrom Peninsula is situated in the centre of the southern coastline of Ellesmere Island. Only when you are within a few hundred metres of where we got dropped off can you see any flat surface. The gravel shore at the bottom of the mountains is about one hundred metres by five hundred metres. The mountain range itself is so high that you can see it from as far away as 160 kilometres. It is no wonder the Inujjuarmiut were shocked to be dropped off in such a place as this.

Where we landed, it was just mountains with barely any vegetation; just shoreline and nothingness. All we had was our camping gear, fit only for east Hudson Bay conditions. No building material to build shelter, only our tents. Arnakallak often recounted how that first day had an ominous feeling to it. When the RCMP boat left, the feeling of abandonment permeated the atmosphere. "Here we were, dropped off, three large families and at least six dog teams with no dog food whatsoever." He never forgot how he went hunting with Inootsiak Muckpa in his little flat-bottomed rowboat. They brought back a single harp seal to feed all three families and all six dog teams.

Dark Season

*I*n times of hardship, my mother would retell the reasons her family were given for relocating and talk about all the promises that never materialized. She would start speaking out loud to nobody in particular, listing all the basic goods we were missing. She'd say the families were told that their lives would improve in the High Arctic, that it was supposed to be a land of plenty, that they were to take only clothes, sleeping bags, hunting equipment, and tents.

"We were told to bring only the barest essentials. We were told everything else would be provided for," remembers Akpaliapik.

Not only were we without basic goods and shelter as a direct result of what the government officials told us, I have found out over the years that those of us who were dropped off at Lindstrom Peninsula were not to be supplied with anything whatsoever! The question of shelter was not addressed as anything serious, so our parents were not told there would be none provided. The organizers had planned for us to live in snow houses. But the High Arctic is like a polar desert and can never get enough snow before December to make a good-sized iglu, especially where we got dropped off.

The mountains are very high, and there are huge glaciers. When the warm air from Europe mixes with Greenland's cold air, the combination can cause deadly strong winds, and the snow does not get a chance to accumulate. In October in Nunavik, when the snow came and was packed enough, my family would move from their tents into igluit. Snowfalls in the High Arctic begin in September, and it will get deep enough that one can drive a sled on top of the snow—but not deep enough to make igluit. The Inujjuarmiut were horrified when fall came and there was not enough snow.

My brother Samwillie recalls, "When fall came and started to get cold, our parents were not worried, thinking they would be able to build igluit once the snow came. It turned out hardly any snow falls in the High Arctic in early winter, plus the high mountains make the winds get so strong, what little snow that comes down is blown away."

The first time I went back to Inujjuak, it was in September of 1978. Snow was already on the ground in Grise Fiord and Resolute Bay, normal each season. When I arrived in Northern Quebec, it was like summer. One can imagine the shock my parents must have felt when they arrived up here.

There was also not enough scrap wood to build sod houses, so my family ended up living in their tents. My brother Elijah never forgot that when they went to bed at night, they'd be wearing their clothes, for it was so cold in their makeshift tents. He said it was like they were always out on a camping trip.

We were forced to insulate our tents with whatever we could find, including buffalo hide donated by the RCMP from Craig Harbour. I remember the black walls of our tents. Elijah said the hides were so stiff, it was necessary to use a hand drill to put holes in them to rope them together. My sister Anna said, "Whenever the pebble flooring got too soiled, it was necessary to replace it with clean ones, which meant opening the tent door. When the outside air came in, you could see the cold fog coming in."

The Pond Inlet families knew what to expect, but Akpaliapik was the only one who got enough scrap wood to build himself a sod house, as he had always done back in the Pond Inlet area. Unfortunately for Arnakallak, there was not enough to do the same for his large and growing family. What they endured throughout the winter is a story of the struggle to survive. The Arnakallak family members have told me they were often cold during the nights. Because of the experience, some of the children became arthritic when they grew up. Combined with the frequent high winds in the fall and how very dry the region was, the relocatees were caught in a dire situation they never forgot about for the rest of their lives.

Alex Stevenson, a government representative, had recommended *Mittimatalingmiut,* people from Pond Inlet, be included as "support families." "When we heard the government was looking for recruits to look after Northern Quebec Inuit, Arnakallak and I readily gave our names," said Akpaliapik. "We thought we would be working. After all it was a federal government initiative. We excitedly talked about the hunting boat we would be buying after two years!"

But both Arnakallak and Akpaliapik said that for the first two years, everyone struggled just to survive, including them. "We were sent to be with the Inujjuarmiut to help them adjust to new conditions, but we all ended up working together to survive the first two years," Akpaliapik recalls. Arnakallak said the same: "The first two years were horrendous, most difficult! It was too much! *Uakallaluaraaluulauqtuq!*"

Stevenson wanted to avoid what he had seen happen in another experiment twenty years earlier. That time, the government had moved families from Kinngait, Pangnirtung, and Pond Inlet to Dundas Harbour on Devon Island. Stevenson had noticed the Kinngait families had found the dark season particularly difficult to cope with. The thing that made me angry was that he never told our parents about the dark season when he moved us in 1953. The dark season was a total surprise to my relatives. This neglect had a lasting psychological effect on the adults. I have no doubt it was one of the contributing factors in shortening my father's and mother's lives.

Our chances of surviving the first two years were increased by the addition of the Pond Inlet families, but the dark season had a devastating effect even for them, although they were moved only a little over four hundred kilometres farther north. In Pond Inlet, the twilights during the dark season are very much brighter than on Lindstrom Peninsula. In the High Arctic, after the sun has set, the days get shorter by twenty-minute increments. Each day gets noticeably shorter. The sun completely disappears by October 28 at seventy-six degrees latitude. The first dark season my relatives witnessed was scary for them! Anna echoed what many others had said at different times when telling about their first dark season experience after arriving in the High Arctic from Inujjuak: "It was such a scary and overwhelming feeling that it soaked me to my innermost being in fear when daylight started to disappear," she said.

My mother told of a time she went out to chop some ice to melt into drinking water. It was so dark she could not tell the difference between a piece of an iceberg that had broken off and a rock covered in frozen ocean spray on the shore. When she remembered this incident many years later, she would smile, thinking about how bewildered her face must have looked when her axe sparked like a flint.

The lack of proper shelter and the dark season were not the only things we had to worry about. Back in Nunavik, the Inujjuarmiut had always depended on stoves for heat and cooking. They used homemade stoves made out of 45-gallon drums, cut into one third of the size. But wood stoves need wood to burn. On the shores of Hudson Bay, driftwood is plentiful. Trees grow all the way up to the northern edges of Quebec, Ontario, and Manitoba, which all touch Hudson Bay waters. On Lindstrom and on most of the southern part of Ellesmere Island, heather is the only available plant for stove fuel, and even then, it only grows in rocky areas of the peninsula. It was a shock for the Inujjuarmiut to have to search for heather among the hills, over boulder-covered ground below the 2,800-foot mountains. On top of that, the stuff is so sparsely distributed that it required many trips just to get a few days' supply. The men had brought along their kayaks, but having heard that they would be hunting walrus after they arrived, they sold one to Qallunaat onboard the ship. Unfortunately, the rest of the kayaks were the first casualties of the wood stoves.

I get tears in my eyes when I remember my mom struggling to find heather all summer with my Aunt Annie and Mary Thamoosie. If it hadn't been for those three women, our lives would've been much colder in our tents. Every time I see the hills on Lindstrom Peninsula, I can see those three women picking heather in silence. One can only wonder what was in each woman's mind. I know my mother's thoughts would've included the broken promises as she struggled.

I often went with my mother as she hunted for heather. When she spoke out loud, citing the broken promises, it was difficult to listen. Where do you go as a young child when your mother is angry? You are not supposed to be concerned at that age about issues of an adult nature, but it was hard not to be. I had nowhere to go. Children copy their parents' behaviour, subconsciously or consciously. I am not one to hold a grudge and avenge myself to those who have hurt me. However,

I have noticed when I get angry, I am very judgemental and start analyzing my situation, as if I'm trying to justify my anger. Others who were children during the time of the relocation have told similar stories about their parents' behaviour. Our parents felt betrayed and had no recourse, and sometimes took out their anger on their children. Zebedee Nungak called it "relocation syndrome."

The shock of a sudden change in diet was also very difficult to get used to, especially for the Elders. Big game like walrus, beluga, polar bear, bearded seal, and ringed seal are readily available in Northern Quebec. These animals have the necessary vitamins to keep Inuit healthy, especially in the more northern areas with less vegetation. The Inuit diet is so complete, doctors have been amazed by our health. We had virtually no heart conditions, and tooth decay was unheard of, let alone toothaches. Only old age caused our teeth to fall out. It was normal for women to have very low teeth by the time they reached their thirties from chewing so many animal skins to soften them. Our plant intake consisted of blackberries, rhubarb, blueberries, cloudberries, and other types of edible plants that supplemented the diet of meat. The *maktak* of a whale provides vitamin C, and seal liver contains multiple vitamins. As well, animal tendons provided sinew for sewing garments. Ujjuk skin is used to make soles for our *kamiit,* our boots, rope for dogs, and material for whips. The meat is delicious when dried; the intestines are delicious when boiled. And 99.9 percent of a caribou is useful— even the droppings were used for making sled runners slippery. After making the runners smooth, slush snow is applied over the frozen caribou droppings.

But in the High Arctic in 1953, caribou-hunting areas were limited to a minimum of thirty miles—about fifty kilometres—away and were heavily regulated. The waterfowl that far north is also very limited. There are snow geese, but no Canada geese, eider ducks, king eiders, red-throated loons, or old squaws (long-tailed ducks). The selection of diet choices is also harder to access than in Inujjuak. In the spring and summer, you have to go elsewhere to hunt different types of waterfowl and to find areas where tides get low enough to collect clams. Inujjuak is on the coast and has lots of lakes. We had Arctic char, lake trout, two different species of cod, sea urchins, and other small sea creatures. We ate mussels, clams, oysters, and different types of seaweed. In the High Arctic, there are very few lakes, and seafood is limited mostly to sculpin and a few sea urchins.

Different kinds of vegetation had also been readily available in Inujjuak for food or to use as insulation. Mountain sorrel is available, but many different kinds of berries, such as blackberries and cloudberries, don't grow in the High Arctic.

"By the time spring arrived, I was just skin and bones because I hardly ate due to the fact I was not used to the diet change while I was breastfeeding my son," Sarah Amagoalik said.

My mother missed eating Arctic char and other fish so much that when Gamaliel Akeeagok brought a bag of it to our home nine years later, she cried. Twice, she cooked dog meat in early spring to eat something other than seal meat day after day. I don't eat seal meat much now because of this. I remember cooking wolf, too, at least once. She remarked how the wolf tasted almost like caribou. It was during those times she would speak out loud of the broken promises, repeating the same story again and again, listing out loud what was not available, contrary to what had been promised. "I thought we were brought to a place of plenty! Where are all those plentiful things? Huh?" It would scare me when she was angry. On some days she would cry, saying she missed her sisters and her family.

Many of the relocatees I have spoken to have shared similar stories. When the Resolute Bay relocatees were landed on shore, they found themselves on an empty, barren, gravel beach. To make things even more traumatic, it started to snow, and the wind was very cold. "While we were putting up our tents, it was so cold, children had to huddle with our dogs to keep warm," remembers Zebedee Amagoalik. John Amagoalik remembered it as akin to "landing on the moon."

* * *

Craig Harbour, about fifty-six kilometres in a straight line from where we were settled on Lindstrom Peninsula, was the closest place to trade. By the time the ice had frozen and was safe enough to travel on, our already minimal supplies were running low. The story of the first trading trip to Craig Harbour from Lindstrom Peninsula in mid-October of 1953 is forever etched in the relocatees' collective memory.

Two dog teams—Joatamie's and Elijah's—left very early in the morning when dawn was just breaking, when everyone else was still asleep. Elijah remembers that they "wanted to be the first, to buy what was left of the canvas material for making a tent, as there had been so little left last summer." When the others—Thamoosie Amagoalik, Akpaliapik, and Arnakallak—finally arrived, Akpaliapik shook hands with the Inuit from Craig Harbour one by one until he reached where Joatamie was standing, and extended his hand before realizing who he was trying to shake hands with. My brother thought that was so funny.

Arnakallak had brought nothing to trade with, thinking he could get a credit as they always had with the Hudson's Bay Company back in Pond Inlet. He was flatly refused. He remembers that the corporal stationed there "was very stern with his refusal at my request for a credit. I could do nothing about it. Everybody else had something to take home except me." Here was a man with many dependents, including his eighty-year-old grandmother. A young constable filled his stove without telling his superior, but Arnakallak never forgot the experience.

Their return trip is also an episode that was never forgotten. What the pioneers did not know at the time was that the cold air from the North Pole comes down Ellesmere Island's high cliffs and can cause gale force winds. When they left Lindstrom Peninsula, the ice was still quite thin in some areas, which strong winds can easily break apart. Based on their descriptions of the conditions at the time of their departure, the air must've been quite moist already, a sign of a storm on the way. When the wind starts to break the thin ice at the mouths of the fiords, it can shred like a soggy cracker. The atmosphere was probably brewing bad weather when they left Craig Harbour, because the mouth of Starnes Fiord was already free of ice. Only the coastal areas of Jones Sound are safe for travel across the ice before January, but even then, only with caution—storms can keep breaking off new ice until then. In 1953, the relocatees did not know these facts. On the way back, the group was forced to detour to the western part of Anstead Point to a flat area. Paulassie Nungaq was on Akpaliapik's sled, the last to land at the Anstead Point area. He remembers that "Akpaliapik and I barely got on a small iceberg for safety just as the ice we were travelling on started to break up."

The group was forced to spend days and days waiting for the ice between them and Lee Point to freeze, all the while using up the precious store-bought goods and food. It was very frustrating for them to have to consume the goods, knowing very well that their families back on Lindstrom Peninsula needed them just as much. The dogs had nothing to eat, and the group was forced to kill two muskoxen, even though they knew they were going to have to report the killing of the "forbidden" animals, which could cost them a $5,000 fine or even get them arrested. When the ice finally became safe to cross Starnes Fiord, they left for home. But before they arrived, another windstorm started. When they arrived at Lindstrom Peninsula, the ice had broken off at the edge of the land, but it was close enough for Philipoosie and Samwillie, who hadn't gone with them to Craig Harbour, to row down with Arnakallak's little rowboat to pick them up.

As the last load was being ferried over to the peninsula, the wind suddenly started to blow hard, and the water started sloshing into the little boat. The men were in danger of drowning as the little rowboat started to fill up with water. In a mad struggle to stay afloat, they were forced to throw overboard the excess load of fox traps and some of the goods they'd worked so hard to bring home. Akpaliapik and Arnakallak were forced to go farther west to look for a narrow passage to land. Another six kilometres farther, they were able to get ashore. "When we landed, we were wet; soaked through in saltwater after spending all day on sea ice; exhausted," Arnakallak said. By the time they got home, they were all chilled to the bone.

A few weeks later, Arnakallak had another close call when he made an attempt to trade at Craig Harbour with young Inootsiak Muckpa just before the sun disappeared for the winter. When Arnakallak told the story, he didn't talk about heroics. He talked about what had happened matter-of-factly, like it was just like anything else that could happen in the North. When he and Inootsiak left, there was a hazy cloud covering and the sun was not shining brightly, but the weather was otherwise good. Halfway to Craig Harbour, they stopped to make tea, but they had neither lighter nor matches. Arnakallak took the front of his telescope lens and used it to light some fuel-soaked paper. He was able to light the Primus stove, and after tea, they resumed their trip—only to find that the mouth of Starnes Fiord was ice-free. It was not possible to get across, so they turned around.

On the way home, Arnakallak caught a very large harbour seal. He was tempted to leave it behind, but at the last minute, he took it. It was only when they were in front of Grise Fiord, just a few kilometres from home, that a very strong wind suddenly picked up. Arnakallak noticed that it was so strong, it was breaking up the ice like broken glass in its wake, and the broken ice was getting closer. The two men were in danger of falling into the water. Luckily, there was a stretch of flat, multi-year ice ahead of them—ice that has been frozen for years, becoming thicker each year as new ice forms on top of old. Just as they got on top of it, the ice they had been travelling on broke up entirely into a multitude of small pieces. Arnakallak and Inootsiak found themselves drifting away towards the middle of Jones Sound. As Arnakallak recalls, "It got dark after 6 p.m. at nights. We were drifting farther and farther away into the middle of Jones Sound. At night, we could see the clear sky and the stars. In the middle of one of the nights, we were surrounded by a large pod of beluga whales. Luckily, we had a tent, and that large seal was our salvation. It fed us and our dogs throughout our ordeal."

The two men drifted so far out into Jones Sound that they could see Coburg Island. Finally, one day the two men found themselves drifting back towards Ellesmere Island, and eventually they hit newly formed ice in front of South Cape Fiord. They tested it with one poke with a harpoon shaft and found that it was thin, but passable in an extreme emergency—and this was an extreme emergency. Arnakallak knew if they waited for it to get thicker, they would be taking a chance: the current and the wind could change direction at any time and take them back out. Both men knew that once they started, they would have to keep moving, knowing that if they stopped, they would fall into the water through the thin ice. They decided to take a chance and make a run for it. They ran with one man on either side of the sled, both holding a rope attached to it. Arnakallak encouraged the dogs to run by fooling them into thinking he'd seen a bear. He did not like using his bear calls to deceive his dogs, but this was an emergency. The dogs spread out in a large fan, knowing that to bunch too close together was dangerous. Once in a while, some of the dogs' paws would poke through the ice, but it held.

After what seemed like an eternity, the two men made it to safe ice. "It was like we had arrived home, although we were still far from land," Arnakallak remembers. "When we finally got home, my grandmother had been very worried and not sleeping at nights. All this adventure because we wanted to buy tobacco!"

* * *

As it turns out, the fact that we were settled a full day's travel away from the nearest place to trade was intentional. An RCMP report from December 1953 says that "it was thought best to have the natives away from Craig Harbour at least by one days [*sic*] sled travel. Being encamped at Craig Harbour might have given these natives the tendency to look for handouts when not absolutely necessary." Every effort was taken to prevent us from relying on "handouts"—including putting us in a place where we needed to risk our lives in order to get basic goods. On top of that, in early spring, starting in April, most of the basic store goods like sugar, flour, lard, and tea would be gone, and the sealift did not come until September. When the RCMP did mail runs to Resolute Bay in April, they would ask some of the relocatees to come along so they could carry goods back to Craig Harbour. I remember that when they returned, we could see the steam from the dogs' breath as far as thirty kilometres away. But even with the goods from Resolute, we had very little. For many years, I did not like the months of April, May, and June because of the memory of what these months were like back then. Until very recently, I have had to struggle to enjoy the spring.

All of the survivors have said at one time or another over the years that the first two years were the most scary and difficult. Each told how unprepared they were to defend themselves against the elements. The stories they told over the years about their struggle were always the same, with very few variations. The government's experiment left many very critical gaps that we paid dearly for.

An article in the *RCMP Quarterly* written by Constable Fryer speaks of how the new people from Northern Quebec looked noticeably better not long after being moved. He described how we were "a depressed, lifeless group of individuals, who were looking for too many handouts from the white man," but that "in a matter of few short months had visibly gained weight and looked so much more alive.

"All the Eskimos, except one old character from Port Harrison, were delighted with their camp location."

4

My Father's Soul

I don't remember the first winter in the High Arctic, when my father—the "old character" that Constable Fryer referred to—was still alive. I only remember the early spring of 1954, in late June, when the ice was starting to melt, just a month before he died.

My mother told stories of my father as being a very outgoing, talkative person back in Inujjuak. Even on the way up to the High Arctic, he was excited about the grand adventure, and curious about the places the ship passed along the way. Philipoosie said his brother would disappear once the ship arrived in a community. There was no place for the *C.D. Howe* to dock in the communities where we stopped on the way up except for Fort Churchill, Manitoba—even today, there are no docks in the Arctic—so barges had to ferry people and goods from the shore to the ship. "My big brother would be nowhere to be seen once the first barge left to go ashore," he said. "He was so curious."

But when my mother spoke about my father after arriving at Lindstrom Peninsula, she spoke of a man whose behaviour had changed. He became unusually quiet, as if he were deep in thought, almost deadly silent.

Anna said that a week before my father died, he fired a rifle with the explanation that he had seen an ujjuk swimming down by the shore—but there didn't seem to be anything to see. He may have seen something that wasn't there, or he may simply have wanted to handle his hunting rifle one more time. It's impossible to say now, but back in Inujjuak, hunting bearded seals, especially through *agluit* with just a harpoon and a line, had been one of his favourite things.

His death stands out the most clearly of all of my early recollections.

My mother told me that she had been making fresh fried bannock on the Primus stove. Before eating, my father got up to go look at the weather, as was custom. After taking his first step, he fainted. He had started to have fainting spells after we arrived in the High Arctic, from the stress, no doubt, so my mother was not alarmed. But he never came out of this one.

My memory starts out with everyone crying. Everyone had come to our tent to mourn. Our tent was a typical Nunavik type, made of a canvas material, circular in shape, and about four by six metres—big enough to accommodate a large number of people. I don't recall any crowding, even though everyone from the Lindstrom camp was inside it. It was the first time I ever truly felt hurt in my heart. It was to be one of many to come over the years as other tragedies befell our family and friends.

What happened next is up to you to decide whether to believe or not. You can call it a grieving child's fantasy or imagination, but I know what I experienced.

I was tired from crying and decided to leave the grieving people behind me. As soon as I opened the door of our tent and stepped outside, I saw my father! I was puzzled, thinking, *How...?*

I had just grieved his death inside the tent with my family. I had seen his form face down. Yet when I went outside to get away from the grief and sadness of losing him, there he was! I did not dwell on the question and ran to him. I was so happy to see him alive! He was lying on his side on some kind of mattress. I had never seen a mattress before, but years later when I went to a hospital, I recognized what he had been lying on. I don't remember seeing him talk, but somehow he told me not to be so sad because I would see him again very soon. When he told me this, I remember looking forward to that reunion. We then played in the sand, making little *inuksuit* out of small rocks and pebbles.

The funeral procession was sombre, everyone walking in a line towards the burial site, mourning in silence. But I remember not being sad at all. Instead, I was thinking, *Why is everyone so sad? We're going to see him very soon anyway.*

I have recently learned from one of Arnakallak's granddaughters that her grandfather knew what was weighing so heavily on my father, what I believe was ultimately the real cause of his death. It was the knowledge that he had made a mistake by agreeing to move. He told Arnakallak that he did not know how to tell his family that he felt he was coerced into relocating. He felt that he must somehow tell them, but he did not know how to do it. He said he was in an impossible situation, that he did not want to sound helpless to his family. I am sure Arnakallak would have told me if he felt he could.

I think my father also felt like he should have better understood the situation. His younger brother William was a special constable. They used to go hunting together, and my father learned early on about the ways of the RCMP. He was also very popular among the Qallunaat because of his carvings. He was very outgoing and talkative, like me, and would party with them in the evenings. I believe he felt he should have known better as a result and that he should have been more vigilant.

Today, after more than sixty years, only the children who were at my father's funeral are left. The question remains: Did I really meet my father's soul on that beautiful July day in 1954? I truly believe I did.

* * *

After my father died, we moved three kilometres farther west, closer to the middle of the peninsula. There were no rivers or lakes for fresh water at the first location, but the move was also to get away from a place of sorrow. Everybody moved that summer in 1954 with Akpaliapik's boat. The little sod house that Akpaliapik built at the first location stood another eighteen years after he moved to Grise Fiord in 1962. You can still see remnants of it today at Lindstrom Peninsula.

Lindstrom Peninsula is mountainous, especially at the spot where we were dropped off, and very few stretches of flat land meant very few places where we could settle. The second site was better. We settled on the east side of the river, and there was enough flat terrain for everyone to choose their own spots. But we stayed in that middle area for only three years. The shore was too rough after the ice froze. The currents in that area push drifting ice to the shoreline, which causes rough ice to accumulate over time. In fact, the whole Lindstrom Peninsula shore area gets rough ice by freeze-up. The Inujjuarmiut were able to make homemade huts with scrap wood frames that were insulated with heather housed in burlap bags, but life was still a struggle for all involved.

That place, in the middle of Lindstrom Peninsula, had some of the most difficult times. During the dark season of 1954, my mother cried almost every night. It was dark outside, and it was just as dark inside of me. I remember Samwillie telling her to stop crying so much, saying her constant lamentations could cause my father's soul to go to a place between heaven and hell. The reminder must've caused her to think twice, because she didn't cry so much anymore after that.

5

Prison Island

My father's death was far from being the only loss the relocatees endured. Unlike Inujjuak, Lindstrom Peninsula was completely isolated from everything, including medical services. Jaybeddie's two sisters died due to a lack of medical attention. Simeonie and his wife lost several infants due to the extreme cold and lack of food. The Resolute Bay group also did not fare well. They had to scrounge for sandwiches, meals, anything edible from the base dump at the Department of Transport six kilometres away and were reprimanded when they were caught. They learned to start going under the cover of night, but Simeonie said that the constable who had recruited them dictated their lives so much that he would check everything they had at their homes when he visited them. He would open their pots and pans, looking for anything he suspected to have been taken from the dump.

The Resolute Bay group also was not X-rayed to check for tuberculosis before the *C.D. Howe* dropped them off, and TB ravaged the people in our camps. The reason given for the omitted X-rays was that the machine was broken. It is a strange thing that such an important piece of machinery, one that is most needed, did not have a backup, considering that one of the main reasons the ship travelled each summer was to check for tuberculosis among Inuit.

Markoosie Patsauq, John Amagoalik's older brother, had come down with the first known case of tuberculosis among his group before we had even left Inujjuak. It worsened during the winter of 1953–1954, and he subsequently ended up infecting almost half of the Resolute Bay relocatees. As a result, Anna's friend, Sarah Salluviniq, as well as Simeonie Amagoalik, Mary Iqaluk, and Sarah Amagoalik, spent many years in a sanatorium in Edmonton. Daniel Salluviniq, Sarah's husband, was a single parent for so long he became good at sewing clothes for his family, including their outdoor garments. Sarah was eventually able to return to her family, but the disease had taken its toll. Her lungs gave out only a few years later.

* * *

The main promise made by the government when they were trying to convince the Inujjuarmiut to relocate was that we could be taken back home after two years. That promise was the foundation of why most people agreed to go in the first place, and starting that first winter in 1953, the Inujjuarmiut took every possible opportunity to try to return to Nunavik. When the "volunteers" realized how far away from home they had been sent, they felt abandoned—exiled in no man's land. But even after all of the loss and the hardship we had endured, none of my parents' requests to return to Inujjuak were ever acted on. My father, although none of my family members knew at the time, requested to go back home the very same summer we were moved in 1953. He was denied. After my father's death, my mother was alone, without a husband, and not able to go home. You would've thought the government would have agreed to take my family back after that, but they did not.

I remember my family making plans every summer to try to tell any government officials onboard the *C.D. Howe* to be taken back to Inujjuak. And year after year, the reply was always the same: "No." I remember one specific trading trip, we were on our way to Grise Fiord—I think the year was 1961, seven years after my father's death. The Craig Harbour RCMP detachment had been decommissioned by then, the new detachment at Grise Fiord having been finished in 1956. My mother and Samwillie were talking about requesting to be taken home while we travelled. I remember them making plans to tell the RCMP that they wanted to go back to Inujjuak. I myself did not hear them speaking to the RCMP, being just a boy, but I will never forget the long faces of my brother and my mother on our return home. We travelled back to camp in dead silence; not a single word was uttered the entire way back to Lindstrom Peninsula.

My mother recalled again and again what the translator had told them back in Inujjuak. She said that he had "made the conditions so clear. In his slow, deliberate, interpreting style, I can still hear him saying, 'If for any reason whatsoever you are not satisfied with your situation, you are free to ask to be taken back.'"

* * *

Sarah Amagoalik remembers that "from the day we arrived, Simeonie's grandmother would pack her things every day, expecting to leave to go back to Inujjuak. She would meekly ask us each time, 'Are we leaving today?'" She did not live very long up in Resolute Bay. She died asking the same question: "Are we leaving today?" Simeonie's grandmother Nellie was eighty-five.

Arnakallak's grandmother Mukpanu was in her eighties as well when she came to the High Arctic. Like my father and Nellie Amagoalik, she wanted to return home almost right away, as she quickly began to miss her usual diet of Arctic char, caribou meat, blackberries, and the other foods she was used to in North Baffin. My mother noticed Mukpanu sitting on the beach nightly, anxiously waiting to board the *C.D. Howe* for the voyage home to Nalluat, their traditional home near Pond Inlet. What hurts when I think about her story is that it should not have ended the way it did.

In the spring of 1955, despite the wishes of one particular officer, Corporal Sargent, Arnakallak decided to move back to Pond Inlet. With Akpaliapik's utility boat, the two men moved all of Arnakallak's equipment to Grise Fiord in preparation for the *C.D. Howe*'s annual arrival. Arnakallak recalls, "I was caught between two people, each saying the opposite to each other for almost two years. My grandmother always wanted to go home, and Corporal Glenn Sargent saying no to her requests. In the end, my grandmother's pleas won out as far as I was concerned. I decided to leave regardless of the consequences."

But Arnakallak's grandmother never got home. She boarded the ship, but when the ship's doctor took her X-ray, she was diagnosed with TB.

"My great-grandmother had been diagnosed with TB even before 1955," Rhoda Arnakallak told me. Mukpanu had first received the diagnosis in 1953 on the way up to Craig Harbour from Pond Inlet. "My father told me the *C.D. Howe* doctors wanted her to leave when she was first diagnosed but Corporal

Sargent argued with the doctor, saying the voyage south would be too hard because she was elderly, and therefore he kept her from leaving all the time we were on Lindstrom Peninsula. She used to be in pain some days. I slept with her since she would have her own tent in summers."

Arnakallak was told his grandmother was going to be taken down south to a sanatorium instead of to Pond Inlet. He had asked the officials to drop him and his family off at Nalluat, and he got his wish. When they arrived, he asked the doctor to let his grandmother go ashore, even just for a few minutes. The doctor refused, no matter how hard Arnakallak argued. It was the one time he became very angry with the government officials. Nothing was heard about Mukpanu until the fall of that year, when Arnakallak went trading to Pond Inlet. He cried all the way back to Nalluat. He became a heavy drinker later in his life.

* * *

Instead of returning us to Inujjuak, the government staged a second relocation in 1955. The families who were moved to Resolute Bay said the RCMP also discouraged them from going back to Inujjuak. Like us at Lindstrom Peninsula, remembering the government's promises, they fully expected to be taken home in 1955. But instead, the government wanted to move their family members up to the High Arctic from Inujjuak. That was not what they wanted, but that is what happened. I believe they were coerced into agreeing, the same way they were coerced into leaving their homes in the first place.

Daniel Salluviniq was moved in 1953; his brother Levi Nungaq was moved to Resolute Bay to be with him. Alex Patsauq was moved in 1953; his younger brother Johnnie Eckalook was moved to Resolute Bay to be with him. RCMP reports state that my father had requested for his stepson Josephie Flaherty to join us, and since my father was denied passage home the same year we were relocated, Josephie was moved to Lindstrom Peninsula instead. The Flaherty family arrived in 1955—after my father had been dead for more than a year!

Josephie Flaherty had led a comfortable life back in Inujjuak before he was told he had to move up to the High Arctic. My family has always wondered why the Flaherty family was sent up after my father died. What was the purpose? It did not make sense to us. Josephie Flaherty was a man with a growing family, and he was an independent person capable of making his own decisions. The consequence of being sent against his will was the pain he bore that transferred to his family. Martha, his daughter, was a young girl and was forced to grow up too quickly.

Back in Inujjuak, Josephie had worked for Environment Canada with good benefits. "I was paid three times better than the RCMP special constables. I made three dollars per day whereas they only got paid one dollar each day," Josephie told me. But once he was moved up to Lindstrom, he was forced to start hunting again.

"It was horrible to have to go with my father on his hunting trips," Martha remembers. "I had to corral seals to him by walking in circles while he waited for them over an aglu. It is not easy to pee outside as boys can. I could not remove my outer garments in the freezing cold when I had to relieve myself! My father had to help me." She said that from when she was seven until she was twelve, she would go hunting with him in -40°C to -60°C weather in the dark season, with no daylight and no food, for days on end. "I was the only son he had until my brother Jamie was old enough to go with him instead," she said.

Josephie, like those relocated in 1953, also tried to return home to no avail. "Josephie Flaherty came to me after he was refused on his request to move to Inujjuak in the spring of 1962. He had tears in his eyes as he spoke," my brother Samwillie recalls. When Josephie spoke of Inujjuak, all he ever spoke about was good things. He'd describe how wonderful it must be in Inujjuak as the months of April, May, June, July, and August passed by in Grise Fiord. He'd compare how it was each month with how it was back home, saying that the Canada geese would be arriving, and listing the other types of birds that would be flocking to the area in the spring. He obviously missed Inujjuak. He didn't live to see it again.

* * *

What the government told us about how things would be in the High Arctic—that it would be a "land of plenty," that our lives would be better, and that if they were not, we could return home—was all wrong. But it was not only what they were telling us that was wrong; it was also what they were writing. The article Constable Fryer wrote for the *RCMP Quarterly* is a good example of this, but the best ones come from Corporal Sargent's annual reports detailing "Eskimo

Conditions" in Craig Harbour. He knew how to convey the requests to return to Pond Inlet and Inujjuak as if they were not really serious, as if maybe we did not really want to go home. In his annual report for 1955, he wrote, "There has been no definite word from any native families to return to their native land." In 1956, he reported:

> No natives have definitely stated they wish to return to
> their former home. Last fall one single native wished
> to return to Pond Inlet. However due to rush conditions
> prevailing last boat time, this was not practicable.
> This native to date has not said anything definite about
> coming sooner. Eskimo family ANGNAKADLAK appears always
> to be in a half a mind to return to Pond Inlet to help
> his aged parents, but hasn't said anything definite. If
> definite requests come in, notification will go forward
> soonest possible.

Throughout the Craig Harbour condition reports from 1953 to 1961, the writers are quick to make reference to how good things were. They would say how requests to move never materialized because circumstances had changed or because the relocatees had been talked out of it. It is clear we were sent to Lindstrom Peninsula with no intention of ever being sent back to where we had come from. It turns out that the *C.D. Howe* did not even stop at Inujjuak on its trip back down south. The relocatees are often referred to as "High Arctic Exiles," and it is a fitting term. It is clear that we were prisoners in our own country, and Ellesmere was our prison island.

In 1959, Elijah made a request to leave Lindstrom Peninsula. He wanted to go to Resolute Bay, where Samwillie was at the time, hoping to find a wife. It's yet another indication that my family wanted to leave Lindstrom Peninsula, to be anywhere but here anymore. The RCMP account of his request looks like this:

> There has only been one man who has indicated he would
> like to move from this area and that is ELIJAH E9-912,

with his wife and mother. This native would like to move
to Resolute Bay and the only reason given for wanting
to move there is to join his brother SAM WILLY E9-913,
who went there last year to look for a wife. The writer
talked to Cst. JENKIN of Resolute Bay detachment by
radio and was advised that SAM WILLY would be leaving
Resolute Bay this Spring and it would not be advis-
able for ELIJAH and family to move. ELIJAH recently
contracted a loan from the Department for a new house.
Now that the house has been built, he should realise
his obligation to repay his debt before thinking of
moving. SAM WILLY seems to be the cause of this problem,
when he went to Resolute Bay last year it was with the
understanding that the prospective wife was available
and that he would return to Grise Fiord that summer or
this coming Spring. It now appears SAM WILLY has no wife
or prospective wife, but wants his mother and brother
to come and live with him in Resolute. The writer is
against such a move as it is known that others from this
area would like to live at Resolute also, and if one
moves it is felt that more will follow.

Not only was Elijah's request denied, the mention that my brother had an obligation to repay a loan he had contracted for a house was not true. Elijah said to
me, "Simon Akpaliapik, my brother-in-law Pauloosie Killiktee, and I paid for our
houses with cash and paid them in full on one payment. Others had to pay in
instalments. The three of us had enough money in our accounts at the trade store."

This report, like many others, also contains a prime example of the government's insensitivity towards Inuit: the references to my brothers in the 1959 report
as "Elijah E9-912" and "Sam Willy E9-913." The government of the day had
noticed that Inuit only used first names to identify themselves to people they
met, a system that did not mesh with things like birth and death certificates, or
welfare and health records.

The Canadian Arctic was generally divided into two areas, west and east. Inuit of the Western Arctic had a very distinct dialect that was noticeably different from those in the east. Eastern Arctic Inuit called them *Ualinirmiut*, "people of the Western Arctic." Usually, this meant from the Cambridge Bay area west—the Eastern Arctic includes the Kivalliq, Nunavik, and Qikiqtani regions. This division is reflected in the "E-numbers" assigned to my family. E1 was for the Baker Lake area, E2 for Kivalliq, E3 for Rankin Inlet and the surrounding area, E4 for Devon Island, and E5 for the High Arctic, including the Pond Inlet area and Arctic Bay. E6 was Clyde River, Qikiqtarjuaq, and Pangnirtung. E7 was Kinngait, E8 was Ungava Bay and the surrounding area, and E9 was for East Hudson Bay Inuit, like Inujjuarmiut. I was Larry E9-1905. I was probably the 1,905th Inuk born in district 9. It was not until 1972 that I was legally Larry Audlaluk.

* * *

When Samwillie decided to move back to Inujjuak in 1978 after my mother passed away, like the people before him from Grise Fiord and Resolute Bay, he was flatly refused. He had worked for the territorial government since 1962, so he used his paid vacation travel assistance to leave Grise Fiord. Before that, Arnakallak was the only one who had successfully moved back home. His grandmother's persistent demands to leave for home won out over the corporal's refusals. He said the corporal was most unhappy, but did nothing to stop him. Why not? Because Corporal Glenn Sargent knew that every Canadian had the right to live anywhere they wished—which means that had we known our rights as Canadians, we could've moved back too!

When we started to pursue the relocation issue, the efforts by the former federal government civil servants to discredit our claims were long and tedious. I have since realized to what extent governments were insensitive to Inuit during the 1950s. The paternalistic attitude was paramount during the time of our relocation. I have been thankful for organizations like the Inuit Tapiriit Kanatami and other Inuit and Indigenous organizations for making us aware of our rights as Canadians.

6

Buried Memories

a lot of what I have written about so far has been from the Inujjuarmiut's collective memory—things that I know, but was too young to remember in detail. My recollection of early events is in bits and pieces, like short chapters in a bigger story. For example, I have the memory of falling into the crack in the ice while playing with Allie and Salluviniq. But I didn't know until later that Ikumak had saved my life that day. She had been up the hill where the women were picking heather when my father shouted at her that I had fallen in. She told me that when she reached the crack and looked down, I was lying on my back at the bottom, underwater, with my eyes wide open. It was low tide, so the water was shallow, but the crack was deep. She had to struggle to get a hold of me. I thank God she didn't give up! I owe my life to her. I never thanked her properly, and have always felt that I should have when I had the chance.

As a child, I wasn't aware of all the politics surrounding my family's relocation, although I suffered the consequences alongside them. I had my own problems to deal with. The place we moved to after my father's death was a place of fear and loneliness for me. When we were still at the first location, I ran into a manila tent rope, causing a permanent injury to my right eye. After we moved, the injury became increasingly painful. I cannot describe how excruciating the pain was! I would literally roll around on the bed in pain, crying. I slept in the daytime as I could not open my eyes when the sun was out. If you have ever experienced a migraine headache, but at the same time had someone pushing on your eye with their thumb—now you have an idea of the pain I felt. I don't like to remember too many details of that place.

Besides that, playmates were few and far between, other than Allie and Salluviniq. I had been friends with them since the government had unsuccessfully tried to send them to Alexandra Fiord and they ended up with us on Lindstrom Peninsula. Martha was a welcome addition after Josephie arrived, but she was six months older, and she says I was too rough with her when we played. I believe that. After being alone so much when I was a little boy, I was ignorant about being careful not to hurt girls.

The pain in my eye was so much that I have blocked out a lot of memories from that time. I also know I buried a lot of trauma during the early years of my life on Lindstrom, which I'm sure has affected my memory. My memories from my later childhood are a bit clearer, but I know I have blocked out parts of certain events. This is one example.

* * *

In the spring of 1957, we moved from our second location to an area farther west that had smoother ground and more room to build houses. This story takes place after our move.

In 1958, sculpin, sometimes called "ugly fish," was the Inujjuarmiut's main source of fish. Eider ducks were starting to migrate into the fiords, and they'd pass by once in a while. My uncle would bring his 12-gauge shotgun along when we went fishing in case ducks passed by. Sometimes the whole camp would go out onto the ice near the shore to fish, starting in May until the ice drifted away at the end of July or in early August. Some years, the ice break-up happened a month early, closer to the end of June. I have noticed that today, with climate change happening so fast, the ice breaks up at this time of year more often than it used to.

Elijah would go sculpin fishing with me and my two boyhood friends, although we boys were never allowed to go by ourselves. The past spring, Elijah and Thamoosie (Allie and Salluviniq's father) had gone on a camping trip past South Cape Fiord, and all of us boys and my cousin Elisapee went along. I don't remember catching any animals, but I was just six or seven years old. That camping trip was the last time we were all together.

Although Salluviniq and I had gone with them that trip, Allie often went alone with his father on hunting trips because he was the eldest. The principal role of boys his age was to help with the dogs—that is how traditional skills are passed on, by watching the father hunt. Salluviniq and I played together when his big brother was away, and we became really close. The boys had another brother, Charlie, but he was just a toddler at the time.

Past events have a way of telling you what is going to happen, but you never know what that is until it's in the past. I believe I was told my friendship with Allie and Salluviniq was going to end under tragic circumstances, but I didn't know we were being warned at the time. As all youngsters, we were typical boys when it came to play. We'd spend all day playing outdoors. One time, we were playing in the home of Allie and Salluviniq. Their parents were not home that particular day, and when we tired of loafing around, we started reflecting on our fears and got to talking about "what ifs." I don't remember what my "what ifs" were, but I remember that we began talking about tragic situations, in particular hypothetical scenarios where the remaining two would be questioned if something bad happened to one of us. We ended up talking about what would happen in the that one of us accidentally caused the death of someone.. How would we explain ourselves? Our conversation went something like this:

"What would you do if you accidently caused or were thought to have caused the death of someone?" I know it was Allie who asked the question, as he was older, but I have never forgotten what he said after that: "You know, I would become so scared even though I know I am not to blame, I would run away and hide or climb the highest mountain even."

How were we to know both boys would be gone by the end of that same summer? The talk we had happened when the weather was getting warmer, I think around April. Thinking back, it was the last time we had such a talk. When I see boys that age, I sometimes envy them, wishing I could go back to that period. Everything seemed so perfect. The weather was serene, and despite the hardships of the years since we were relocated, life was good. We had better shelter. We no longer had to live in insulated tents in the winter. I was just a boy, eight years old, with no responsibilities or cares.

Every time boating season came, we boys gave our parents a difficult time, wanting to go with them. The canoes had limited space, and Elijah would ask Elisapee to take us sculpin fishing so he and Thamoosie could go boating. Although I don't know if that was the reason she took me that fateful morning, I know it was a typical summer day with clear skies, no wind—perfect conditions to go fishing. Anna told me that the ice had broken up that very day.

It was warm, almost hot. Our tents were pitched at the eastern corner of the flat area of Lindstrom Peninsula. We headed west of our home. Elisapee initially wanted to go fishing with only me, but we were walking below the big hill above the tents when we passed by Thamoosie's wife, Mary, one of the three women who had scoured the hills for heather with my mother. She saw us and said, "Wait up! I want my boys to go with you."

Elisapee groaned, said, "Oh, no," and stopped to wait. Since Mrs. Amagoalik was an adult, she obliged. When Allie and Salluviniq caught up with us, she told them right away that we were going to fish sculpin for only a short time and go home when the tide started coming in. The place we were headed for takes only ten to fifteen minutes to reach, and the area at the edge of the ice where the shore meets the water—where we planned to fish—is very short, not even half a mile in length. Where the mountain cliff goes straight down into what looks like black, bottomless sea marks the end of the good sculpin-fishing area.

We fished for a short time as planned. As soon as we reached the sheer mountain cliff, my cousin said she was quitting and going home. As we'd had fun on what seemed like a very short fishing trip, Allie said he wanted to fish a little bit longer by going farther, past the cliff along the ice edge. I naturally wanted to go with them, and in fact started to follow the two boys. As we started to walk away and disappear behind the sheer cliff, my cousin shouted at me, "*Anitsaarualuk qaigit*! My cousin, come back!" I did not want to obey her, but she was older than me, so I reluctantly turned back. Before the two boys went on, she told them we were going to wait for them on the hill. "We will wait for you up here collecting *qunguliq*," she said. Allie said, "Okay, we will be right back. We will not be long." It was the last time we ever saw the two boys alive. How were we to know?

Elisapee and I went up the hill to collect rhubarb as promised, and I filled my hat full of it. After over an hour, Elisapee said she could not wait any longer and headed for home. I don't remember what happened after my cousin and I decided to go home. My next memory is being awakened by my mother.

"Wake up, Laari, get dressed. Your *qatangutiapik* is dead," she said, referring to Salluviniq as my little cousin. It was the second time in my life I felt that burning feeling in the pit of my stomach, as if there was a knot inside, and then fear took over my very being.

We lived in tents all spring and summer, and it's a time of constant brightness, with twenty-four-hour daylight. Like the time of my father's passing, the weather was beautiful: warm, no wind, and the sun bright in a clear sky. I must have slept all day, because by the time my mother woke me up, they had already found Salluviniq's body.

Anna remembers what happened while I was asleep. "Mary came to visit our tent, bringing two very badly plucked murres," she said. "She said her two boys hadn't come home yet. When my uncle Philipoosie came back from a hunting trip by boat after midnight, we told him the two boys had been gone all day and were not back yet. He was instantly alarmed and chastised us, shouting, 'What is wrong with you people?! Don't you realize something is wrong?!' He was tearful, as if he knew something terrible had happened, and he was right."

The RCMP were told that same night, and a search was started right away. Two or more canoes were used in the search for the boys. Special Constable Lazarus Kayak was in one of the canoes with Thamoosie when he saw a body under the water, but he just drove away lest Salluviniq's father see it. It was Paulassie who "first" saw it from the second canoe. It was near the shore where Elisapee and I had last seen them alive. When they examined the body, they said there was a bruise on his forehead. Allie was never found. Many, including his mother, don't think he died from drowning.

I do not have any memory of what happened between the moment of our last contact as four youngsters until the moment my mom woke me up, but I know I blocked out the traumatic events. The RCMP investigation compelled my parents to ask me questions. I told them everything about how close we were. One of the adults must have thought to ask me about how Allie and Salluviniq's state of mind had been from as far back as I could remember. I told them the story of our "what ifs." People started looking for Allie in the hills. Samwillie even climbed the 2,800-foot mountain looking for him. He remained in hiding.

In Nunavik, it was the custom of most families to discard the personal possessions of the deceased—my mother threw away my father's reading glasses, telescope, Bible, and clothing when he died. I remember after the funeral for Salluviniq, my mother came home, tearfully recounting how she had just burned all of Allie's and Salluviniq's new clothing. The RCMP expected us to dress our best at ship-time—they wanted us to be described well by the people onboard. And so, because we feared them, we did. The clothes that my mother burned were being saved for the boys for *C.D. Howe* time. She said, "All spring and summer the two boys wore tattered clothes, all the while new clothes were put away, just waiting, to be worn for special occasions; so sad!"

What happened to Allie and Salluviniq? We will never really know; however, I have always thought they were so busy fishing sculpin, they forgot about time and the tide coming in. Changing tides can cause the separation of floating ice from the ice frozen to the shoreline, creating an expanse of open seawater called a "lead." Learning they were floating away, Allie might have jumped to the safety of the shore. Salluviniq was two years younger and very much smaller than his big brother. Allie was very fit physically, often out hunting with his father, even in the coldest of winters. Jumping across a lead that was opening fast might've been almost effortless for him, but Salluviniq was not as fit. He was much bigger than I was, even though he was just a boy like me, still with soft red cheeks. He was big for his age, but most of it was not muscle like Allie. Paulassie said that when Salluviniq's body was found, his arms were in a reaching position, but his hands were in a holding position, indicating he had held on for a long time. On his forehead was a bruise. He may have jumped with his big brother at the same time, or jumped right behind him, but didn't get across, and managed to grab hold of something like a rock or ice, bumping his forehead in the process. The edge of the ice on the shore at Lindstrom Peninsula is usually pretty high at low tide; Salluviniq may have fallen in the crack and out of Allie's reach.

Allie may have gotten scared and hid after watching his brother drown. As often happens to older children in a family, he likely felt responsible. I remember that Allie was afraid of his father; Salluviniq was the favourite son of the family. I know Allie would have been scared not only of his family, but of the authorities as well. I have always believed that is what probably happened after Elisapee and I parted company with them for the last time more than sixty years ago now.

I do not think Allie drowned or floated away on a piece of ice. Before the annual supply ship came each summer, we used to go to Grise Fiord to wait for it to arrive at least a couple of weeks in advance. While we were there, the men would go back home to feed and give water to their dogs. Elijah remembered what Thamoosie would say after coming back from giving his dogs food and water: "It's very strange, my dogs were neither hungry nor thirsty." He reported the same thing all throughout that summer. It is most likely Allie came out of hiding when everyone was at Grise Fiord. He would have not only fed their dogs, but lived off the seal meat meant for dog food.

His mother once told my sister Anna that she believed he was still alive because the family had noticed missing things around their home that could only have been taken by Allie. Sometimes the dogs would suddenly get up in the middle of the night and start to make noises as if they recognized someone outside.

Fear can destroy people's lives completely in an instant, as I believe it did to Allie when his brother drowned. He lived through the summer, but he would have been slowly dying. In the fall, Tatega Akpaliapik, Simon's wife, heard someone crying in the hills to the west of where they lived. It was very cold then. Allie was probably dying of starvation and cold. Each fall, when the weather gets cold and snow is coming in Grise Fiord, I will look over to Lindstrom Peninsula, thinking about how horrible it must have been for him, slowly freezing to death! Tears well up in my eyes when I think of him, living in fear, too scared to go home. I have always wanted to scour the hills of Lindstrom Peninsula to look for his body. He was never given a proper burial, nor was any funeral service held for him.

In the spring of 1968, I went for a snowmobile ride on my brother's Ski-Doo to the place where Salluviniq is buried. I saw an Arctic hare sitting next to his grave. I had Samwillie's .303 Lee Enfield rifle with a 10-shot clip with me at the time. I shot at the hare until I ran out of ammo, but not one of the bullets hit the animal. I thought I was shooting too high and thought nothing of the fact that I missed my target ten times. Just a few years ago, I was having a conversation about that Arctic hare with another hunter when he told me a similar story. He said he was hunting with his brother when they saw an Arctic hare at the same gravesite. They were using a .22 and also could not hit it. Was the Arctic hare a representation of Allie's spirit visiting his brother's grave? According to Inuit belief in spirit animals, it is possible this means that his spirit needs to be given proper ceremonial closure.

* * *

Naturally, the whole camp requested that summer to be taken back to Inujjuak. The RCMP had their typical "wait and see" attitude, hoping everyone would forget in time. The annual report for 1958 reads,

> After the sudden death of THOMASSIE'S two children,
> morale was at a very low ebb at the native camp. These
> natives still have their superstitions and several men
> stated they wished to move from this area. Also at this
> time staple food articles such as flour, rolled oats,
> sugar, milk and tobacco were depleted in the trading
> store, so that the natives were not happy to start with.
> However with the arrival of the C.D. Howe and trad-
> ing store supplies and especially the arrival of two
> new families to the area, old superstitions were soon
> forgotten and the natives were quite happy again.

7

Snapshots

*a*fter the loss of Allie and Salluviniq, I found myself suddenly with no one to play with. Their younger brother Charlie was too small. I tried to play with him a few times the first winter after my friends were no longer with us, but he was simply too young.

Before my big brother Joatamie began work as a special constable for the RCMP in 1958, I played with my half-niece, his daughter, Lizzie Amagoalik. But when Joatamie left for Alexandra Fiord, I had nobody else my age once again. I also used to play with Tookashie Akpaliapik, but the Pond Inlet and Inujjuak families had separated by then. Arnakallak had left with his family, and when Akpaliapik went back to the first site in the fall of 1955, aside from Lizzie, I only had Allie and Salluviniq for playmates.

The only time I had anyone to play with after they died was when we went to Grise Fiord to trade. Special Constables Arreak's and Kayak's children were welcome playmates there, but it was only for brief periods. Of the Arreak brothers, Benjamin, Juilie, and Lazarus, Juilie seemed the friendliest. During one visit there, we played "dog team." The four of us took turns being the "dog-team driver," giving commands to the "dogs" pulling the sled. Ben was my lead dog, with Juilie and Lazarus making up the rest of the team. Of course, Lazarus was the youngest, so he had the shortest rope, and had to pull the hardest. I also learned to look forward to Special Constable Kayak's visits to where we were living on Lindstrom Peninsula. He would come to make sure that everyone was doing okay, and would bring his son, Moses. Although Moses was very much older than I was, he was gentle, kind, and soft-spoken. I see him every once in a while either in Pond Inlet or Iqaluit, and when I do, I thank him for being there when I needed a friend.

The two years following the loss of my friends were so lonely for me! I learned to use my imagination so skilfully, I could invent alternate realities. I went on a walrus-hunting trip with other hunters. We chased a herd, excitement in the air, trying to harpoon one before we shot it so it would not sink before we got to it. I went on long, airborne journeys, exploring unknown places, places too incredible to describe. You know what it's like as a child to have no friends your age? Sometimes I would just sit or lie in the snow and stare at the sky all day.

Once Charlie Thamoosie grew older and "caught up" with me in age, we became inseparable. We sometimes went sliding on the hills all day. One favourite outdoor game Charlie and I never forgot about was our make-believe dog-team trips, which we talked about long after we grew up. We assembled our "dogs," harnessed them, tied the ropes to our sleds, and away we went. Oh, the journeys Charlie and I went on, incredible odysseys with our dog teams. The "dogs" were all empty cans we collected from the dump. We had nothing to use as sleds at first, but later we started using our own sleds that the adults had made for us to go sliding. Charlie and I would be sitting side by side on our sleds with our can dogs in front. Now and then we would pretend to run alongside of our sleds, prompting the "dogs" to go faster. Every once in a while, we'd pretend our dogs fought each other, and we'd have to stop them before they got hurt. Charlie's dogs fought each other often, and he would have to discipline them. My favourite lead dog was either an empty Magic Baking Powder can, a Honey Bee can, or a Fort Garry coffee can. My "boss" dog was an empty Klim powdered milk can because it was the biggest. The dog that had the shortest rope was the Export tobacco can. I always had twelve dogs, whereas Charlie only had seven dogs, just like his father. These memories with Charlie are worth more to me than golden treasures.

* * *

Even though I don't remember much in detail about our life in the years after my father's passing, I do remember my friends. I also have a few other vivid memories of that time. I may not have the full picture in my memory, but I have snapshots. Even in the midst of trauma, there are moments of amusement, too.

The insulation of our sod house was heather covered in burlap material. Samwillie used to sleep in the middle of our home, facing the opposite way as the rest of us. One morning just before he got up to dress, a caterpillar dropped right down onto his head from above! It had obviously been alive and well inside the heather.

Another memory I carry to this day was saying the Lord's Prayer each morning and night. Once, when I was four years old and too young to follow the prayer, we were praying before my brothers left to go on a trading trip. So instead of saying the words to the prayer along with everyone else, I did my own version and repeated: "Just before my brothers go on a trading trip, just before my brothers go on a trading trip..." Everyone burst out laughing before they could finish praying.

There were also some happy moments for our family in the form of weddings. I can't remember the dates exactly, but my sister Minnie tells me that it was probably in September of 1955 that Anna married Paulassie. Akpaliapik and Tatega got married at that time too. Elijah did not have a church wedding with Elisapee until 1968, but it was in the mid- or late 1950s that they became common-law husband and wife.

Also among the things that stand out in my mind from that time is the visit from the Inughuit from Siorapaluk, Greenland, when I was six years old. Of course, I did not know at the time that their presence had anything to do with why we were there in the first place. These were the people that one of the RCMP inspectors called "poachers on Canadian soil." Minnie says our first contact with the Inughuit was in March of 1954, but my first memory of them is from the second time they visited in mid-March or early April of 1957. When they first arrived, in 1954, the people at Lindstrom Peninsula were so happy to see the Greenland visitors, they held a prayer service to mark the important occasion. The first Greenlanders we met were Qulutanguaq Jerimisson, Kisunguaq Kristiansen, and Qauggunnaq. I have heard it said that the hunters had lost many dogs to starvation by the time they arrived in Craig Harbour. Moses Kayak said he took Kisunguaq to Lindstrom with his father's dog team to introduce them to us. The two other Greenlanders must've used their own teams.

We were living at the last spot on Lindstrom Peninsula the second time they came. I remember one morning, before we all had a chance to get dressed, the dogs must have been making sounds like they do when there is a polar bear around. My brother looked out to see what the commotion was about. As he looked out the window, he said that dog teams had arrived and were stopped on the ice. He described their short sleds with upstarts—two pieces of wood attached vertically to the back—and how short their dog ropes were. As he looked on, he said the men were approaching, carrying something under their arms. We learned later that it was the four brothers-in-law, Maja and Massauna Petersson and Sigluk and Qaulluqtuq Miunge. Apparently, they were the first of two groups of polar bear hunters from Siorapaluk.

Elijah and Josephie have each told me the story of the Inughuit's journey to Lindstrom Peninsula from Greenland. The story is essentially the same, although both of them told it to me separately. It goes like this:

Imina was an Inughuit hunter descended from Qidlarsuaq, the leader of an Inuit group that migrated to northwest Greenland in 1859. Imina's sons were very good polar bear hunters, with dogs so well trained they could hold a polar bear with their teeth and keep it from escaping to the open sea at a floe edge. No one questioned them when they dictated how a hunt should go. Maja's group was told they were to hunt near the shore area on the way to Canada while two of Imina's sons, Kulutanguaq and Kisunguaq, hunted near the floe edge. Traditionally, hunters from northwest Greenland would hunt along the stretch between Greenland and Ellesmere Island. The terrain they had to go through required crossing great ice caps and rocky landscapes, and the dogs had to be highly trained to go through twisted trails and the huge, mountain-sized pressure ridges between Greenland and Ellesmere Island. The need to keep their dogs well fed made them highly skilled seal hunters. When Maja's group decided to bring some extra walrus meat for dog food, they were told it was excess weight, that Canada was a good hunting area. "What are you taking all that extra food for? Don't you know where we're going is rich in game?"

The two groups did not see each other again until past the Cape Norton

Shaw area. Maja's group was travelling slowly, hugging the east coast of Ellesmere Island, going through some deep snow. One day near Craig Harbour, they came across dogsled tracks, which they recognized as belonging to the other team. At first, the sled tracks seemed normal. But farther on, they noticed human footprints running alongside the sled tracks, indicating slow progress. Inughuit rarely run alongside their sleds when their dogs are healthy. Later, it became clear the teams ahead of them were not travelling normally. Maja's worst fears were confirmed when, up ahead of them, he saw a dead dog. Just before arriving in Craig Harbour, they caught up with the other team resting. Josephie used to tell me that they were cooking a dead dog! Maja and his companions learned that the other hunters had not seen a single polar bear since they had parted company. There were no polar bears near the floe edge. Maja and Massauna and their two brothers-in-law had caught eight polar bears. They gave some of their dogs to the other team so they could continue going to Craig Harbour. It is never wise to get too confident in the Arctic.

* * *

Sigluk gave my mother his *kamiik* that had torn for her to sew. She was amazed at how different the style of their kamiit were from ours, yet simple in design. My niece Alicee was only two years old when the Greenlanders were visiting in 1957. By the time they left, she was calling her mitts "*aiqatik*." My brother Elijah benefited the most from that visit for two reasons. First, he picked up the idea of having upstarts, which could be used to push the sled from the back, on his *qamutiik*. But the most beneficial outcome was having exchanged dogs with Maja. Elijah gave Maja one of his dogs and in return was given a white female dog. Maja's dog bore a litter of puppies that were half Inujjuarmiut, half Greenlandic. When he started using them as a team, nobody could keep up with him. His travel speed doubled. By the time he was returning from a day's trip, his companions who had left with him in the morning were just arriving, ready to make camp.

Another Greenlandic hunter, Aron Duneq from Qaanaaq, came to Grise Fiord regularly to visit. He would come with his younger brother, and sometimes with other Inughuit hunters. In 1968, when he was twenty-two, Aron and a group of hunters were near Coburg Island hunting for polar bear. The group he was with had not originally planned to go to Grise Fiord, but Aron convinced them to visit. I was away at school at the time, but I have seen old photos from their visit. While they were here, Aron climbed a nearby mountain with Isaac Akpaliapik and Seeglook Akeeagok. Since then, this mountain has been called "the Greenlander mountain."

Aron told us that the Inughuit called Coburg Island "*Appaqsuit*," meaning "many murres." In Inuktitut, we call it "*Qurvik*," which means "washroom," because there are so many droppings there from sea birds!

We looked forward each year to the arrival of the Inughuit hunters from Qaanaaq (formerly Thule) and Siorapaluk. Some of them were direct descendants of the Greenland explorers. Even today, we reminisce each March about how we looked forward to their arrival. My mother would describe how she could understand the Greenlanders at the start of their conversation, but when they spoke in longer sentences, she couldn't understand them anymore. Having first seen them when I was six years old, and later read about the North Pole expeditions, I was thoroughly fascinated by these people.

8

Ningauk

I remember things in greater detail after my beloved brother-in-law came to be with us. I became more relaxed, and I felt safer and happier.

Minnie says she first met her husband, Pauloosie, while we still lived in the middle. I always thought he had arrived after we moved to the last spot on Lindstrom Peninsula, but since I was only six years old at the time, I cannot contradict her memory. I do remember clearly when he and Elijah arrived from Alexandra Fiord. It was a beautiful spring day, and I started to call him "stranger." My sister told me right away to call him "*ningauk*," brother-in-law.

The story of my brother-in-law Pauloosie is full of good memories. Pauloosie's parents were Ningyou and Atagootsiak from Pond Inlet. His grandfather Killiktee had served as a special constable for the RCMP during the 1930s in the Bache Peninsula area, just a few kilometres northeast of Alexandra Fiord and Craig Harbour. Ningyou started following in his father's footsteps early on—a 1936 RCMP report describes a patrol led by Killiktee that took place from Craig Harbour to Fram Fiord. His sons Atagootak and Ningyou, who was just seventeen at the time, were with him. The men drove two dog teams. Killiktee was injured when one of the sleds ran over his legs, and Ningyou had to take him the sixteen kilometres back to Craig Harbour while Atagootak and the corporal who was with them continued hunting for caribou.

Ningyou started working as a special constable in 1948. His first posting was in Dundas Harbour on the south side of Devon Island. He served in Pond Inlet,

Craig Harbour, and Alexandra Fiord from 1953 to 1958, Pond Inlet again from 1958 to 1960, and finally in Grise Fiord from 1960 to 1968.

I have no doubt that when Ningyou became a special constable, as his father had been before him, the police knew they had hired someone with a solid reputation. When he was stationed in Dundas Harbour, Alexandra Fiord, and Craig Harbour, it was necessary to make mail runs to Resolute Bay and Eureka each March or April by dog team. The trips from Alexandra Fiord sometimes took them to Eureka via the Sverdrup Pass and on to Resolute Bay. The round trips were almost 2,400 kilometres each year for five years. Only Special Constable Arreak served in Alexandra Fiord longer, by three years.

While Ningyou was posted in Alexandra Fiord, a US Air Force B-27 bomber crashed near Pim Island. He and the rest of the RCMP were dispatched by the Thule Air Base in Greenland to investigate the crash site. It had been on a routine air patrol in the North Pole area. The flight may have originated from the Alaska USAF base or it could have been returning to the Thule Air Base when it ran into a pingo (a permafrost hill) that was directly in its flight path. When the RCMP search patrol found the missing aircraft, there were no survivors. The crew had been thrown clear on impact. All of their boots had come off, and their bones had shattered like windshield glass.

Aron Duneq had passed through the crash site few times on his way to Grise Fiord and had noticed how deep the engines had ploughed into the ground on impact. He told a story about a time on one of the RCMP's summer boat patrols that a corporal had moved one of the wheels of the wreckage. The wheel rolled down the hill towards where their boat was anchored and missed the RCMP boat by inches! The Inughuit no doubt visited the site every now and then to salvage anything useful.

Ningyou and Pauloosie helped to build the RCMP detachment at Alexandra Fiord. Caleb Sangoya, a minister from Pond Inlet, saw the foundation on one of the buildings in Alexandra Fiord when he visited the then-abandoned detachment one summer in the early 2000s. He was amazed by how much work had been put into it: a large section of a solid rock had been removed to make it big enough for a house. Instead of finding a better spot, the RCMP had decided to chip away at the uneven rock to make it flat. He said Ningyou and Pauloosie must've been in pretty good physical health to do such a monumental task.

It was while Ningyou was posted at Alexandra Fiord that my brother Joatamie was hired to work for the RCMP. Elijah escorted Joatamie to Alexandra Fiord by dog team, but had no one to travel back with. It so happened that arrangements had been made for Pauloosie to go to Grise Fiord to wait for the *C.D. Howe* for summer passage to Pond Inlet, along with Inootsiak Muckpa, at the same time that Elijah was heading back from Alexandra Fiord. The Inuit special constables were subjected to transfers every two years like the regular police members, and the government booted out the children of their Inuit staff when they became of legal age. Once Pauloosie reached that age, Ningyou would have had no choice but to send him back to Pond Inlet to find a wife. If I know my brother, I wouldn't be surprised if he told Pauloosie all about our sister on the journey from Alexandra Fiord. Somewhere along the way, Pauloosie made a decision to go see her, and by the time he arrived in Grise Fiord, he was ready to head to Lindstrom Peninsula to ask for Minnie's hand in marriage.

From what I saw in their marriage, I know it was love at first sight for both of them. Early photos of my sister and Pauloosie show how beautiful and handsome the couple were. When they met, they met all the traditional requirements to become common-law husband and wife. With my new brother-in-law's arrival, a new chapter started in our lives on Lindstrom Peninsula.

* * *

Before the introduction of the steering wheel in the front of canoes or boats, it was necessary to have someone control and steer the boat with the motor tiller. It was difficult to shoot and steer at the same time alone in a canoe with an outboard motor. It was better to have someone to sit in the front of the boat and be the "shooter." Ammunition is never cheap to purchase, and the shooter would end up doing most of the actual hunting in this fashion. The owner of the boat, most of the time, did the driving and the steering, but it did not matter who caught the animals on boat hunts as long as everyone in the family and the camp benefitted.

Before my ningauk came into our lives, Elijah's hunting companion was Thamoosie. In the summer, he was Elijah's shooter, sitting in the front of the boat.

My brother sometimes had other hunters come with him, but most of the time it was Thamoosie who sat in the front. I guess Elijah felt most comfortable with him as a hunting companion.

When Pauloosie joined our family, he became Elijah's front shooter exclusively. My ningauk was very quiet, but very outgoing in his quiet way. By 1960, he had bought his own 20-foot canoe fitted with a 7.5-horsepower Evinrude outboard motor. It was the first time I ever saw a logo encased in fibreglass. Man, that was such a cool logo. The wide stern of the canoe was something new, and it made the craft seem so big it was like a ship in comparison to the lake canoes they had. Oh, the speed that craft could go—and with only 7 horsepower!

Pauloosie was one of a kind to me at my impressionable age. He became our lay reader. My mother said his sermons were like a breath of fresh air compared to my uncle's teachings. When the hills in the immediate area ran low on heather, he would take us by canoe to collect it in other places. He also worked on outboard motors in our little community, and it seemed like he could fix anything. One time, Isa Naqtai and his brother Mososie came paddling home from Harbour Fiord when their 7.5-horsepower motor stopped running. It took Pauloosie no time to fix it. I still have the propeller he repaired when both blades of his own motor broke off after hitting a rock.

The year after Pauloosie got his boat equipment, Elijah upgraded to an 18-horsepower Johnson and gave Pauloosie his 10-horsepower motor, which let Pauloosie travel much faster. He told a funny story about the first time he saw a smooth wake at the back of his boat. He had installed the new motor and was out hunting with Thamoosie. While waiting for seals to come up to breathe, he shot one from where he and Thamoosie were waiting atop a piece of floating ice. He went to retrieve it with the boat while his companion remained behind on the ice. The seal had drifted away a bit, and when he sped up to catch it, he noticed the smooth wake behind him and was fascinated by what he saw. The next thing he knew, he was on top of another piece of ice. He spent the next couple of hours trying to get the boat back in the water, all the while with Thamoosie waiting, helpless to aid his companion.

In 1960, Elijah worked for the Geological Survey of Canada. With the money he earned, he bought a 21-foot wooden boat with a 4-horsepower

Briggs & Stratton engine. The boat was a step up from the tiny lake canoes, but the motor installed was for slow speeds, to be used by fishermen. The engine turned four times for each propeller rotation; in other words, it was a four-to-one ratio. Elijah said it used to take them half a day to reach Grise Fiord and just as long to get home—about as long as it would take to walk. He would laugh when he talked about how Philipoosie had the honour of being designated "driver" of his new boat.

"The boat was so slow, some days my uncle would turn around and drive the boat facing backwards. We'd be nowhere to be seen for hours, but people could hear the engine echo over the mountains miles away before we appeared in sight," he said.

When Samwillie came home from Resolute Bay, he bought his big brother a 10-horsepower Evinrude outboard motor. Elijah removed the Briggs & Stratton engine and shaft, covered the hole in the back, and installed the outboard motor. Then he could travel at speeds that were more normal!

* * *

Like Elijah, Pauloosie also worked for the Geological Survey of Canada. They hired my ningauk and Gamaliel Akeeagok as guides for two of their geologists. The plan was for the two men to go to Alexandra Fiord and work in the area and come back that same spring. Akeeagok accidently cut his finger while preparing walrus meat with an axe, and was forced to give the job to his eighteen-year-old brother-in-law, Ookookoo Quaraq. Since Ookookoo's dogs were still too young, he had to use Akeeagok's dogs.

"I was so young; when my sled over-turned, I could not upright it alone," Ookookoo remembers.

I remember reading in my brother-in-law's diary about the survey work. One of the entries was about a time when his dogs almost mauled one of the Qallunaat. It's likely that when the geologist was coming back from a field trip carrying rock samples in his hands, Pauloosie's dogs thought he was carrying food and was coming to feed them. Exactly the same thing happened one time when Allie Amagoalik was walking towards my uncle's house carrying his toy sled—the dogs thought he was carrying dog food and ran at him.

When Pauloosie and Ookookoo left for Alexandra Fiord, they followed the traditional trail along the southeast coast of Ellesmere Island via Craig Harbour, Cape Norton Shaw, past the mouth of Makinson Inlet, and then along the west coast of Pim Island. Instead of passing Makinson Inlet on their way home once the work was done, Ookookoo and Pauloosie went into it. They almost did not make it back.

The inland trail from Pirlirarvirjuaq Lake to Starnes Fiord was not familiar to Inuit of Canada and Greenland at that time. The last three quarters of the way into the inlet, they turned into a valley, making camp on the lake. It was spring, and with the deep snow getting soft fast, there was no trail to follow. What made it even harder was the fact that both men had never been on this route before. The only information they had was from the Inughuit from Siorapaluk who told them about how Qidlarsuaq's group had starved at that lake almost one hundred years before.

Ookookoo said his companion tried to make a hole in the lake but gave up as he only had a harpoon shaft for an ice pick. After camping one night, the two young men proceeded to follow the winding valleys below the mountains. The farther they travelled, the narrower their passages became; the trail has many passages that can confuse first-time travellers in the valley. They couldn't turn back as their dogs were in danger of starving, and the snow was melting fast. When they made camp, exhausted and lost, Pauloosie told Ookookoo to dream about a safe passage as they prepared to go to sleep in their tent, as if he were an apprentice shaman.

"I dreamed we continued travelling through a narrow passageway in which some places it got so narrow, it was necessary to put our sleds sideways in order to keep going," Ookookoo told me. "After a while, the trail got wider. Farther on, we came across polar bear tracks."

When they woke up, he told Pauloosie about his dream. When they hit the trail, Ookookoo's dream came true. The men continued travelling through a narrow passage, so narrow in some places it was necessary to hold their sleds as they went to keep them from tipping over. Soon, the trail widened again, and they came across polar bear tracks—just like in Ookookoo's dream! After that day, they arrived safely on the sea ice in Starnes Fiord and made it home not long after.

9

Qallunaat Nunangat

*T*he injury to my eye from the manila rope had made me very susceptible to sickness. When we moved to the last area on Lindstrom, my eye stopped hurting, but in the winters, my body was not strong enough for me to go hunting with my brothers. I missed learning some crucial hunting skills. Unlike Allie Amagoalik, Imooshee Nutaraqjuk, and Isaac Akpaliapik, I could not be out in the cold too long. I remember spitting blood when I coughed while playing outside. It turned out I had tuberculosis.

The RCMP was getting instructions via high-frequency radio from a doctor in Pangnirtung, and by late summer in 1958, I was scheduled to leave for a hospital. The date of my departure was scheduled for March or April of 1959. The RCMP's de Havilland single-engine Otter would pick me up during its annual detachment visit. Being just an eight-year-old boy and naive, I was excited. The prospect of going on my very first airplane ride, wow! I could not even envision what it was going to be like, but the very idea was thrilling. How was I to know that once the excitement was gone, I would rather be home? How was I to know it would be but the first of hundreds of airplane rides to come in the next fifty or more years?

My mother and I were taken to Grise Fiord from Lindstrom Peninsula. We stayed at the empty special constables' apartment next to where Special Constable

Kayak and his family were. We slept on the floor in the living room. The stove was out each morning, and I enjoyed the cozy atmosphere when it was being lit, the heat coming back on while I was still in bed. Before I left, we must've gone home to say goodbye to the rest of my family, because the day the aircraft was to leave, Gamaliel Akeeagok took us back to Grise Fiord to board the plane. The doctor from Pangnirtung, who was to be my escort, had checked everyone in the days prior to our departure. He had come to our camp on Lindstrom Peninsula with the police plane to inoculate everyone. It was one of the few times a doctor visited the community by aircraft.

At last, the big day! Everyone from Grise Fiord was on the ice to see us off, my mom included. What happened next was a total surprise for me. Everyone who was leaving with me on the plane started to board. Right up until I was lifted up into the aircraft, I had no worries, but as soon as I was put on the plane, I suddenly realized I was leaving my mom. I burst out crying, trying to get back to her, but the door was closed just as I was calling out to her. I could hear her moaning in emotion; even now, I can still hear her crying. It was the very first time in my life I had been separated from her.

However, I did not cry for very long. The doctor spoke perfect Inuktitut, which was a comfort and helped alleviate my fear. The people who knew me at that age have said I was very intelligent for a small child. I am sure the excitement around me and the novelty of being inside an airplane must have distracted me quickly. Onboard the aircraft were two other policemen besides the pilots. One of the things I remember very clearly as I got on the plane was how full it was. Not so full the windows were covered, but there was enough stuff inside that one of policemen had to sit on the floor in the middle, holding onto something during takeoff. As soon as the loud engine sound started, and my curiosity took over. When the pilots started the takeoff run, it was the first time I had ever heard such a loud sound. It was as if the whole world was going to blow up! I marvelled at everything around me—what a sight to see us become airborne! Looking up ahead to the pilots, I could see they were staring out ahead of them into the clear blue sky. It was as if we were heading for heaven, eternity, a journey into make-believe, like the song by The Moody Blues: "Nights in white satin, never reaching the end..."

First we flew to Resolute Bay, for how long I didn't know, but when I flew the same route as a teenager, it took three hours. I remember the panic I felt when I had to pee. My escort must've been asleep because I remember that the policeman who wore a Western Arctic–style parka, with the hood not pointed at the back, was the only person awake. I could not speak English, so I spoke the only language I knew, Inuktitut. I said, "*Quisukkama,*" and to my pleasant surprise he understood and helped me pee. I now know I peed into an air sickness bag.

My next recollection is being inside the airport base at Resolute, the long, narrow corridor, and the huge dining room with all the people inside. I think we only stayed there one night. I was taken to Jackoosie Iqaluk's. The Iqaluk family had been part of the 1955 relocation. When I entered their house, I saw that they lived like Qallunaat: the clean floor, even almost shiny; walls painted light blue; that clock that chimed every half hour! The house itself must've captivated my mind so much I don't even remember the people. I slept on the couch. A couch in an Inuit family home! I thought, *Wow.* The family might as well have been millionaires. The warmth of that couch was so comfortable. I had never slept so well.

I have no memory of our trip to Pond Inlet, but that is where we went to next. I stayed with Special Constable Benjamin Arreak, who was now stationed there. I had my own room and slept on the floor. We were in Pond Inlet for about a week while the doctor went on his rounds to the local camps with the police plane giving inoculations. I got a bit anxious to leave Pond Inlet; I found the place almost too quiet. Perhaps Resolute Bay with the airport base had already spoiled me.

Our next stop was at Cape Dyer, although it was very brief. I remember landing right in front of the detachment, the houses just above the tidal edge. We got off the plane, and right above us were the RCMP houses. The special constable apartments were the closest. The Pijamini family was waiting on the ice to greet us, standing next to each other, from the head of the family right down to the youngest, a boy, and also the smallest. The whole family wore white outfits. We were invited into their house, and they all willingly allowed the doctor to give them their needles—until it was time for the youngest to get his shot. Of course, he had other plans. That was when the drama started. He ran to the bedroom crying. With the doctor holding the needle and the whole family following him, he got on the bed and tried to get under the pillow! In June of 1962, Special Constable Abraham Pijamini was transferred from Alexandra Fiord to Grise Fiord. I recognized the whole family immediately as the same ones we had met in Cape Dyer. It turned out the little boy who had tried to get under the pillow was none other than Looty Pijamini, who, starting when they arrived in Grise Fiord, became a lifelong friend.

The next place we went to was Clyde River, where the walk to the village was long from where we landed on the ice. The place was bigger than Resolute, Pond Inlet, and Cape Dyer, but it was just as quiet as any of those communities. In those days most Inuit still lived in traditional homes. I stayed with the Jaypoody family and slept on a bed with their daughter, Leah. It was the first time I had ever seen an Inuit family who was part Qallunaat. Years later, when I went to Churchill Vocational Centre for school in Fort Churchill, I recognized Leah Jaypoody. I met Mr. Jaypoody again thirty years after we had stayed with the family, and he still looked the same. He didn't seem to have aged!

Our next stop was in Pangnirtung. It was brief, and I did not enjoy my time there. The man of the family we stayed with seemed friendly at first, although his wife never spoke or smiled. It ended up that my stay there was the first time I was sexually abused. The man made me shower with him and hold his penis. It was not right. It was confusing as an eight-year-old to be made to fondle an erection. Anyone who does this to a child should be locked up for life with no possibility of parole. The trip to Iqlauit was a relief for me.

When we landed in Iqaluit (or Frobisher Bay, as it was called at the time), I couldn't believe how small our aircraft looked on that huge runway! In the other communities, we'd landed on ice, and I knew we were on skis. As I watched out the window, not knowing that aircraft skis could be elevated for landings on gravel or paved runways, I got scared, thinking we were going to land on solid ground on skis. To my amazement, as we touched down on the paved runway, we landed on wheels! I was comparing everything I saw to my home on Lindstrom Peninsula. My first impressions are no different than any other Inuk's stories about venturing out into the "world" for the first time. The waiting area at the airport was the biggest room I had ever been in. It was so enormous, it seemed empty.

My next recollection is looking at all the lights in Apex Hill as we were coming down the hill in a vehicle. I must've spent most of the day at the hospital getting a checkup, because I know we arrived in Iqaluit mid-morning but didn't go to Apex Hill until it was after dark. I was relieved to be taken to Charlie's home. He was married to Leetia, my cousin and stepsister.

The house Leetia and her family lived in was a triplex, which they shared with two other families, one on each side. The building is still standing today. Apex Hill had been established as an experiment by the federal government in the late 1950s. It was meant to be a model town and was populated by Inuit from all over the Eastern Arctic. Many of the residents had ailments like polio and other medical needs that required them to be near a hospital. The government ran the town and offered training programs in jewellery making, cooking, carpentry, and metalwork. It had a recreational community hall, a fire hall, and a Hudson's Bay store. It felt like I had arrived in a city.

As soon as Leetia and Charlie learned who I was, the first question they asked was how my father died. Was it while he was hunting walrus, as they had been told?

I explained to them exactly how he had died at home one morning, but they kept asking over and over if what I was saying was true. This was my first inkling that some of our relocation story had been fabricated. I found out that *Time* magazine had run my father's obituary, as he had been known in other parts of the world for his soapstone carvings. The obituary said he "slipped from an ice floe while hunting walrus off Ellesmere Island." I believe the RCMP gave them this information to show that the men were out living off the land and engaging in hunting exploits, making the relocation appear "successful." How else would *Time* have even found out about his death?

About a week or two later, my trip to southern Canada resumed. I was now going to go to *Qallunaat nunangat*—the land of white people! My escort for this leg of the journey was a young man who had very light brown hair he'd soaked with Brylcreem, the likes of which I'd never seen. He spoke convincingly like a real Inuk. I was amazed. After *Inuktitut* magazine came out, it ran an article in the early 1960s about young men and women the Department of Natural Resources had hired as interpreters and translators with pictures of the newly recruited young Inuit. Each picture showed the person's name and hometown. I recognized my escort: Charlie Watt from Kuujjuaq (formerly known as Fort Chimo) in Nunavik. In the 1970s when I met up with him again, I asked him if he remembered me from the time we went to Quebec City. He said he remembered me as an easy assignment with no problems to escort, and very bright.

We got on a DC-3 aircraft, and when we arrived, I was taken to a small hospital in Quebec City, and I remember apple trees outside. All the Qallunaat spoke French. I'd never heard French before, and the fact that I could not understand a single word anyone said made the whole experience even scarier. That was when the realization that I was far from home hit me! I cried and cried, until my roommate got sick of hearing me and started to say, "Shut up, *sacré bleu*, shut up!"

I was given an orange and an unfamiliar red fruit. I had seen and eaten an orange before, but it was the first time I had ever seen an apple. Naturally, I tried to peel it. The skin was so thin I wasn't even halfway done when to my pleasant surprise, an old friend came in: the eldest daughter of Special Constable Kayak, Mary Panigusiq! I must have looked funny to her, trying to peel an apple, because she told me I didn't have to peel it. After her visit, I don't recollect crying much.

After that first hospital, I was taken to an outpatient home that had an apple tree outside, too. I overate apples there. Even today, I still can't eat too many apples. Worse, that outpatient home was so dry, I dreaded seeing a nurse. Every time someone touched me, there would be an awful static *craaackle!* and it hurt like hell. I learned to hate the daily baths the nurses gave me because of the static. I also had to be inoculated every day for the TB.

I don't know why I was moved around so much, but next, I was sent to a big hospital in Ontario. The people there spoke English only, and I started to slowly pick up a word here and there. I actually enjoyed being in that hospital. Almost from the day of my departure from Grise Fiord, I had been captivated by all the new sights and people I saw. I met a person from Arctic Bay, a man named Qavavow Laisa who had also been in a hospital in Brandon, Manitoba. It was the first time I ever saw an animated motion picture. I was amazed by *Pinocchio*, and I also loved *Bambi*. It had lot of open scenery, which reminded me of the open space back home. *Snow White and the Seven Dwarfs* was an interesting movie, but it had so much forest imagery that it made me feel closed in.

It was during my stay at that hospital that I first experienced lightning. One day the sky became overcast, and then it started to rain. I was fascinated to see rain like that. I had never seen the world become so wet in my entire life! The next spectacle was the awful lightning, accompanied by such a loud bang. I truly thought the world was ending! I started to cry, and I could no longer sleep. I was alone, with no roommate, and I was terrified. Finally, one of the nurses put my bed in the centre of my room, away from the window.

It seemed some days, when I became lonely for Mom, like I was never going to get home again. The homesickness felt unbearable at times, but I never cried again like the time I had in Quebec City. One day while I was alone in my room, a Roman Catholic priest walked in. I recognized him right away from the descriptions my mother used to tell me about them. She had always told me to be suspicious of these priests, and a deep mistrust took over. But then he started to speak Inuktitut. The joy of hearing somebody speak Nunavik dialect erased all my suspicions. We talked for a while, and then all too soon, he had to go. But before he left, he asked me if I could read and write. I didn't need to be asked twice. He gave me a piece of paper and a pencil and said I could write home. He said he would make sure my mom got my letter. And indeed, after I got home, Mom showed me that one-page letter. The words were slanted to one side but were quite legible. She treasured my letter, keeping it safe in her Bible for many years.

My next memory is leaving the hospital and being on a plane ride to somewhere. There were other Inuit onboard. It turned out we were on our way to Fort Churchill via Winnipeg. All I knew was that we were going west. I was always aware of what direction I was being taken, from the day I left home on that RCMP plane. I have never forgotten how pleasant that airplane ride was. We were in a huge aircraft, with passengers sitting in what seemed like endless rows of seats. I must've walked around a few times in the aisle because I remember being told to stay in my seat. I remember watching the farmlands below as we journeyed west.

After we landed, I went to an Inuit community called Akulliq in Fort Churchill, Manitoba, to wait for the *C.D. Howe* for passage home in July. I think it might have been just before Christmas, because I seem to remember going to the military base there to celebrate—I remember being inside a huge metal building. That was the first time I ever saw a cat, and learned they were delicate creatures that are indoor house pets. Someone put it outside just to see what its tracks on the snow would look like.

Akulliq is at the northern border of Manitoba, near Nunavut (Northwest Territories at the time). The winter wasn't as cold as it was in the High Arctic and it didn't last as long, but so much moisture in the air made it feel much colder, especially when it was windy. I stayed at a boarding home for children run by a woman and her family who were originally from Kinngait. Mrs. Qarjuraqjuk was a warm, kind woman who looked after the children under her care as if they were her own. She was very protective of me. She was a big lady and her husband was not, and her authority was never questioned. She did not dominate him or intentionally make his life hard, it was just that when Kuppapik came home from the bar at the base, she made sure the children were not disturbed. Knowing she was protective of us, we felt safe.

Even though I was of school age, I did not attend school. But I did meet boys my age while in Fort Churchill who were originally, I learned later, from Kuujjuaq. I became good friends with two boys named Tommy: Tommy Gordon and Tommy Berthe. Both boys were kind to me. I was especially close to Tommy Gordon, who was very quiet. He was the first Inuk I ever saw with freckles. I used to give him ten cents to buy me Pink Elephant popcorn when they came back from the Hearne Hall elementary school at the base. Tommy Berthe was very outgoing. I looked forward to being with them when out playing. I met lots of other boys from Akulliq who were originally from the Kivalliq region and other places, but I was closest with the Tommys. I guess I felt close to them since they spoke a dialect I could easily understand.

I remember many other people from my time in Fort Churchill, like Gordy Kautak. He was from Resolute Bay, but when I met him, his family lived at the south end of Akulliq. He had a home that was right at the edge of the community. I also met Iqualaaq, who ran an adult boarding home. She was partially of African descent, and her skin was so dark that the very first time I saw her, I didn't know she was Inuk. What personality, what energy she had! Her youngest son, Leopold, was quite a challenge for her. He was constantly getting into trouble. The boarding home was always full of people, but it had a homey atmosphere I enjoyed being in when I visited. It was probably because Iqualaaq made people feel at home away from home. When I started going to meetings at Nunavut Tunngavik (the organization that oversaw Nunavut land claims) in the mid-1980s, I found out that she has many descendants in the Kivalliq region. I'm proud to know and be friends with some of her grandchildren.

I have many good memories of that time. I remember playing out in the woods on warm spring days when the summer was coming, watching streams flowing, and noticing how beautifully the flowers bloomed. Far away in the distance you could hear the train whistle once in a while.

The summer of 1960, I left for home on the *C.D. Howe* when it arrived in Fort Churchill. I have no memories of leaving Mrs. Qarjuraqjuk or saying good-bye to Tommy Gordon and Tommy Berthe. I think I had learned to block out tearful farewells at an early age. Oh, how I enjoyed the thrill of standing at the front of the ship before we left, looking out at the huge grain elevator and the ship's boarding ladder. To my pleasant surprise, there were two Inujjuarmiut families aboard, the Nowras and the Ningiuks. Josie Nowra, who was a special constable with the RCMP, was being transferred to Grise Fiord. Davidee Ningiuk, whose hip had been crippled by polio, was being moved with his family to Apex Hill to be near a hospital. The Inujjuarmiut on the *C.D. Howe* all asked me how my father had died, just as my family in Iqaluit had. "Did he die while hunting walrus in a kayak?" they wanted to know. I had to tell them the truth.

I struck up a friendship with Louisa and Jimmy Nowra right on the first day. Jimmy and Louisa and I played hide-and-seek on the ship, and I thought it was genius when I saw how they cooled their pop by hanging the bottles outside the port windows. What made it even more special was that their parents told me we were related. Jimmy was my qatangutiapik. I liked his happy-go-lucky attitude right away. It was as if he was always in a hurry, as if there was no time to lose. It turned out his life would end only twenty-four years later in an untimely death in June of 1984. Perhaps his essence knew he would not be with us for long. I miss him sometimes. They say good people don't live for very long.

The trip from Fort Churchill to Grise Fiord took all of August because the ship was on its annual Eastern Arctic patrol, stopping at every community along the way to offer services like medical checkups, missionary visits by the

Anglican bishop, and anything else that needed to be done, including taking patients to southern hospitals. The medical team from the ship was received with mixed feelings by the people in the communities. TB was rampant, and nobody knew what their X-rays would reveal. For those who had the disease, it meant a trip to the sanatorium in Hamilton, Ontario. Some Inuit patients never came back home. Children sometimes came home not recognizing their own parents and not able to speak Inuktitut. Occasionally, authorities wouldn't know which community to send someone back to, and some children ended up being adopted by southern people.

My friend Mary Panigusiq was one of the interpreters onboard the summer I was on the *C.D. Howe*. I hadn't seen her since my stay in the hospital in Quebec City. She was often worried I was going to fall overboard. I must have been quite a handful for her at times.

Finally, we arrived in Resolute Bay. Samwillie was there, and I stayed with him in his summer tent for a few days. Around that time, I had developed a strange leg ailment and could not walk very well, so Samwillie would put me on his back when we went to go visit other families. After we left Resolute, we stopped in Pond Inlet in the middle of the night. I went to sleep after the anchor dropped, before I even saw the community, as it was September and already dark. When I got up the next morning, we had left Pond and were on our way home. I noticed a whole bunch of new people who had boarded in Pond. It turned out to be the Killiktee family on their way to Grise Fiord. Special Constable Ningyou Killiktee, Pauloosie's father, was being transferred to the RCMP detachment there. All the beds where I usually slept alone were full of his family members, including his son Roger. Jimmy and I became good friends with Roger, and we played around the ship a lot before we reached Grise Fiord.

It was a beautiful, warm early September day in 1960 when we arrived. The ship anchored so close to the settlement, I remember looking at the RCMP buildings and being able to recognize some of the people. It felt like you could jump off the ship and land on the beach. Elijah wanted to take me home right away, but he was told a doctor would have to discharge me first. Still, I was happy to be back. After my time away, I very much appreciated that there really is no place like home!

10

The Best Years

The early 1960s stand out as the most memorable period in my young life. Those were the best years of my childhood, and in the lives of our family as a whole. My brother Elijah seemed the happiest during those years. Pauloosie had joined our family, and not long after, Louisa had as well: Samwillie had determined that he would marry her right from the day he first saw her when the Nowras arrived in Grise Fiord. She became Louisa Elijasialuk.

Our homemade shacks had been replaced by houses brought from the south, and best of all, I was back home from hospital. I did have to take a ton of TB pills. Eight brown pills every three hours, totalling thirty-two pills each day. The side effects were horrible: fear, anxiety, and a general feeling of doom and gloom. This lasted almost eight years after I stopped taking those pills. The TB came back in 1971, but luckily it was only two pills per day and only lasted for one year.

But mostly, everything seemed perfect. I was a month short of my tenth birthday when I returned home. My sister and Pauloosie, who had lost their firstborn son, Joanasie, when he was only a few months old, had welcomed a second baby, named Samwillie, that May. The new houses seemed so big compared to our old homes, which were now used as storage sheds. The winter storms seemed a distant memory in our sturdy new house. Our shelter needs no longer in question, I noticed my family was no longer tense. They were not worried anymore about what was going to happen to them in the coming winter, and their body language reflected that. I'm not saying they had stopped asking to go home; far from it. A year never went by without them asking for passage home. The answer was always the same, but life after those little houses came was much more bearable.

I enjoyed watching men repair their hunting equipment and the recreational activities like soccer games. It was an activity that pulled the community closer together. My uncle Philipoosie would be the goalie for the opposite team. Unfortunately, he had begun having fainting spells as early as 1957. He often fainted when exerting himself, but that did not stop him from participating in a game he loved. Right up to his bedridden days, he enjoyed soccer. When the CBC televised sports, he enjoyed watching the rare soccer games.

I have many wonderful memories from when life was good in that last place on Lindstrom Peninsula. The houses were small, but that did not stop people from having the rare square dance. The dances would be held at my uncle Philipoosie's house. The 78 rpm record player we had was the hand-wound type. When the spring broke, it was never repaired. Instead, a person would be designated to turn the record with a finger. My uncle would have the job of keeping the record turning with his fingers.

The RCMP staff were changing at the time, too. Corporal Glenn Sargent was leaving after nine years in Craig Harbour and Grise Fiord. Constable Bob Pilot was promoted to Corporal. Special Constable Lazarus Kayak was leaving after eleven years in Craig Harbour and Grise Fiord; the Inujjuarmiut would feel his absence for quite some time. My relatives remembered the kindness he and his family showed us during our struggle to survive those first few years. Special Constable Ningyou Killiktee had come back to the High Arctic. It was a happy time for Pauloosie, who was now able to be near his family.

My relatives and the other Inujjuarmiut were also happy to have the Nowra family as an addition, although they lived ten kilometres away. In 2007, my sister-in-law Louisa told me her father had misunderstood the RCMP when they asked him if he wanted to be transferred to Grise Fiord back in Inujjuak. He was hard of hearing. When he realized his mistake, he felt he could not change his mind. Subsequently, his later postings included Alexandra Fiord, Pond Inlet, and Kinngait. I'm glad they came because my family gained a daughter-in-law, a wife for Samwillie.

* * *

It was in 1960 when Elijah, Thamoosie, and Akpaliapik got AM/shortwave transistor radios. Elijah would fiddle with his radio, listening to whatever station he could get, into the wee hours of the night. We suddenly had access to radio waves from around the world! The AM signals are best heard at night even today, although not so clearly some evenings; the signal depends on atmospheric conditions. It can get frustrating when a good song is being played. The shortwave signals are usually stronger but seem to have a vibrating sound and are never as crystal clear as AM.

We could hear the military air base in Thule, Greenland (now known as Qaanaaq), even in the daytime. They broadcast the *Grand Ole Opry* live on Friday afternoons. It was the best show. It exposed me to some of the greatest country music singers with songs like "Walk On By" by Leroy Van Dyke, "I Fall to Pieces" by Patsy Cline, "Miller's Cave" by Hank Snow, "Tennessee Flat Top Box" by Johnny Cash, and "I've Got a Tiger By the Tail" by Buck Owens. The list of my favourite country tunes is endless. My all-time favourite DJ announcer was Wolfman Jack, who played the latest popular hit songs such as "The Lion Sleeps Tonight (Wimoweh)" (Pauloosie's favourite song), "It's My Party," and "Hit the Road Jack." A song by The Four Seasons, "Walk Like a Man," is my all-time favourite. Over the years, Wolfman Jack influenced many other DJs to follow his style. A conversation he had with a caller just before the song "Hit the Road Jack" became his trademark. I remember the original phone-in request when the guy called in, and Wolfman Jack had to cut him off due to the time constraints of the phone-in show—the guy was calling just to talk about his girl problems, which had nothing to do with a song request. I was surprised when years later, I heard the same phone-in call, now being used as part of his show. All these great songs are exclusively by American artists. The British invasion was yet to come.

Late at night, we could hear WWVA from Wheeling, West Virginia, which would start every broadcast with "The Cat Came Back." On Saturdays, the Greenlandic stations would broadcast variety shows, including Kalaallit (western Greenlandic Inuit) comedy. On Sundays we could hear Kalaallit radio. Pauloosie could understand the Sunday services, as he had learned the dialect from the Inughuit from Siorapaluk.

One day while I was visiting my brother-in-law, Elijah came in excitedly, saying he heard an Inuk speaking on the radio. It was Annie Padloo, broadcasting from the CBC in Montreal. It was the start of a new era for Inuktitut-language broadcasts. The broadcasts became our favourite shows to listen to, with news in our very own language from Monday to Friday in the evenings from 8:30 to 9:00 p.m. for many years. When Annie was away, Mary Panigusiq would substitute for her. Having a line of communication to the outside world suddenly made us feel not quite so isolated. We now could hear about world events in Inuktitut!

Here are some memorable news items Mary Panigusiq read that I've never forgotten: One was about a jet plane that flew around the world. I believe it was the first flight around the stratosphere in a jet, part of the American-Russian space race. There was one about a policeman who was shot in the chest but survived because the bullet was stopped by his police badge! There was also the most heart-wrenching human interest story about a very loving doctor who died of cancer. The way she related these stories, you could almost see the events as they happened. When Russians sent the first spaceship into orbit by launching "Sputnik," which started the space race with the United States, we first heard about it on the CBC. Mary read that story too. She would probably have been trying the best she could to make what she was reading understandable to Inuit, who had no grasp of what a spacecraft was. It was the first time I heard the expression "the world is much smaller now." I thought the world had literally shrunk. I could not figure out how it could get smaller.

The introduction of *Inuktitut* magazine around the same time gave us a chance to get new reading materials besides just the Baffin-dialect Bible and the prayer book we were used to. Some of the articles in the magazine were very interesting to read. I especially liked the legends some contributors sent to the editor; it was the first time I read about Atanaarjuaq, Kaugjagjuk, Kiviuq, Lumaaq, and other well-known Inuit legends.

The CBC on shortwave was available to listen to all day without too much interference. The signal actually got poorer at night with so many other signals coming from around the world. I grew to love listening to *The Max Ferguson Show* and the classical music on *Gilmour's Albums*. Both radio shows were 100 percent Canadian.

Radio plays, like *Dick Tracy*, on shortwave were an interesting change on the weekends. When CFFB began broadcasting CBC programs from Iqaluit, they aired a variety of Inuktitut radio shows hosted by Jonah Kelly. When I met Inutersuak Udluriak from Siorapaluk in 1984, he told me he and his wife listened to those shows and loved listening to the Inuit Elders telling stories and legends. CFFB was the first station from our region to broadcast Inuktitut singers, like Dominique Angutimariq with songs like "*Niaquvinikuluk langala langala*," Etulu Editlui with his beautiful love songs, and Tumasi Quissa's "*Angijuuliruma maliqattalaaramali.*"

Every Monday evening, the Akeeagok family would walk almost five kilometres to our house from their home in the middle of Lindstrom Peninsula to listen to the CBC broadcasts in Inuktitut. Some evenings the signal was too poor to hear anything. Even so, it was a good way to socialize in those days. When Paulassie and Pauloosie got their small black radios, the Akeeagoks would visit them instead. Oleesee Akeeagok and Anna liked each other's company, so this was welcome for Anna. After the broadcasts we would talk about what we'd heard.

* * *

When I came home in 1960, I resumed playing with Charlie. When we visited with the Akeeagoks, he and I would play with Imooshee, Seeglook, and Peepeelee. Imooshee and I would play all day together. Once, we took our parkas off and left them by the edge of the water. The next thing we knew, they were floating away with the incoming tide. Our big brothers had to use a canoe to retrieve them. I had even more reason to look forward to going on the trading trips to Grise Fiord, because then we could play with Jimmy Nowra and Roger Killiktee. The visits seemed to end all too soon. With Jimmy, Charlie and I had an extra *Inuujuarmiuq* to play with—someone who thought like us and was crazy like us.

If there ever was a boy with an imaginative mind and a hyper personality, it was Jimmy Nowra. Jimmy stuttered very badly when he was younger. He and Louisa had spent time in the Hamilton sanatorium. When he was there, a group of Cree boys would put him in a closet and lock the door, giving him a bad case of claustrophobia that caused him to be scared of everything and anything when he was alone, including his own shadow. The experience impeded him from speaking normally until he became an adult. He acted older than his age, maybe because his time with us would be short. I was stunned years later when I learned that he was actually younger than me. He was a natural leader with lots of ideas. He was a good storyteller, too.

I have a couple of particularly funny memories of Jimmy. My family used to go to Grise Fiord for Christmas. We would stay upstairs in the special constable apartments. The upstairs bedrooms of each apartment had a manhole-sized square vent right above the coal stove. The ventilation hole was perfect for drying clothes. Sometimes it was completely covered by a sleeping bag or a sheet. This particular day, Roger and Aksakjuk Ningiuk were drying a sleeping bag, and the vent was completely covered. Jimmy came speeding into the room, running from someone. He was probably playing tag. The next thing Roger and Aksakjuk knew, he was gone—*SWOOSH!*—right down the vent! The loud noise caused everyone to go to Ningyou's apartment to see what the commotion was all about. He had landed square on his butt on top of Atagoosiak's teakettle where it was sitting on the stove, and bounced to the floor. The only damage was to the spigot and Jimmy's dignity— and I'm sure the only pain he felt was the tongue-lashing from his parents!

Another time, in 1961, we were spending the spring camping at Lee Point. Special constable families from Grise Fiord and the Lindstrom Peninsula folk would go there each spring until 1965. Some days, it would get foggy right to the ground, and we couldn't see anything beyond sixty feet—and in the North, where everything is white, objects can get distorted. Only two people were outside on this particular spring day when Jimmy cried out, "*Ummimmaaluk!*" A big muskox! Everyone dashed out to see the muskox, but Jimmy and Atagoosiak were the only living creatures around. People asked him, "Jimmy, where is the muskox?" He looked around, confused, and then glanced in the direction of Atagoosiak, where he thought he had seen the animal. What he had seen was actually her, bending down to work on putting wooden pegs on a sealskin that was stretched out to dry. With the fog shrouding her, Jimmy had thought he had seen a muskox. When he cried out "Ummimmaaluk," she stood up, and Jimmy's muskox disappeared!

After Samwillie became Jimmy's brother-in-law, Jimmy would hunt with us, especially in the summer by canoe. He was a crack shot with a .22 long rifle. In the fall, we used to go hunting for ptarmigan. He could shoot a bird's head or neck with ease. I would still be struggling to aim, and he would already have caught three of them, all the while laughing away in excitement. He used to stop to wait for me, because otherwise I would have nothing to shoot at.

* * *

When we lived on Lindstrom Peninsula, we lived off the land. We relied on the animals for food and used the hides and skins to trade at the store in Grise Fiord. To an outsider, the way Inuit hunted animals in great numbers in the fall would seem excessive, but they were catching as much as they could to last the winter, and Elders always reminded hunters to harvest only what was needed. In the High Arctic, April is the turning point for winter. The temperature goes below zero by mid-September, and it isn't until after the third week of April, when ocean currents begin to move in the opposite direction, that spring starts. Before then, the currents are at their weakest. When tidal highs occur in the winter, the pressure of the sea rising will crack the ice, but in April, tidal cracks don't open at all. Seal holes become very large, making it difficult to hit the seal when it comes up under the dome of ice that is created by the splash of the seal coming up in the same spot. The land animals seem to disappear in April, too. It's almost as if they are on holiday. Most starvation occurred in April because a hunter had run out of cached food. If a hunter is forced to dip into his cache in the middle of winter, he might run out by April. This might happen because he miscalculated the amount of food to be put away, or the winter hunting was bad due to frequent storms, or the hunting in the fall may have been poor. If it rained in the autumn, a layer of ice would form over the snow, and caribou would starve because they could not get through the ice to access food.

After a successful hunt, if the hunter had no room left on his sled or in his boat, he would cache the extra food for later retrieval. He would go back for it within a few days; the earlier the food was retrieved from the cache, the less chance polar bears, wolverines, wolves, foxes, and ravens had to get at it. It's no wonder Inuit always stuck to the same annual cycle, following the animals' migration patterns very carefully. Their own survival depended on it.

In the summer and fall, hunters harvested whales, walruses, and seals for the winter, although there were plenty of seals available year-round, so we had no need to collect many other mammals. From mid-November to mid-April, it was fox-trapping season. It was a busy time. Each week, men went out to check their traps, leaving Monday and returning by Friday. While the men went out to their traplines, I stayed with Minnie until they came back. She was good friends with our neighbour, Alicee Naqtai, and the women visited each other quite a bit while their husbands were on the trail. When the trappers were expected back during the dark season, Minnie and I would stop to listen for dog teams while we were heading home after visiting Alicee. We would listen for dogs panting and the sled runners on the snow, waiting for the hunters to return. When there was light, we'd look for the dog teams far in the distance. I loved listening to Elijah's stories of how the week's trip went. He would give us a day-by-day account.

Hunters would usually skin the foxes as soon as they were brought in from the trapline, but frozen foxes had to be thawed first. Catching a fat, greasy fox was a good omen, indicating that there were plenty more foxes to come from that trap. The foxes were cleaned on Saturdays, and when all the foxes were cleaned, they would be put on wooden racks to dry. The racks would be hung from the ceiling or leaned against the wall. It was normal to see a lot of skins drying inside our house. Everyone rested on Sundays, with evening services held at my uncle's house.

One season in the late 1960s, Elijah and Paulassie left to set fox traps about thirty kilometres into Starnes Fiord. Unknown to them, the ice near the shore of Anstead Point had opened up and some of the trail was gone. At this time, hunters had started using snowmobiles to pull sleds instead of dog teams. Elijah was ahead of his companion, quite a distance from Paulassie. Since it was dark, he could not see very far ahead. He suddenly saw open water, but he had no time to turn or stop. He skidded ahead, and the machine fell through the newly formed, paper-thin ice. He quickly tried to swim back to the safe ice, but his foot was caught in the sled's tow rope. He had no choice but to dive to remove the rope from his foot. The snowmobile sank, but the sled and the empty 10-gallon fuel container kept it from going down any farther. After removing the rope, Elijah tried again to swim back to safe ice, but the thin ice was stopping him from going forward. The distance he had to swim was no more than thirty feet, maybe not even that, but the water was starting to freeze, making it almost impossible. He was in a desperate situation. That was when he thought to pray for help.

Remembering the story of Moses from the Bible, he prayed at the top of his lungs, "God, if you still answer prayers like you did when Moses prayed loudly to you, I am praying now for help!" He tried swimming for a third time. Suddenly, he could hear ice breaking, almost like the sound of an icebreaker ship. He was able to get on top of the safe ice.

When Paulassie finally caught up with him, Elijah was standing there shivering, starting to become hypothermic. Paulassie quickly removed his outerwear, put him in the sleeping bag he had with him, put him on his sled, and rushed home the five kilometres back to Grise Fiord. Elijah used to say the power of prayer saved his life.

* * *

When the days got longer in early April, the trappers went on long-distance hunts for polar bear. The hunts would last as long as two weeks. On the way home, they would remove any fox traps, along with any final foxes. They also hunted caribou and birds from spring until the fall. The Inujjuarmiut had to get used to having a limited selection of birds to eat. The coast of Hudson Bay has so much variety. The families from Quebec longed to eat Canada goose. The spring and summer also seemed such a short time to hunt migrating birds; my family could not get used to the short summers in the High Arctic, often comparing it to Nunavik.

Hunters had to adhere to rules when hunting each species. A good example is whale hunts. The hunt for whale when they pass by in the summer is carefully planned. The first pod of whales that goes by is known as the "leader group" or "pathfinders." The pathfinders are allowed to pass without being hunted because this pod is few in number and separated from the main group behind them. The Elders stress the importance of never chasing the first pod of whales that passes by. If the hunters attack this group, some will turn back to warn the main group to detour through a different route.

Another rule we were told by our Elders was about hunting walrus on haulouts, the places where walruses come up onto the land to give birth, die, or mate. They stressed that after harvesting on a walrus haul-out, it is important to make sure no trace is left of the carcasses. Otherwise, the herd will leave that particular haul-out and not come back for a long time. I have seen that happen on a haul-out sixty kilometres west of Grise Fiord. Some walrus carcasses were left behind, and for the next thirty years, no walruses went on the land near that area.

Narwhals did not always pass by the south end of Ellesmere Island every summer. If the north end of Devon Island became ice-free first, they would migrate west along the south side of Jones Sound, and we would not see them at all. If both the north and south areas of Jones Sound became ice-free evenly, then they'd migrate on each side of the sound. It could happen that we would not see any for three or more summers. The first time my relatives saw narwhals was in 1960. It was also the first time my uncle ever tried removing their tusks.

With my brother-in-law's guidance, the first catch was substantial. Elijah and Pauloosie came in with five narwhals in tow. With so many more to chase, the two men asked Philipoosie to butcher them. Pauloosie told my uncle to remove the tusks without giving him any instructions on how to do it. When the two hunters came back with their second catch, my uncle was still on the beach. My brother-in-law noticed he was holding a hacksaw. He then noticed the five narwhals' tusks had been removed. He burst out laughing. My poor uncle. How was he to know you first had to remove the head, *maktaaq,* and meat before removing the tusks with an axe?

With the help of our beloved brother-in-law, we learned how to hunt and remove their tusks properly, although not before my uncle made that funny mistake. In those days, there was no quota on narwhal. Hunters could harvest as much as they wanted, but they only took what they needed. Each hunter's harvest was cached, calculated to last to the end of April the following year.

In the summer, Elijah, Pauloosie, and Thamoosie shared their catches, although sometimes everyone pitched in. Paulassie and Philipoosie each had their own cache. We had a limited number of hunting canoes and outboard motors, but no hunter was left out when it came to sharing food. The main source of income in the spring and summer switched from fox to harbour sealskins. During this time, the seals were caught at agluit and on top of the ice. Bearded seal hunting took place from May until the fall, and the men caught as many as they could. The thick skin of the bearded seal was used for kamiit soles, rope for dog harnesses, whips, and harpoon lines. Adolescent walrus hide made good kamik soles, too. Paulassie used to say he liked kamiit with walrus-skin soles. He said he never got cold feet in the winter wearing them. Anna made kamiit for him from beluga whale skin once in a while, too. The colour was almond-chocolate, and interesting to look at. Harp sealskin is not as thick as bearded sealskin for soles, yet they last much longer. The Northern Quebec Inuit used the bearded sealskin for water-proof kamiit, using a double-stitching style, with just the hair removed. Later, other Inuit in the Eastern Arctic adopted the same style.

I used to love watching my brother-in-law make new dog harnesses out of strips of bearded sealskin. First, he'd cut the skin into strips of the desired width. Then, he would soften them one by one by chewing them—very tedious, but necessary. Once all the strips of hide were soft enough for him to make into a harness, he measured each piece and cut them into the correct size. Instead of sewing them together, he tied them with homemade leather strings, made from the same skin, into a harness. Each season, he could make a complete new set of twelve harnesses in a day. After the harnesses were all made, he made new dog ropes for each individual dog. The bearded sealskins had already been cut to size while still raw, then dried. It was a simple matter of softening them, although this was no small task. Each piece of the rope material is so dry, it's stiffer than card-board. Once tender and soft, they were cut to the desired length.

I got my first seal the same summer I came back from the hospital. I went hunting with Elijah and Pauloosie a few weeks after my return. I even had my own .22 rifle during the hunt! I felt so mature. We were on top of an ice floe waiting for seals to come up, as was our custom when hunting by boat through-out the summers in those days. We were in a valley a few kilometres west of our home. We had not been waiting long when a huge harp seal came up. I was aiming at it when a small ringed seal appeared. My brother-in-law said, "Hey, try shooting this one instead." So I did, and my bullet hit the ringed seal point-blank! I heard my ningauk cry out, *"Aukataalungani!"*—oh my goodness!—in perfect Inujjuarmiut dialect. The two men hurried to get the seal onto our boat. I had shot my first seal! I could not stop smiling that day. As my godfather, my uncle Philipoosie took over the whole tradition of organizing the community feast. I was forbidden to eat from my first seal, as was custom. Good memories.

Since I was a boy, I have always loved the time in the fall when there is snow on the land, but the sea has not frozen yet. The days are mild with low clouds in the sky. The days are getting shorter every day and it's necessary to leave early in the day in order to hunt longer, unlike in August. The sea is very salty and the seals float after being shot. You don't have to hurry to retrieve them. When there is little daylight, the whiteness of the snow reflecting off the smooth water makes it possible to see seals when they come up. After the ice is formed and there is no snow, the seal holes are easy to find. Wearing over-boots called *mannguat*, it's possible to walk up to an aglu without the seal hearing you. The mannguat muffle the sound of your walking. You can also hear the seals from quite a distance when there is no snow on the newly formed ice. Elijah said you can hear the seals in the Grise Fiord area easily compared to the ones in east Hudson Bay when they come up to their breathing holes.

One looks forward to freshly killed seal, butchered right after pulling it out of its hole. The Primus or Coleman stove is brewing fresh tea while the hunter is cutting up the seal. Drinking fresh tea with iceberg water, having bannock instead of bread, yummm! Nothing like hunting seal in winter—what a life!

Kumaguak, my great-grandfather on my mother's side,
in the mid-1800s.
CREDIT: Avataq Cultural Institute

My mother, Mary Aupaluk, me, and my father, Isakallak
Aqiatushuk, leader of the Exiles. Here, we are in a tent lined with
buffalo hide on Lindstrom Peninsula in the winter of 1953–54.
CREDIT: Glenn Sargent

My mom's younger sister Annie's daughters, Mina and
Anna, in Inujjuak, late 1950s or early 1960s.
CREDIT: Inukpuk family photo collection

Above: My mother, Mary Aupaluk Aqiatushuk.
CREDIT: Bob Pilot

Right: My mother (left), Special Constable Lazarus Kayak (middle), and Mary Panigusiq (right), where the relocatees were dropped off on Lindstrom Peninsula in 1953.
CREDIT: Glenn Sargent

Below: Grise Fiord in 1954 or 1955.
CREDIT: Bob Pilot

Mary Thamoosie, mother of Allie and Salluviniq,
who scoured the hills for heather in the early years
on Lindstrom Peninsula.
CREDIT: Glenn Sargent

From left to right: Paulassie Nungaq, Elijah Nutara, Thamoosie Amagoalik, Philipoosie Novalinga, Samuel Arnakallak, and Moses Kayak during one of the first caribou hunts.
CREDIT: Bob Pilot

Craig Harbour, sometime between 1953 and 1955.
CREDIT: Bob Pilot

My uncle Philipoosie Novalinga, who prevented my brother Samwillie from being separated from his family, in 1954 or 1955.
CREDIT: Bob Pilot

(Left/Below) My brother Samwillie during a caribou hunt in the early years on Lindstrom Peninsula.
CREDIT: Bob Pilot

Samuel Arnakallak's wife, Qaumajuk (left), and
grandmother, Mukpanu (right), who convinced
her grandson to leave Lindstrom Peninsula. Photo
taken around 1956, in the second place we lived on
Lindstrom.
CREDIT: Bob Pilot

Special Constable Lazarus Kayak (left) and
Thamoosie Amagoalik (right) with an RCMP
boat at Craig Harbour in 1954 or 1955.
CREDIT: Bob Pilot

Thamoosie Amagoalik (foreground) and Josephie
Flaherty (background) during a caribou hunt in the
mid- to late 1950s.
CREDIT: Bob Pilot

From left to right: Elisapee, me, my mother, Elijah,
and Minnie, Christmas 1955 or 1956.
CREDIT: Bob Pilot

Allie (left back), Salluviniq (left front), Mary Thamoosie (middle), Charlie (middle front), and Thamoosie Amagoalik (right), Christmas 1955 or 1956.
CREDIT: Bob Pilot

From a spring hunting trip in 1955 or 1956, somewhere in the area between Craig Harbour and Fram Fiord.
CREDIT: Bob Pilot

RCMP detachment at Grise Fiord, probably around 1956.
CREDIT: Bob Pilot

My mother in the second place we lived on
Lindstrom.
CREDIT: Bob Pilot

Me at age seven or eight outside of our tent on
Lindstrom Peninsula.
CREDIT: Bob Pilot

Joatamie, Ikumak, and Lizzie, before Joatamie
became an RCMP Constable.
CREDIT: Bob Pilot

Ikumak and Joatamie getting ready to leave after a
spring trading trip.
CREDIT: Bob Pilot

My ningauk Pauloosie Killiktee in the mid-1950s,
before he met my sister Minnie.
CREDIT: Roger Killiktee photo collection

Pauloosie chipping off ice for water in
Alexandra Fiord.
CREDIT: Roger Killiktee photo
collection

Louisa Elijasialuk, Samwillie's wife.
CREDIT: Family photo collection

Group shot from the early years on Lindstrom Peninsula. From left to right: Ikumak, Joatamie (holding me), my mother, Minnie, Elisapee, Annie Novalinga, Glenn Sargent, Philipoosie, Allie Amagoalik, Rhoda Arnakallak, and Moses Kayak.
CREDIT: Bob Pilot

Isa Naqtai (background), Akpaliapik (left), and Elijah (right) getting trade goods from Resolute Bay, sometime around 1958.
CREDIT: Bob Pilot

Akpaliapik (centre) in
northwest Greenland in the
late 1950s, with Inuhuit hunter
Qaviganguaq (right) and
Qaviganguaq's wife (left).
CREDIT: Bob Pilot

Inuhuit hunters in Grise
Fiord, 1958. From left to
right: Sigluk Miunge, Maja
Petersson, Qaulluqtuq
Miunge, and Massauna
Petersson.
CREDIT: Bob Pilot

My ningauk Pauloosie between Brume Point and Lee Point on the way to Fram Fiord on an annual caribou hunt.
CREDIT: Bob Pilot

Annual caribou hunt to Fram Fiord, 1959 or 1960. Elijah standing at the back, Lazarus Kayak in front of him, Isa Naqtai leaning, and Moses Kayak at the front of the boat.
CREDIT: Bob Pilot

From left to right: Elijah Nutara, Inootsiak Muckpa, Josephie Koonoo, Simon Akpaliapik, Mososie Naqtai, Pauloosie Killiktee, Ookookoo Quaraq, and Imooshee Nutaraqjuk, between 1958 and 1960 during sealift time. My brother Elijah is smiling here. He was happy when Pauloosie was still alive.
CREDIT: Killiktee family photo collection

My brother Elijah Nutara with his accordion in the early 1960s.
CREDIT: Killiktee family photo collection

Little Sam Killiktee, early 1960s.
CREDIT: Killiktee family photo collection

Seeglook Akeeagok (left), Josie Nowra (centre back), Sam Killiktee (centre front), and Peter Flaherty, mid-1960s.
CREDIT: Killiktee family photo collection

Isa Naqtai with his daughters Sarah and Maggie on Lindstrom Peninsula, sometime before 1962.
CREDIT: Minnie Killiktee photo collection

(Above) Glenn Sargent, Bob Pilot, Lazarus Kayak, and Josephie Flaherty on the 2,000-metre ice cap on Devon Island, late 1950s or early 1960s.
CREDIT: Bob Pilot

(Right) Me (right) and Sam Killiktee (left) with a sealskin in Grise Fiord, 1967.
CREDIT: Minnie Killiktee photo collection

Minnie Killiktee and little Sam, not long after Pauloosie's death in 1962, just before the move to Grise Fiord.
CREDIT: Bob Pilot

My cousin Elisapee and Louisa Elijasialuk, around 1963–64, in front of their home in Grise Fiord.
CREDIT: Minnie Killiktee photo collection

Mososie Naqtai (right) with his wife and his daughter, Nellie, in front of their home in Grise Fiord, 1963.
CREDIT: Minnie Killiktee photo collection

Schoolteachers leaving Grise Fiord on a Nordair plane, 1963 or 1964.
CREDIT: Bob Pilot

Minnie Killiktee, 1963 or 1964.
CREDIT: Minnie Killiktee photo collection

Sam Killiktee, 1963.
CREDIT: Minnie Killiktee photo collection

Minnie and me, 1965 or 1966, in Grise Fiord.
CREDIT: Minnie Killiktee photo collection

The two Samwillies, my nephew and my brother. A rare moment when my brother was standing still.
CREDIT: Minnie Killiktee photo collection

Elijah Nutara during a fishing trip to Makinson Inlet in May 1968.
CREDIT: Family photo collection

Me in a photo booth in Winnipeg in 1969 or 1970.
CREDIT: Larry Audlaluk

Me in Winnipeg, 1975.
CREDIT: Annie Audlaluk

Me with my first dog team in the mid-1970s,
untangling their harnesses.
CREDIT: Annie Audlaluk

Me, mid-1970s, on a Ski-Doo.
CREDIT: Larry Audlaluk, taken with a self-timer.

My sister Anna with her husband, Paulassie Nungaq, and
their son Joanasie in Grise Fiord, 1979.
CREDIT: Annie Audlaluk

Samwillie in Grise Fiord in the mid-1980s.
CREDIT: Larry Audlaluk

Group family photo taken in the mid-1980s. My
brothers and sisters and their children.
CREDIT: Family photo collection

From left to right: Samwillie, Elijah, and Anna.
CREDIT: Family photo collection

My dog team in the early 1990s.
CREDIT: Annie Audlaluk

Me during the height of the relocation hearings in the 1990s. Here, I am putting on a face for the camera.
CREDIT: Annie Audlaluk

This photo of me was also taken during the relocation hearings, but here, you can see how I actually felt at the time.
CREDIT: Annie Audlaluk

My wife, Annie, in the late 1990s or early 2000s.
CREDIT: Larry Audlaluk

Present-day Grise Fiord.
CREDIT: Vincent Desrosiers

Me in Nuuk, Greenland, in May 2018, providing
entertainment during the Pikialasorsuaq
Commission Knowledge Workshop.
CREDIT: Vincent Desrosiers

A Family of Widows

*T*he passing of our beloved ningauk Pauloosie is one of the saddest chapters in Inujjuarmiut family history. Just as I have told the story of our lives with him, I will tell what I remember of his passing. I never liked to delve into it, yet it has to be told.

The RCMP discouraged my family and the rest of the relocatees from hunting near Fram Fiord, including the Lee Point area. Caribou were hunted only in September each year and only under RCMP supervision. We were told we could hunt Peary caribou west of Lindstrom Peninsula any time of the year, but Fram Fiord was a very restricted area. I remember a caribou was taken one summer from somewhere near Harbour Fiord, and my family told me to keep my mouth shut. It was a very hush-hush affair.

The hunters in our area had heard about caribou being available in the western area of Ellesmere Island, near Goose Fiord. Four hunters, Elijah, Pauloosie, and Mososie and Isa Naqtai, left sometime in late March or early April of 1962. Goose Fiord is about 160 kilometres away from Grise Fiord in a straight line. By dog team, at an average of thirty kilometres a day, that worked out to five nights. The caribou hunt to Goose Fiord was the first time I had ever known hunters to travel that far away. There were trails to the Baumann Fiord area through Goose Fiord, and routes the special constables used, but nobody from Grise Fiord had discovered them yet.

The day they left, Minnie and I followed her husband to the first trapline, three kilometres west of where we lived. The trapline at Naqsakuluk, or 8 Mile

Valley, was the closest to home, and the women of our community had traps there throughout the trapping season. When it was time to part company, my sister went with her husband's sled to say goodbye while I waited. She had their son Sam, who was a month short of his second birthday, in her amauti. She said, "I did not want to leave the sled. My husband said he took all of his medication with him, saying he was going to be very healthy when he came back. He told me I better get off, otherwise I was going to have to walk too far. I did not want to get off. I just wanted to be with him." It was the last time she saw her husband alive.

I remember clearly that it was still daylight when we got home. I don't know how long the hunters were away, but we celebrated Easter before they came back. We'd never had Easter celebrations before, but that spring the first celebration games were held on the ice. We'd held games during Christmastime, but always indoors. Special Constable Ningyou was in charge. We hadn't been on the ice very long when we noticed a dog team approaching. Everyone walked over to see who it was. It was Isa, his empty sled turned upside down to anchor the dogs and keep them from running off. He looked at Ningyou and shouted, "We have lost someone!"

Ningyou asked, "*Kina?*" Who?

Then, Isa uttered the most painful word, which I will never forget for as long as I live: "Pauloosie!"

Elijah's account of what happened was painful to hear, but it's only right that I tell what I heard.

Shortly after arriving at the end of Goose Fiord, before they had even made camp, the hunters saw a herd of caribou and harvested them right away, planning to hunt for more the next day. It was a joyful time.

Elijah recalled with tears in his eyes, "My ningauk seemed the happiest. Even when his mannguat got bloody, he did not seem to care. He just laughed at his bloody footwear as if it was the funniest thing. What struck me with sadness afterwards was that he caught a young fawn he said would be for his son to play with. He became ill shortly after, very quickly."

He fell sick the same night and was quickly confined to bed. Elijah expressed his alarm and wanted to head for home. Of course, the Naqtai brothers were not receptive to heading back at first, not yet having had a chance to go hunting as they had planned. It was also not the first time Pauloosie had become ill while out hunting. In fact, one summer one of the doctors on the *C.D. Howe* had told him he needed to go to a hospital for medical attention, and he had refused. He was given medication instead of going away for an operation. But as he had always recovered before, the brothers were not immediately alarmed.

Several nights later, in the middle of the night while they were camped, Elijah was awakened by the sound of someone calling him.

"Ningauk!" It was the voice of Pauloosie, who always called Elijah "brother-in-law." When Elijah got up to check on his sick companion, he seemed to be asleep. He checked his cheeks, and they were cold. Elijah knew he was gone.

The men had to head back, now with three sleds, one of which carried the body of Pauloosie Killiktee. Seeing the body home was Elijah's responsibility, on top of which he had two sets of dogs to manage. Goose Fiord is often windy, and it is one the longest fiords on the southwest coast of Ellesmere Island. It has very little snow on the surface of the ice in the winter because of the frequent winds. I've travelled there in the summer as well, and it's just as windy. A huge storm had arisen, and my brother described how he literally had to hang on to the sled for dear life during the blizzard while trying to get out of the fiord. They must have encountered gale force winds. I get tears in my eyes even while writing this story. The men did not make camp once the entire trip home! One can only imagine the weight Elijah carried on his shoulders.

My brother had to explain everything to Pauloosie's parents, his wife, and to all of us. I never heard Elijah tell the story again. Roger Killiktee told me that after Elijah had moved back to Inujjuak in 1989, he sent Elijah a blank cassette tape and asked him to record the story, and he did, although I'm not sure where the tape is now.

When we heard the news, we all went to Ningyou's house to mourn. I don't remember the trip home. I was too stricken with grief. The pain was back; the same pain I felt when my father, my two best friends, and Pauloosie and Minnie's first child died. I can't forget my mother lamenting, "Seems to me my family is destined to be a family of widows; why?"

Some of the saddest moments were after two-year-old Sam noticed his father was not around. We would cry when he opened the door, looking to see if his father was coming back on his dog team, calling out, "*Ataata!*"

Corporal Terry Jenkins investigated the cause of Pauloosie's death. It was found that his appendix had burst, and the toxic contents had spread throughout his body. The right side of his thigh was dark blue! Markoosie Innualuk is said to have remembered that my mother suspected Pauloosie had been murdered. She even looked for bullet holes in the body. Of course, when my brother told us exactly what had happened, her mind was put to rest.

This was the first time we learned that in the Baffin region, unlike Nunavik, families took their departed loved one's things. We gave all of Pauloosie's hunting equipment to the Killiktee family, with the exception of the fair exchange of his canoe for a wooden boat they had. The boat and canoe stayed in use until the 1980s. Aksakjuk Ningiuk inherited Pauloosie's dog team, but the team was never as fast as I remembered them before his death. It seemed they slowed down to a walk from their pacing speed. As is part of our tradition, and common practice even today, I believe dogs should be put down if their master dies.

The worst thing was the way Pauloosie was buried. It had a lasting effect on all our lives, including on some of his siblings. Only four men attended the funeral: Elijah, Thamoosie (who read the burial text), Ookookoo Quaraq (who donated the plywood and built the coffin), and one RCMP officer. "I carried that plywood from our camp strapped to my back," Ookookoo said. "He had been one of my good friends. I was honoured to help in a time of sadness."

"My father told us he was not going to attend his son's funeral at Lindstrom Peninsula. He told our family he felt it would be better this way," said Roger Killiktee. Nobody else attended the funeral. It was one of the strangest events. Even my mother and uncle did nothing to stress the importance of attending. I'm not sure why. I have come to realize that we did not have proper closure with one of the most beloved members of our clan. I was angry with Ningyou for many years for this, but I never had the guts to tell him so. He may not have been in agreement with Pauloosie's marriage to a former Inujjuarmiuq in the first place. After all, Pauloosie had been on his way to Pond Inlet to find a wife when my brother took him home; Ningyou may have wanted Pauloosie to marry someone from Pond Inlet instead. When Ningyou was in his eighties, a few years before he passed on, he came to visit Grise Fiord for the last time. When my chance came to tell him, I suddenly saw how frail he had become. I silently forgave him without saying anything.

For many years, I dreamed Pauloosie was still alive. Sometimes I would awaken crying because I had dreamt about his death. The dreams indicated that I had never properly grieved at his grave. In the early 1990s, Levi Killiktee came to me asking if I could look into having a minister come in to do a proper burial procession over his brother's grave on Lindstrom Peninsula. It would be another few years before we could grant his wish. Sadly, Levi himself had passed on by the time we finally got Caleb Sangoya of Pond Inlet to read the funeral passages from the Anglican prayer book. Finally, my sister and I could cry at this second ceremony. The family from Pauloosie Killiktee included Josephie Koonoo, Qaumajuannu Koonoo, Isigaittuq Phillip, Roger Killiktee, and their families. Ever since the ceremony, my spirit has been at peace. Attend funeral services of loved ones if you can.

Family dynamics are so much better when in-laws are there to make life stronger for the whole family. Life when our brother-in-law Pauloosie Killiktee was with us was so much better. After he died, I saw our family unity start to fall apart. It was so sad to see it start to unravel almost from day one. All of a sudden my brother Elijah seemed to have lost his right arm, he looked so dejected. He had to start all over trying to find a hunting companion he was comfortable with. Life completely changed after our ningauk died. In May, we started getting ready to move to Grise Fiord. It was a welcome distraction.

12

A New Era

In the late 1950s, the government started telling Inuit families living in their traditional homes to move to the existing trading posts in the Eastern Arctic. The families were told that schools would be built in these places. Some Inuit were told it was mandatory to move, or else family allowances, old age pensions, and other benefits would be stopped. When we first heard a school was going to be built in Grise Fiord, everyone thought we would all go to school from where we lived, travelling each day by dog team in the winter and by boat during ice-free months to attend classes. But we were also required to move. Like all changes, it was exciting. It was such a new concept, and the subject of much discussion. The school building supplies were dropped off at the edge of the pond next to the RCMP staff houses in Grise Fiord. I remember Roger Killiktee telling me what all the building material was for while I played outside with him during trading trips in the winters of 1961 and 1962.

Before we moved from Lindstrom Peninsula, our parents were very excited about the school coming and the fact that their children were going to attend. I remember Simon Akpaliapik one time while he was visiting telling my brother how classes were to be conducted. He told us how it was necessary for students to put their arms up each day when they came into class. He demonstrated by putting both arms up like someone in a cowboy movie who had a gun pointed at them. When we started school, the teacher would do roll calls. We'd sometimes raise our right hand in response. I smile when I think of how Akpaliapik understood it.

Before we moved, in late April or early May, a filmmaker arrived to make a story about life in the High Arctic. He arrived with the annual RCMP visit in their de Havilland single Otter aircraft. Constable Bob Bacchus and Corporal Terry Jenkins were the police in charge of the Grise Fiord detachment at the time. We were told the filmmaker was going to come scout for actors to be in his film. I remember my mother's excitement at the prospect of being in a film.

My family had been involved with cinematography for quite a long time. My uncle Philipoosie got a part in the North's first feature film, *Nanook of the North*, by Robert Flaherty. It was filmed in Inujjuak in 1920. It's ironic that the very first film ever made about Inuit was filmed near where I was born. In the movie, Philipoosie is playing tug-of-war with another boy using an ujjuk flipper. He was thirteen at the time. He and his wife remembered that Robert Flaherty had to film the movie twice because the first version accidentally burned during the editing process. In 1966, our teacher Roger Cousins brought in the movie and showed it to everyone in the community. My uncle would get up to point out on the screen who was who. It was interesting to watch with someone who was there during the filming.

I have never really cared for *Kabloonak,* the movie about the making of *Nanook of the North*, starring Charles Dance as Robert Flaherty and one of my cousins, Adamie Inukpuk, as Nanook. The film has some good cinematography, but I don't care about the story. Like any typical Hollywood-type production, it portrays Inuit as drunks at a party. Robert Flaherty is portrayed as a womanizer and some-one who was making Inuit get drunk. My uncle remembers Robert Flaherty quite differently. To him, Robert Flaherty was a man who was great with children, often making homemade candies out of molasses, a skill my family still practiced when I was growing up on Lindstrom Peninsula. He was also my stepbrother Josephie's biological father. Josephie's mother, the Inuk actress who played "Nyla" in *Nanook of the North,* married my father's younger brother Elijasie. When Elijasie died, my father adopted Josephie, as well as their daughter Leetia.

Since I was a boy, I have been fascinated by film cameras and still photog-raphy. It comes from Corporal Sargent and Constable Bob Pilot at the Craig Harbour and Grise Fiord detachments. They were into black-and-white film developing. Leah Qumangaapik and Mary Panigusiq would send photos to my family with their father, Special Constable Kayak, whenever he visited Lindstrom Peninsula. My interest in movies and photography as an art form was kindled at an early age. It was probably further embedded after watching *Nanook of the North*.

Mom made her children wear our best outdoor clothes the day the RCMP plane landed on the ice. There was much excitement in the air. I suppose the memory of *Nanook of the North* may still have been fresh in my family's mind. The chosen cast included Simon Akpaliapik and Louisa Elijasialuk, with Ookookoo Quaraq as Akpaliapik's son-in-law, married to Louisa. My mother played Thamoosie Amagoalik's wife. The cast also included Markoosie Innualuk as one of the storytellers mentoring young Imooshee Nutaraqjuk, and even my sister Minnie and young Sam were extras. They shot at several locations, including Lee Point, Brume Point, and the floe edge in front of Craig Harbour.

The film starts with Ookookoo going to the Grise Fiord detachment to report the illness of a child at Lindstrom. An RCMP patrol, led by Ningyou Killiktee, leaves Grise Fiord for Lindstrom Peninsula to attend to the sick child. On the trail, the teams have to camp. It was funny to see them put caribou skins on the ground outdoors, sleeping in the open with bare chests and just their caribou pants on. I don't know why the filmmaker decided to do this. It is true that in specific conditions, in twenty-four-hour daylight when it's not windy, it's not necessary to put up a tent—but it was still funny.

Constable Bacchus was said to have gotten tired of the producer's demands throughout the film shoot. After the filmmaker left, the move to Grise Fiord started in earnest.

* * *

Most of the houses from Lindstrom Peninsula were moved to the raised beach east of the school in the present-day Grise Fiord community. In May, our little homes were placed on top of sleds and taken by dog team. It took two sleds for each house. I will always remember travelling by dog team to Grise Fiord with Samwillie, Mom, and Alicee Nowra on a beautiful spring day, the Naqtai brothers travelling off to the southwest of us, with one of their houses being pulled by two dog teams. A new era for the relocatees had begun.

I don't remember when the construction crew came, but it must have been with the Nordair DC-3 charters in June that moved the RCMP transfers. The one-room school was a prefabricated type and easily put together. At the time, it seemed like such interesting technology. The crew first assembled what was to become the power plant for the school. They were in Grise Fiord the rest of the spring and summer. By late spring, one of the crew had been fired. With no other place to sleep, he stayed with the crew, but he did not shower often and smelled pretty bad. We started to call him *Mamanngittuq,* the smelly one. He was a nice person, though, and the people in the community liked him.

In late summer, an old military aircraft PBY flying boat arrived to pick up the crew and brought the electricians: Newkinga Kilabuk, Nutarariak "Jumbo" Evaluardjuk, and the chief electrician. The evening they arrived a big storm came up. A hole was punctured in one of the PBY's pontoons by the rocks at the shoreline, and the whole community was put to work to pull it up to shore for repairs near the police workshop.

One of the PBY crew members was cross-eyed. Mischievous Roger Killiktee let the poor man know it, making all kinds of faces at him. Roger had a characteristic trait that would get him into situations once in a while as a teenager; he was always up to something. He was older than most of us, so we would find ourselves in some difficult situations. When he teased the man, I felt embarrassed and scared, yet the man did nothing in response. Unfortunately, I'm sure he was used to being made fun of.

The *C.D. Howe*'s annual trip in 1962 brought our first government mechanic, Hallas Shaw, and his wife, as well as our first schoolteacher, Peter Scott, his wife Barbara Scott, and their two boys, Timmy and Larry. Civil servants rarely ever went home for holidays in those days, and the additions to our population were welcome.

Not long after the fall of 1962, electricity was introduced to the community. I remember visiting my uncle Philipoosie's home when Samwillie and Hallas came to the little house and installed the light bulb in the ceiling. With a flick of the switch on the wall near the door, presto—Mister General Electric had arrived! All of a sudden it seemed possible to see everything, even at night once the poles were fitted with streetlights. We can't imagine now how we lived up here without electricity before 1962.

Work for the RCMP had been the main source of income for Inuit for many years in the Grise Fiord area, although Inuit would sometimes be hired as guides by the Polar Continental Shelf Project. Zebedee Amagoalik, one of the Pond Inlet relocatees, was flown to Mould Bay with his whole family to be a guide. Mould Bay is located on one of the northernmost islands in the Northwest Territories. While they were there, one of his daughters became deathly ill. A medical evacuation aircraft was sent to take her to the nearest doctor. Sadly, before the aircraft arrived, she died. In the 1970s, a group of weather station personnel and researchers was stationed at Mould Bay. The cook would visit the little grave every day after work. She felt compassion for the deceased child and became very attached. Before leaving Mould Bay, she made up her mind to change her will. She wrote in her will that when she died, she wanted to be buried next to Zebedee's daughter to keep her company. In the early 2000s, her wish was granted. There is now a second grave next to the child's in Mould Bay.

When the school was opened, it needed maintenance, which meant more employment opportunities. Casual workers were required to haul ice for the water supply. Until proper equipment to haul ice was introduced, local dog teams and their owners were hired. The mechanic and his wife ran the power plant, but it needed a janitor to keep it clean. The plant needed servicing too, including fuelling the generators daily from the 45-gallon drums. When Samwillie went to Resolute Bay in the late 1950s, he gained valuable mechanical skills, so he was hired as the new school janitor. Quickly, the workload got to be too much for him. The government hired Markoosie Innualuk to clean the school and Samwillie ended up working at the power plant, the job he loved most. Hallas must have been impressed with his interest in generators. Eventually, Samwillie hired Ookookoo as a casual worker, and the two men became lifelong friends.

The territorial government introduced settlement life with low-rental housing, which required a board of directors elected by the local people. When the settlement council came, it was run the same way. The traditional homes we had left behind had been run in similar fashion as the "new" way of life the government was introducing to us. The social welfare system is nothing new to Inuit. Inuit always made sure nobody starved. Ever since we can remember, we have understood the importance of sharing food, helping those in need, and the concept that someday we too might be in the same situation. This philosophy is no different from the Biblical philosophy, "Do unto others as you would have them do unto you."

The low-rental housing program also provided new jobs, with workers needed to take out the "honey bucket" toilets, fill the heating fuel tanks, and deliver water. In 1968, two Bombardier Muskegs were brought in, each specially fitted with a wagon, and another machine with a fuel tank for diesel oil to service the houses. The first Housing Association Board was formed after the houses were built, and Elijah was the very first chairperson. He was given the task of going to each house at the end of every month to tell the tenants the responsibility they had to clean their homes. He and some other board members would inspect them the following day, after cleanup.

Square dances became a common event on Friday or Saturday nights at the Federal Day School in Grise Fiord. Dances were held occasionally when we lived on Lindstrom Peninsula, but we didn't have a proper dancing space. I remember only one such dance at my uncle's *qarmaq*. When we went to Grise Fiord during Christmas, the dances were held at the RCMP workshop and the porch of the staff houses. Elijah provided the dance music with his harmonica until 1956, when Alicee Naqtai joined with an accordion. With the new school, space was now available to hold square dances without the worry of overcrowding. It seemed there was now endless space to dance! We used the school record player for music. It was exclusively Don Messer records, and with the proper sound equipment, the fiddle tunes were nice and loud—so loud that you could hardly hear other people speak.

The best square dancers I have ever seen were Mososie, Isa, and Alicee. Even today when I watch dancers from different parts of the North in person or on TV, nobody can match their talent. I can still see that trio dancing: Mososie's head all sweaty with his long hair hanging down, eyes staring straight out, Isa a bit more kempt but equally talented, and Alicee, the best female dancer I had ever seen.

I tried to learn to play harmonica as well as my brother, but I could never match him. He had a style all his own. Had he lived during the computer age, I know a recording of his talent would have been of professional quality. For a long time, he was the only musician to host square dances. Each dance averaged thirty minutes, with about five dances in a night. He had learned to play tune after tune from start to finish over and over again to keep the music going continuously. Elijah's ability as a harmonica musician was a classic example of his "practice makes perfect" attitude. Later, he bought a guitar, and not long after that a piano accordion, but his real love was playing Yamaha keyboards.

That year, 1962, was also the first time most of us ever saw recreational ice skating. Our principal and the rest of the Scott family all had skates. The senior boys would take turns using the principal's skates. Those of us who couldn't fit into Timmy's skates would put on a pair of duffle socks and wear Mr. Scott's skates. The thrill of sliding on skates once you learned how! And the comfort of loose feet after you took the skates off! Roger ordered his own through the Eaton's catalogue, and he became my best friend when it came to skating. When the school got a supply of skates the following year, we could all find a pair that fit us properly. I had to get used to wearing skates that fit right, since my first impression was that wearing oversized skates with duffle socks was normal.

Our principal was an outdoorsman. He was also a Second World War veteran, and owned a custom .303 Lee Enfield rifle. He loved going out hunting. If a pod of whales swam by, he would leave our class so fast. The next thing we knew, he would be running down the beach with his rifle in one hand, wearing his green checkered jacket, black woollen hat, and hiking boots, with a pipe in his mouth. If you did not know it was him, you'd have thought he was just one of the local hunters running after the whales along the shore. Class dismissed!

In the spring, he would sit around with the men along the shore in front of the RCMP houses to wait for seals to come by. When a seal came up in front of the men, it was a race to see who would get it, although sometimes nobody knew who shot it. Peter Scott would fire away, albeit a few seconds slower than most of the rest of the men. After the smoke cleared, most of the men would burst out laughing at the slowness of his reaction. He laughed the loudest of all!

In the evenings after work, the men went hunting by boat, including the two Inuuk electricians from Iqaluit. It was the first time we heard Arctic char had been seen swimming at the end of Grise Fiord. It seemed incredible at the time, yet over the years, people from Grise Fiord have seen char swimming in front of the community. Our knowledge of our area was very limited, especially in those days.

When the snow came, ptarmigan would come out of hiding, blending in with their natural camouflage colours. As boys, we used to love going hunting for small game like ptarmigan and hare with Peter and Timmy on the nearby hills behind Grise Fiord. Although other boys would come along on occasion, most often it was just me and Imooshee who accompanied the father and son. After we came back to their apartment, we'd clean our rifles and have cookies and hot chocolate as we talked about our adventure. Boy, those cookies sure tasted good. Of all the times I went with them, Timmy never once shot a hare.

Ningyou once told a story about hosting a hunting trip with Peter and Timmy one summer. Seals can be very plentiful some summers around Jones Sound, especially in the fiords. Hunters never put fish nets out in the sea for fear of seals getting caught and damaging the nets. With so many seals coming up in all directions of the canoe, Peter Scott, not realizing they would have to come back up to breathe, would shoot without aiming before they went back down. The son and father were using a military direction system where Timmy would say, "Dad, six o'clock!" *BANG!* "Dad, twelve o'clock!" *BANG!* "Dad, three o'clock!" *BANG!* He couldn't hit any of them. Ningyou thought it was hilarious to watch! He said it was so comical to watch the teacher shooting away at seals, never hitting any.

When the ice is newly formed in September, there is no snow to obscure the agluit, and they are easy to spot. Polar bears can find them easily, which makes September an ideal time in Grise Fiord to go polar bear hunting—they're all close to the community, looking for seals. In the fall of 1962, it was no surprise when a medium-sized polar bear was sighted near the little islands across from Grise Fiord. The men took off on foot, rifles in hand. Our principal was with them (in those days, even Qallunaat could shoot polar bears). When he saw the men running on the ice with their rifles, he had run to his apartment to put on his hunting clothes and grab his rifle. Ookookoo was the hunter of the day, and people stood around the fallen King of the North to admire the first bear of the season. Just before going back to class, Mr. Scott said that he had been so excited that he forgot to put on his outer pants, and pointed out to everyone how he was dressed: just his shoes and long johns. Everyone burst out in laughter!

Timmy Scott was the quiet one of the two boys. He loved to draw pencil sketches. I used to love watching him draw aerial combat scenes. Boys being boys, one will test another's skill in physical abilities like wrestling. I could never beat him, no matter how hard I tried. Larry Scott was quick to get into trouble, and seemed often to get into fights with his peers. He may have been the one to teach the rest of us how to fist fight.

Those of us who were eight years old and up found it difficult to stay in school all day long, from 9:00 a.m. to 3:15 p.m. It was most difficult to concentrate on school lessons when the weather was good outside. Roger and Imooshee would get into mischief the most often in our class. It was funny how Imooshee would call Mrs. Scott *Nikujjaaqtuqtuq*, which means "the one who walks with her heels raised." People who wear high-heeled shoes can develop a habit of walking with their heels raised even if they are wearing just sealskin slippers. Imooshee would imitate her walking style when she wasn't looking, and the class would burst out laughing. One day, Imooshee was doing his imitation walk behind her, and the principal caught him. The class started to snicker and at the same time, Mr. Scott looked up. "IMOOSHEE!" he yelled. Of course, Imooshee earned an hour of detention after school, which included cleaning the chalkboard.

Roger's practical jokes were of a more serious nature. He was once sent to the RCMP by the principal for poking Timmy in his rear end. I remember Timmy being very upset, to the point of tears. It was the first time I ever saw him so upset. I don't know what the visit to the RCMP yielded at the time, but today, with very little tolerance for any type of assault, he could have easily been charged and taken to court.

The Scott family left Grise Fiord a couple of years later. I was in the south for medical reasons when they left. When I got back, Imooshee told me Timmy had finally shot a hare. In 2000, we were finally able to get in touch with the family. Seeglook and Mimi Akeeagok received a letter from them, and we learned that Larry Scott had passed on many years prior. It was such hard news to get.

* * *

Before school came, at least in our region, it was common for non-Inuit to learn the Inuktitut language because most Inuit did not understand English. It was necessary if they were to be able to communicate. Some were fast learners, while others took much longer to pick up our language, but it was common for most to become quite fluent, with very little accent. As youngsters, we used to imitate some Qallunaat who had terrible accents, although the RCMP were the only Qallunaat we saw the first nine years we lived on Lindstrom Peninsula, and most of them spoke like ordinary Inuit. I don't recall if any of the schoolteachers or the Department of Public Works staff ever learned to speak Inuktitut; however, Timmy and Larry became so fluent you would not have known they were not Inuit. Larry especially got so good it was uncanny to listen to him speak. He played with a group of boys who spoke Inuktitut exclusively.

When school started, our principal hired Louisa Elijasialuk to be the school interpreter. Her job lasted only a very short time as we learned to speak English quickly. And in the Grise Fiord area, most of my generation already knew how to read and write syllabics from the Eastern Arctic Holy Bible and the prayer book written by the Diocese of the Arctic.

At first, the changes were welcome. And they came rapidly. As an eleven-year-old youngster, I now had more play-friends, which was exciting. There were more varied store goods and canned goods, and frequent mail service started not long after the move, although the annual Christmas drop would continue for a couple more years. The community of Grise Fiord grew, with new buildings being put up, and more manpower needed to maintain them. It was a new lifestyle. But our parents quickly realized that the long-held tradition of passing on one's knowledge of hunting, sewing, and other skills was under threat. Boys could no longer go with their fathers whenever they wanted. It was necessary to make special arrangements with the principal to be allowed to miss classes, although, unlucky me, I was still too sick with frequent eye trouble to go out hunting like some of the boys.

Inuit throughout the North experienced the same change. The transition from the hunting and gathering way of life to the "modern" way of life had a very high price tag. Education was offered at "no cost" to Canadians, including Inuit, yet the "no cost" system was the most expensive: the price was a way of life lost. It meant Inuit parents giving up control of their children to strangers (teachers) who did not know nor care to understand their pupils' way of life. In fact, for many, their mission was to eradicate it. Survival skills on the land, sea, and ice, honed and preserved with some of the strictest guidelines in one of the harshest environments in the world, were lost in a mere forty years in some regions. I watched some fathers going out on hunting trips alone. When we lived on Lindstrom Peninsula, it was normal to see their sons sitting on a sled behind them. The mothers suffered similar frustrations, not only with passing on their sewing skills, but with other important skills, such as being a midwife and knowledge of traditional medicine. There is a whole generation of women who don't know what their mothers knew about child rearing.

After I started going to school in Fort Churchill, Manitoba, when I was older, I remember my brother Elijah asking when I would finish school. I answered, "I don't know yet, brother. Sometime soon, but I can't tell you when yet." He did not say much in protest and fell silent, but I could read his face and body language. He never asked me again after that. I felt helpless not being able to help him when he went out on the land. It's one of many things I regret, not having been with him when he was out on the trail.

13

Montreal

The year 1963 was a year of many changes for Grise Fiord, me, and the world. In fact, the 1960s has been considered a decade of change by many historians—although, unfortunately, it was also a time when children in our community were stricken with whooping cough. The illness claimed the life of Isa Naqtai's six-month-old daughter. I was not prepared to face yet another death, but then, who is ever prepared? A few months before the tragedy, my uncle had caught a polar bear by chasing it on foot. For a while people said the polar bear had brought the sickness upon our settlement. What we sometimes do to justify bad things when they happen.

It became normal to see jets flying by in the direction of Iceland. A jet would appear from the southwest. Sometimes another one would appear from the southeast and connect with the first, flying together for a while, then flying back toward where it came from while the first one would continue, going directly over Grise Fiord. They may have been using the Grise Fiord non-directional beacon to navigate. What we saw could very well have been linked directly with the Cuban Missile Crisis that peaked in 1962.

Regular mail service started in 1964 when Welland "Weldy" Phipps formed Atlas Aviation to cater to the High Arctic communities. He had first gone to Resolute Bay a few years after the Polar Continental Shelf Project was formed when he flew for a charter company based out of Edmonton and ferried one of their single-engine aircraft to Resolute. In the summer of 1963, we saw just how skilled he was as an off-strip pilot when he came up on a medical evacuation mission and landed the little single-engine, canvas-covered aircraft on the beach in front of Grise Fiord at low tide. In late September, when the daylight was disappearing in twenty-minute increments each day, he repeated the feat once again, only this time on the ice. In 1964, he had a little dirt strip made four kilometres east of our community. It was always an exciting event when he came to bring passengers and mail once every two or three weeks in the spring and summer. He landed on the ice in the spring and on the little dirt strip when it was snow-free. People would walk the distance to the strip just to watch the spectacle of an aircraft landing. Even my sister Anna, though she could not walk, was carried to the little airstrip to see the scheduled flight come and go. Weldy Phipps started coming at first with a single Beaver aircraft and later with a single Otter. Dick Deblique was his chief pilot later. We called him "the one with a pipe," *Supuuqtuutilik*.

* * *

In 1963, my eye injury became a problem once more, although the pain was not as intense as before. I could not look at the fluorescent light in the schoolhouse during the dark season. Fluorescent light has the same effect as sunlight on my injured eye, even today. As a result, I missed a lot of school, although I enjoyed it when my classmates would come bring my schoolwork after classes.

My brother Joatamie had left the RCMP, and his family had arrived on the CCGS *Labrador*, the only ship that could go to Alexandra Fiord. The family had lived in Alexandra Fiord since they left to join Joatamie after he started work as a special constable. I was excited to see my niece Lizzie once again after seven years. I was very happy to see them home once again—only to learn that due to my eye, I would be leaving on the *C.D. Howe* on its annual visit. I remember thinking, *My niece Lizzie is back and now I have to leave! Fate sometimes can be so cruel!*

During the summer of 1963, one of the interpreters on the ship was Parnee Noah. I remember noticing that she was wearing a sealskin jacket. The voyage started off terribly. Before I left, the dentist removed a lot of my teeth and did not use enough freezing. I cried out with each pull, and he slapped my face to quiet me down, ignoring my pleas to numb my mouth. It hurt so much afterward, and the bleeding started again during the first week of our voyage from Grise Fiord. I remember the ship headed in a straight line towards Devon Island on calm seas. Then suddenly, I was so seasick I feel I would have died had it not been for Parnee's help. I could not eat anything solid, so she would bring me noodle soup and literally spoon-feed me. I am eternally thankful to her, even now. I stayed in bed for almost ten days from seasickness and sore gums.

After we were past Resolution Island, we had to stop because of fog and snow. The ship was completely covered in snow. While the ship was waiting for the weather to clear, a whole flock of ptarmigan landed on the upper part of the ship. The crew had a field day catching as much as they could for food. The birds were dead tired from their migration and were easy prey. We heard later that the cook was very happy to offer a change in the menu.

As we passed by the southeast corner of the coast of Labrador, we experienced very rough seas. An Atlantic storm hit the coastline of the area with some of the highest rough waters. It was the middle of the night. All the lights were turned off and we were in the pitch dark in bed in the front quarters. When the front of the boat hit the waves head on, we would've flown off if not for the safety racks of our beds. The kitchen's pots and pans were flying all over the floor, an awful racket that made sleep impossible all through the night.

The next morning everyone was up on deck, all excited to see the houses in the towns we were passing along the coast before we entered the Saint Lawrence between Newfoundland and Quebec. I had seen trees before, the first time I had gone south, and I realized I was happy to see them again. Even today, I like being in a city in autumn because of this very joyful sight. To see leaves changing colour in Canada is an experience tourists come from around the world to view. It was interesting to hear the other Inuit passengers "ooh" and "ahh" upon seeing forest for the first time.

The weather was so beautiful when we arrived in Quebec City. Suddenly the *C.D. Howe* did not seem so big, looking back at it docked at a pier. We had never seen such infrastructure as there was at the edge of the Saint Lawrence River. So many buildings and other man-made things compared to the open country we were used to. We were taken to a train station for a train ride to Montreal; it was one of the highlights of the journey.

My memory fades after the train ride. I ended up in a boarding home where only a few other people were staying. It was an old building. The man in charge was grey-haired and elderly. He told me I was going to sleep in the same bed with him. I knew right away what he was up to and spoke up in protest. Speaking out against authority, let alone Qallunaat, was not common in those days, but I knew something was not right. Memories of the experience I'd had with the man in Pangnirtung were still very fresh. I told him there were plenty of other rooms upstairs, but he did not listen. Just as I feared, during the night, he tried to molest me. When I shouted my protests, he backed off and left me alone. I was so relieved the next day when I was picked up by a social worker and taken to billet with an English-speaking Montreal family for the remainder of my time in medical care.

I never forgot the Dobinson family, who took care of me as one of their own. Mr. Dobinson worked at a train yard. George, the younger of the two Dobinson sons, was eighteen or nineteen. I used to enjoy listening to his record collection. One album I particularly liked was by Montana Slim. When I came back to Montreal for hospital care the third time, a few years later, George gave me the album. His older brother Brian was married and lived in another part of Montreal.

Brian Dobinson and his wife used to drive me around in their little Volkswagen. I always told them their car sounded like it was crying, with its distinct engine sound. I loved being given a tour of the city. I enjoyed being shown skyscrapers, bridges, roads, highways, the asphalt jungle of Montreal. It seemed Montreal was a world all on its own, and as a thirteen-year-old boy, the scenery was dazzling! It was around that time that escalators were introduced to the city. Wow, what new technology! It seemed as if I were in one of Isaac Asimov's fictional futuristic books!

My time with the Dobinson family gave me a glimpse into how southern Canadians lived. I felt safe and secure, and all those houses around us helped make the feeling of security real. My real home seemed millions of miles away on another planet! I drank in everything around me with gusto. Unlike during the trip south I took in 1958, I don't remember being homesick for Grise Fiord. I enjoyed playing in the backyards of our neighbourhood with some of the neighbourhood boys. When I started going to school, I would walk to classes with a boy named Johnny, who lived in the same neighbourhood. Johnny's parents were of Indigenous origin. Since he was younger, I was rather rough with him sometimes. Walking to school every day taught me how to cross streets safely. Since English was my second language, I was not required to attend French classes. Not realizing I was missing an opportunity to learn the language, I enjoyed the daily "free periods." I now regret having missed the chance to learn.

There was a corner store just down the street from where we lived. I enjoyed going there on errands for the Dobinson family. I would be given money to buy cigarettes and a new *TV Guide* once a week for them. I had to give back the bills, but I could keep the coin change to buy what I wanted. With a quarter, I could buy a twelve-cent comic book, a ten-cent soda pop (Coca-Cola), and be able to save the extra three cents for the next week, so I could buy a six-cent bag of candies—or wait until I had saved enough pennies. I was always guaranteed twenty-five cents for running errands, although I would get more once in a while. I never failed to buy a comic book each week, though. By Christmastime, I had a good collection. Since the classic comic books cost fifteen cents—sometimes twenty-five—I would sometimes save my change to buy them.

I loved watching television in the evenings when prime time shows were on. We would watch shows like *The Fugitive, Bonanza, The Rebel,* and *The Carol Burnett Show.* On Saturday nights: Hockey Night in Canada. I was a Montreal Habs fan at that time, when hockey legends like Stan Maikita, Jean Béliveau, and the Richard brothers were playing. On Sundays, a Walt Disney movie was shown at 5:00 p.m. and 7:00 p.m., and we never missed *The Ed Sullivan Show.*

I did not start going to school until after Christmas, so I would spend time watching cartoons during the day. Most of those who remember the assassination of John F. Kennedy can tell you exactly what they were doing and where they were when it happened. As for me, I remember that I was at home alone watching cartoons. All of a sudden, the test pattern with the drawing of the Indian (as they said then) wearing a feather headdress appeared on the screen. Next, Walter Cronkite from CBS was on, with "NEWS BULLETIN" written in bold letters across the screen. I did not understand right away what was going on, yet I remember exactly what was said as clearly as if it had been said today, even though it has been more than fifty years: "The President of the United States has been shot!" Eyewitnesses tearfully described what they had seen. There are two particular witnesses that I have always remembered from that day. One was a woman who was crying so much you could hardly understand what she was saying. The other was a soldier who was there on leave with his family. His wife was wearing those white-framed sunglasses that were in style at the time, and they had two children with them. The soldier was giving his assessment of the situation, pointing to where he had heard the gunshots coming from. I remember how sure he seemed of what he heard and saw. It was obvious his military training had taught him how to react in dangerous situations.

* * *

That Christmas stands out as one of best I'd ever had. My mom had instilled in me the meaning of Christmas as the time of the birth of Jesus Christ. I noticed the Dobinson family did not celebrate the holiday the same way as my family did. I did not dwell on the differences for too long when the Dobinsons gave me my presents. I had never had toy guns before. When I was eleven, little Sam Killiktee was given toy guns from the Eaton's catalogue, and I was green with envy. As children in Grise Fiord, we could not go to a department store to buy toys. With the Dobinsons, I could finally have my own toy guns. I was in a toy heaven! Toy guns, toy soldiers, and a cowboy hat and shirt. One toy I treasured for a long time was the Daisy air rifle. I kept it for five years. It was just a noise-maker, but I would insert a wet Kleenex into the front of it and shoot at homemade targets.

I also had a toy telescope. I don't remember if I got it for Christmas, but that thing had a story all of its own. When I was home again, I took that telescope with me every time I went on a hunting trip with my family. In 1967, Ekaksak Amagoalik was in Grise Fiord during the spring. He decided to go on a seal hunt with Samwillie's dogs and took Imooshee Nutaraqjuk, Jimmy Nowra, and me along with him. All through the day, Jimmy and I were the managers of the dogs while the two hunters stalked seal without success. We were travelling along Lee Point's big lead when we spotted a bearded seal on the edge a bit farther away. Jimmy and I were told to keep the dogs still while they stalked the seal. The dogs were trained to watch while they waited and to come running as soon as the hunters stood up from their crouched hunting positions. Before the two hunters could get close enough, the seal went down into the open lead. As soon as the men stood up, the dogs took off towards them, sled in tow. As it went, the sled got closer and closer to the edge of the open lead. We managed to keep it away from the edge for a while, but we lost control, and the sled plunged off the edge and into the water. My beloved telescope was inside the box in the back. Man, I'm telling you, Ekaksak sure was mad at me and Jimmy! When we pulled the sled out, the contents of the box were gone, along with my precious telescope. It was made by Tasco, and it is the first thing that comes to mind every time I see any merchandise made by them. On that same trip, we were headed for home when all of a sudden there was loud *BANG!* from the back of the sled. It turned out someone had forgotten to remove a live round from the chamber of the .30-30 Winchester rifle that was on top of a box behind us, and it had suddenly discharged. Lucky for all of us, the barrel was facing away!

Just before Easter, a social worker brought a bag of clothes I had left behind at the boarding home. When we opened it, we were pleasantly surprised to find seven crisp, new one-dollar bills! It was the money my brother Samwillie had given me the day I was leaving. He had come onboard just before the ship weighed anchor to give me the money. Not being so conscious of monetary value, I had put the bills in the bag and then promptly forgotten about them. I'd also earned some money carving while onboard the ship. I was suddenly rich and could buy things to send home. The Dobinson family helped me shop and send gifts by parcel post. I got some records for my brother and some Easter chocolate and candies. A funny story was told to me about what happened when my family received the package. Nobody had ever seen chocolate in the shape of a rabbit, so naturally, my mother thought the candy was an ornament and put it on a shelf in her bedroom. The candy was on the shelf for quite some time until one day it was accidently knocked down and broke into pieces. That was when they discovered it was chocolate that had been sitting on her shelf.

Sometime after Easter in 1964, I was told I would be going home. Although I was happy that I was going to be with my family, whom I missed dearly, part of me did not want to go. I had gotten used to city life. I had gotten used to living in Montreal, eating varied types of food instead of just seal meat, maktak, tea, and bannock. In Grise Fiord, there was very little of everything. I had gotten used to things like television, telephones, and corner stores, but the conveniences had to come to an end.

With just days to go before leaving Montreal, the Dobinson family was excited for me and went about brainstorming what gifts would be best to take home. The Dobinsons had made my time there so enjoyable by showing me what life was like in the city. I can't remember when I parted company with them. I'm sure I have blocked the memory out of my mind since it would've been an emotional one.

My flight was direct to Resolute Bay on one of those four-engine transcontinental aircraft with three rudders in the back that are so slow and noisy you could still hear the engine sound in your ears almost a week later. Since I was a minor, I required an adult escort, just as I had in 1958 when Charlie Watt had been my escort. One of the RCMP from the Grise Fiord detachment, Constable Bob Curry, was flying back from his holidays, so he was to go with me. Thinking back, the young constable must have been eager to go to a bar for the last time before leaving "civilization" after we were checked in. He knew that in Grise Fiord there was no bar. I drank 7-Up while my escort drank Scotch on the rocks. The flight from Montreal to Resolute Bay was eight hours. The noise of the aircraft engines was deafening, but I slept most of the way. At last, it was good to be with my family once again.

14

Apex Hill

*I*n late March or early April of 1964, Simeonie Amagoalik arrived alone with a dog team to get his stepbrother Thamoosie. Back in 1953, when the officials were dividing up the families onboard the *C.D. Howe,* Simeonie had protested against being separated from Thamoosie to no avail. Finally, Simeonie was able to take Thamoosie with him to Resolute Bay, where he should have gone in the first place. Samwillie and Louisa went with Thamoosie and Charlie as far as the end of Viks Fiord. I had always thought Simeonie left ahead of them, but Louisa told me they left at the same time. A year before he passed away, Simeonie told me how he and his brother had travelled together all the way to Resolute after Samwillie turned back. They came across a food cache just before crossing Wellington Channel. Charlie, being just a youngster, had raided the sweets, including bags of raisins. On the trail, Thamoosie was having trouble catching up with Simeonie, and Simeonie began to wonder why he was stopping so frequently. When they finally caught up, Thamoosie explained that Charlie had had a bad case of the runs. The raisins and the sweets at the cache were the source of his trouble.

I remember Simeonie's departure as clear as day, yet I have no memory of Thamoosie and Charlie leaving. I may very well have suppressed the thought of losing one of my best friends, whom I'd known for as long as I could remember.

In September of the same year, a government-run school called Churchill Vocational Centre (CVC) was started in Fort Churchill, Manitoba. It offered academic classes, home economics, and shop classes, including courses on basic arc welding, sheet metal, carpentry, small engine repair, and drafting. Those who scored higher grades at the start of the school year went to Duke of Edinburgh High School. The few who were twelve years of age and under attended Hearne Hall. Both of these schools were also in Fort Churchill, and students from CVC, Duke of Edinburgh, and Hearne Hall lived in the same dormitory complex. At CVC, students came from the Eastern Arctic region as far south as Sanikiluaq, as well as Nunavik, Baffin Island, Keewatin, and Arviat. Roger Killiktee was the first student from Grise Fiord to ever attend CVC. I will never forget seeing Roger leave Grise Fiord. He walked the four kilometres to the dirt strip carrying his standard blue-coloured trunk and an army surplus sleeping bag. He was wearing his black covered parka. I was so envious, wishing I could go too.

When the 1964 school year started, I was still having spots of eye trouble, although they were not as intense as when we lived in the Lindstrom Peninsula area. In January of 1965, I had to have my tonsils removed. A medical charter was scheduled to come up in January when the moon was full—when there was as much light as possible during the dark season. There were five us, including me, Joatamie and Ikumak, Odluviuvik Nutaraqjuk, and Hanna Quaraq. I'm not sure why the others were going except for Joatamie, who I think was heading there for dental treatment. We flew direct to Iqaluit in seven hours. It was an uneventful flight, which I thoroughly enjoyed!

After our arrival, we were taken to a boarding home run by the Mukpaluk family. It was a multi-room house with many beds. My room was with four other people and I was on top of one double-bunk bed. Just as we were just about to fall asleep, in came Mary Panigusiq to say hello.

The boarding house wasn't always full. In fact, for the few months before I went home, hardly any patients were there. It was during this quiet period that Manasie Audlakiak from Qikiqtarjuaq came to stay with us. He became a good friend, and we have remained good friends ever since. He is two years older than I am, but we went everywhere together in Apex Hill. He reminded me a lot of Salluviniq. We got ourselves in big trouble one day. One of us had gotten the idea to throw snowballs at cars passing the bridge. A bus was passing by when we threw snowballs at it. It stopped and out came the head of the driver to tongue-lash us. We learned our lesson!

I have many pleasant memories from my time in Apex Hill, which is about five and a half kilometres outside of Iqaluit. I met many *Iqalummiut*, some of whom have become lifelong friends, although sadly, over the course of time, some have passed on. Not unlike my tenure in Montreal, I soon started school in Iqaluit. What a clean school Sir Martin Frobisher was. It had those long, long hallways! We were taken to school each morning by bus. There were two different bus drivers, Napatchie Noah and Charlie Sagiatuk. Mr. Sagiatuk was very vocal and seemed to know each and every student. His routine was: "*Kinauvit? Nanimiugugavit?*" "What is your name? Where are you from?" In order to get on the bus, I had to answer both questions. I looked forward to the morning bus rides because I would sit next to my first-ever girlfriend, Elisapee Michael. It was just puppy love, and we did not date for very long. We were very young at the time.

When I started school, I said I was in grade five, even though I was in about grade four back home, which was a mistake. The courses were way beyond my comprehension, but my grades were never questioned. Our homeroom teacher's morning greeting was: "Good morning, class! The sun is singing and the birds are shining! What a wonderful day!"

I enjoyed the softball games we played near the fire hall. Since I was a pretty good runner, I was often chosen as one of the team members. One of the fastest home runners was Oleepika Veevee. I seem to remember that Oleepika and Billy Joamie were a young couple at that time. The fact that she had a baby on her back did not slow her down at all. Boy, could she run! Good times. When we had nothing else to do, I played under the bridge with the younger boys. There was a rope hanging under one side of the bridge, and we'd grab hold of it and swing over to the other side. What thrills!

Not all of what I was exposed to during that time was morally right. It was the first time I was suckered into substance abuse. I was looking for acceptance from older boys, so I was easy prey to suggestions. One time, we went into a beach cabin where there was a container of gasoline. It seemed exciting and dangerous, but when the euphoria wore off it did not seem so fun anymore. Another time, looking for excitement, I was involved in taking Adamie Ningiuk's bicycle from the front of his house. A few of us decided to go into Iqaluit so we could coast downhill near the town. The two-mile walk up the hill was long, but the prospect of coasting downhill made it all worthwhile. Since I did not know how to ride a bicycle, I rode on top of the handlebars once we started going downhill, with my friend Aapa pedalling. The steeper it got, the faster we went. It was exhilarating at first—until we came to the steepest part of the hill above the water treatment station. As our speed increased, I became nervous. Aapa was telling me not to panic, but that is exactly what I did! He was yelling at me to stop fidgeting or we were going to crash. I remember being scared out of my mind! Sure enough, we crashed. The pain was excruciating! "You stupid son of a #@$%& Larry!!" yelled Aapa. Here I was, a thirteen-year-old kid, crying like a baby! My crying only made him cuss at me more. I wanted to stop crying but my behind hurt so much! We did not see each other again for a long time after that.

I also learned during that time that just because you are young doesn't mean you can't be friends with adults. I used to enjoy visiting Noah, who was Parnee's father. I sometimes stopped to chat with him when he was coming back from hunting ptarmigan. We'd just be talking away, and all the while he had a .22 long rifle slung over his neck, held in place with his left arm. Today, you cannot go around carrying hunting rifles in Iqaluit. If a bylaw or RCMP officer saw you do what was normal back in 1965, you'd be charged with public endangerment.

* * *

The first Toonik Tyme Festival happened in the spring of 1965 during the Easter holidays. Toonik Tyme is a major festival in Iqaluit even today. Bryan Pearson, Iqaluit's first mayor, and the Apex settlement council have been credited with the idea of holding an annual spring festival. Spring festivities were not new in the North; it was already custom to celebrate when spring arrived to give thanks for surviving another harsh winter. An extra-large iglu would be built to celebrate life, and the festivities would be held for days. It was the time to start a new year and to let go of any emotions of animosity or any grudges that had built up during the cold winter. Different ways to alleviate tension were demonstrated, including tests of strength and drum dance duels, but mostly it was a time to have fun.

The first Toonik Tyme was held on a lake halfway between Iqaluit and Apex Hill. It was after the new fiscal year had started, and the Conservatives were in power. Former prime minister John Diefenbaker came up to officially kick off the newly incorporated event. There I was, standing slightly to the left of the podium with a "front row" spot. He was wearing his famous brown fur coat. I can still see his curly hair, those intense eyes as he spoke.

The events included a snowmobile race to Kimmirut, traditional tea and bannock making, iglu building, dog-whip demonstrations, a harpoon throw, and countless other events. Nowdlak Kilabuk won so many races to Kimmirut he was given the name "Flash." The festivities closed with the arrival of the honorary Toonik arriving from the hills. When he was sighted coming over the hill, he caused quite a stir, he looked so authentic.

My wife has many fond memories of musicians who have come up from the south to perform at Toonik Tyme. Some are famous now. The Smilin' Johnnie Show was the main musical entertainment attraction that spring. They played on the lake. In later years, other musicians, like Gordon Lightfoot, Creedence Clearwater Revival, April Wine, Mahogany Rush, Blue Rodeo, and many others, have made guest appearances at the Toonik Tyme festival.

* * *

In June of 1965 I learned we were finally going home. Like the other times I returned home after being away, I had mixed feelings: happiness at returning to my family, memories of hardship on Lindstrom Peninsula. Just before we left Iqaluit, the CVC students arrived from Fort Churchill. It was good to see Roger and other friends. People still smoked rolled cigarettes back home, and I remember Eli Panipakochoo giving Roger two cartons of Peter Jackson cigarettes even though the co-op store was closed. Funny what one remembers. We all boarded the Nordair DC-3 charter plane. We landed on the ice in each community and stayed at the transient centre in Pond Inlet. (Transient centres were like a prelude to airport hotels: government-run lodgings for people like construction crews who would have nowhere else to go in the community during their stay.) Poor Manasie; when it was time for him to go home, it took him more than a week before he finally made it to Qikiqtarjuaq. It was early June, and it often gets foggy in the spring in the Arctic, which prevents planes from being able to land. He would get word that the fog had cleared, go to the airport, and fly out, only for the fog to come back and force the plane to turn around. He lost track of how many times he flew right over Qikiqtarjuaq. He'd given up hope of getting home before summer ended, but he finally made it. It would be another three months before I would see him again in Fort Churchill.

* * *

It was so good to be home again. People's faces looked so darkened from being outside so much in the springtime, when the sunlight reflects off the whiteness of the snow. I noticed that Paulassie's face especially was very tanned. It meant he was hunting a lot. He almost looked like an African Inuk! It was good to be with Roger and Looty again, my best friends. I pumped Roger for information about CVC. I had always enjoyed his company, but in the spring of 1965, he suddenly seemed so cool. Since he was Pauloosie's younger brother, I felt we had a family bond—I feel that way even today.

He once told me a funny story about experiencing the strange sounds eider ducks make while feeding underwater. In the spring from 1960 until about 1966, families would go to the Lee Point, Anstead Point, and Fram Fiord areas, which are good for hunting bearded seal. After the school was built in Grise Fiord, they would go when school finished for the year. Roger told me how he had found himself all alone one year after most people had left in June or July to go to back to Grise Fiord. Just before he left, he suddenly heard strange noises in the direction of the open water near the shore. He was really scared, convinced the sound was a supernatural phenomenon. He packed his gear in a hurry. Just as he was leaving the shore, he saw the birds come up in an open lead. Much to his relief, his "ghosts" were nothing but eider ducks!

The summer after he came back from Fort Churchill, Roger had apparently been trying to learn how to swim. The lake, which is behind where the RCMP buildings are today, used to be the only place to swim. It's only three feet deep. It was so cold, we would put up a tent with a Primus stove inside it so we could warm up after we were in the water. One day, out comes Roger wearing nothing but shorts and a pair of waterproof boots. He asked me to measure how far he moved underwater, and he dove in. After a few seconds he came up, having moved no more than a foot or two. When he surfaced, I was thinking, *Should*

I tell him he didn't move ahead very much? He'd ask, "Did I move much ahead? Huh?" Not wanting to disappoint him, I'd answer, "Yes, you moved ahead." After he got out of the water, I burst out laughing when I saw his kamiik, which looked like balloon feet full of water. Every time he took a step, water would squirt out. Such a funny spectacle. I don't think he ever learned to swim.

The summer of 1968, there was a lot of multi-year ice. One day in September, Roger, Looty, and I went for what was essentially a joyride. I remember we spent more time speeding around the Skerries, little islands about thirty-five kilometres west of Grise Fiord, than we did hunting. Near Landslip Island, we were busy talking amongst ourselves when Roger yelled, "Look out!" We saw a large sheet of multi-year ice less than twenty feet in front of us. Roger made an extreme right turn. We hit part of the ice, narrowly avoiding hitting it head on. When the side of the canoe hit the corner of the ice, we tipped about sixty degrees! Man, I'm telling you, that close call scared the living daylights out of us! After that near collision, there was simply too much old ice, and we decided to turn around.

By September, the sun sets a bit after 7:00 p.m. We fuelled up the gas tank with the 46-gallon barrel we had brought with us before we started for home. That was when Roger told us he did not think we were going to have enough fuel to get all the way home. He told Looty and me that the twenty-three litres he put in the tank from the barrel was all there was left of our fuel. It was after 5 p.m. when we started for home. As we neared where we had first landed back in 1953, Roger said he wanted to go ashore to see if there was any fuel cached. He told us there was less than a quarter left in the tank as he lifted it to demonstrate how light it was. He did not think we would make it home. It was already dark by that time, and home was about eight kilometres away in straight line. We drove on the left side of the little islands. Once we saw the community lights, Roger turned the throttle wide open. Being young, we did not know that the faster you go, the more fuel you use. We were still about two kilometres away when we ran out of fuel. Grise Fiord is often windy in September, and the wind blowing outward from the fiord helped us paddle faster. When Roger lit a rag to attract attention, Ookookoo and another hunter came to tow us home. Lessons learned by trial and error.

15

Churchill Vocational Centre

I left home to attend my first year at CVC in September of 1965. I was fourteen when Roger Killiktee, Tookashie Akpaliapik, and I left to attend the residential school. Leaving Mom behind was something I never got used to. It got to a point where I dreaded ever having to tell her I had to leave. Still, I was excited by the change. After living in extreme isolation on Lindstrom Peninsula for nine years, moving to Grise Fiord had been exciting. It suddenly seemed that there were so many people in one place! Leaving Grise Fiord to see new places and new faces was an excitement I did not want to miss for the world. I found myself looking forward to a change of diet as well, knowing there would be different types of food to eat. Although CVC was very difficult to get used to because of the rules, it was a chance to experience a new way of life. My first year was a journey of new discovery.

Instead of having to walk to the airstrip like Roger did the year before, we went by canoe. It was the first time I left home not as a hospital patient. Imooshee was supposed to come with us, but he was stopped from coming at the last minute. I could see him running down the beach to get in the DPW canoe that Olaf Christiansen, the Atlas Aviation agent, was using to take us to the plane. Olaf shouted at him from the door of his apartment, telling him the bad news. I'm not sure why he did not go and why Tookashie went instead. It was either a mix-up in communication or Olaf was talked into replacing him with Tookashie for some reason. The strange thing is, there was no quota for how many students could go from each settlement. On the flight from Grise Fiord to Resolute, there was plenty of room, with only three passengers. It was heartbreaking to see Imooshee walking back home with his head down, dejected. He had been so excited as he ran down the beach with his brown suitcase in his white duffle parka with no cover.

Atlas Aviation's route to Resolute Bay sometimes took us to Truelove Inlet on Devon Island to refuel. Weldy Phipps was the lone pilot that day. It took three hours to get to Resolute. When we were flying over Cornwallis Island, thirty minutes away from Resolute, I noticed with interest how smooth and brown the tundra down below was. When we had flown the same route in 1958 on the RCMP's single Otter, it had been winter. I have flown the same route so many times since then, today, I don't even look at the ground below on some flights. In fact, I can tell you on Twin Otter flights where we are just by looking at my watch, even if we are above clouds or it's during the dark season. But it did not matter how long our flight was that day. For an excited fourteen-year-old boy, the thrill of new adventure removed the passage of time.

We spent a few days in Resolute Bay. I stayed at Minnie Allakariallak's and had my own room. I noticed how big Joannie Iqaluk's house was. It turns out the houses Inuit had there were homemade from scrap wood collected from the base dump. Comparing them to how we lived in Grise Fiord, they may as well have been castles! I remember being impressed by how big Joannie's record collection was.

Next, the charter flight took us directly to Iqaluit. The students from Pond Inlet, Arctic Bay, Grise Fiord, and Resolute Bay seemed so many in number when we boarded the aircraft that took us down to Iqaluit. There, we took on more students, then flew to Kuujjuaq. At the airport it was a pleasure to see Ken Cresweller, who had taught us in Grise Fiord after the Scotts left. The energy of all the students congregating at the airport terminal and outside was intoxicating.

The students from Resolute who were going to CVC and the high schools for their second year were Annie Nungaq, Minnie Nungak, Phillip Nungak, Mary Eckalook, Jimmy Naummialuk, and Jopee Tongaaluk. When we arrived, the girls were taken to their dormitories and we went to ours. In our dorm there was a roll call and Imooshee Nutarqjuk's name came up. I was in awe to hear his name mentioned. I got up to explain what had happened.

When we arrived at the school, we had to get crew cuts, no exceptions. The delousing was also mandatory, but we were able to argue successfully with the big honcho of CVC, Ralph Ritcey, to remove the requirement. The Duke of Edinburgh High School and Hearne Hall students were exempt, and we so envied them! Jonas Alloloo was CVC's designated barber. When he said, "Larry, time to get your hair cut," I knew I was going to get a haircut whether I liked it or not. We used to hate it when he set the time and date, because you knew he was going to come and get you for your hair's judgement day. The man had a photographic memory! We could not hide from him. I rejoiced in 1970 when I learned the haircut rule had been abolished!

We were given our first "free time" that evening. My head was spinning with excitement. There were so many students walking around outside in groups. All those girls! It was good to see my friend Manasie Audlakiak once more. But we were dumbfounded by all the rules the supervisors started drilling into us. There were more "don'ts" than "dos." It turned out that the introduction was just the first page of numerous rules that would be indoctrinated into our very beings. Charlie Watt and Tagak Curley were the only Inuuk supervisors in 1965, which I thought was unusual. Sometimes I see the two men today, and I look older than both of them. I liked Tagak because he was not hung up on enforcing rules. But many years later, it turned out that what we perceived to be brainwashing at the time had profound positive outcomes. Most of those who attended CVC take their responsibilities seriously.

From Monday to Friday, our day began at 6:00 a.m. The wake-up calls were literal. If you did not get up right away, the supervisors pulled off your sheets, took your leg, and pulled you off the bed! We would shower before lining up for breakfast. The lineups were in the fashion of an army march, complete with monitors who acted like military sergeants. The marches to the dining hall through the dormitory corridors were coordinated with precision, timed to the minute. During the long lineups at meal times, the boys admired the girls and vice versa. After breakfast from 8:00 a.m. till 8:45 a.m., we had to clean our rooms, make our beds, and prepare for classes. Those having to do shop time left ten minutes early, as it took fifteen to twenty minutes to get to the shops. Shop time included basic carpentry, drafting, welding, that sort of thing. Every two weeks, the students who had been in the shops switched out with the others. For lunch break, we could not just go directly to the dining room. We had to go back to our dorms, wash our hands and faces even if we had cleaned up at the shop, then line up for marches to the dining room. After school, we took our books to our rooms and had one hour and fifteen minutes of free time. We could do whatever we wanted before supper. After supper, we had a mandatory study period from 6:00 until 7:00 each night.

The free time from 7:00 to 9:00 each night was something we all looked forward to. Aside from the weekends, those two hours to ourselves were the only remnant of what we had given up once we enrolled at CVC. I'm not saying life was hell in Fort Churchill; far from it. But daily conduct was modelled after a regimental, army-style system. It seemed like 90 percent of our lives were under government control. In fact, some students were sent home for not being able to conform to this type of lifestyle. It was obvious that those who had recently come from traditional homes near places like Pangnirtung and Pond Inlet found it shocking. I used to hear them speak about how difficult it was being at CVC in the first months. Some were on the verge of tears as they spoke.

Friday nights were dance nights. By my second year, I had learned what to expect on dance nights, and I started to become conscious of how I looked and dressed. I had seen how boys would go all out to date their girlfriends on Friday nights, putting on their best clothes, shining their latest-style boots, combing their hair with Brylcreem. Some even borrowed articles of clothing from others in a desperate attempt to impress their girls. My seniors in 1965–66 looked and dressed in such stylish clothes. I thought they looked so "cool" and "with it." I was struck by the cool music I heard from the 1950s and '60s rock 'n' roll era with groups and artists like The Dave Clark Five, Chubby Checker, The Bobby Fuller Four, Chuck Berry, Elvis Presley, Buddy Holly, The Big Bopper, and the early Beatles music. It was a type of dancing—to music that was not for square dancing—that was so interesting to see for the first time. Some of the senior students and supervisors were really good at it. Whenever I play "Baby Don't Go" by Sonny & Cher, memories of my first year come back; good memories.

The CVC had its very own group called The Harpoons, whose original members were Michael Kusugak on guitar and vocals, Jose Kusugak on drums and vocals, John Tapatai on bass, Eric Tagoona on guitar, and William Tagoona on lead vocals. The group had started in 1964, and by the 1965–66 school season, they sure sounded professional. The songs they sang were the latest pop tracks of the day. I loved listening to their cover of "I Fought the Law" by The Bobby Fuller Four and "Young Love" by Sonny James, with the guitar solo played by Michael Kusugak. It's interesting how one remembers past moments with sounds.

I can never forget how good William Tagoona was. He must have been no more than twelve or thirteen when I first laid eyes on him. I can still picture him standing in front of the mic, his head held high, both hands on the microphone, wearing the latest pop-musician style. He is wearing pointed shoes with high heels. The mic and the stand are way too high for him, so he has to hold his head up. His rendition of "Barbara Ann" is perfect. His cheeks are red because of his youthful appearance, but his singing skills make up for it.

The Harpoons did not just play at our dances; they would also play at special events all over Fort Churchill. I may have been one of The Harpoons' original fans. I used to love hanging around some afternoons watching the group practice. The inspiration I picked up watching William practice the songs had a lasting impact.

The other group at Fort Churchill were called The Excels. They played at the CVC dances once in a while. William remembers that they all had jobs at the National Research Centre in Fort Churchill. They became so good they went to Winnipeg to cut an album. We were shocked when we heard they had been in a tragic automobile accident on their way to the recording studio. Their drummer was the only member who survived.

On Saturdays, we were given an extra hour of sleep, which I looked forward to. However, we had to be up for the morning cleanup. We had to clean not only our rooms, but the entire dormitory we lived in. After the cleanup, the dormitory administrator and our supervisor would inspect our rooms with a checklist to mark each point. Beds had to be made tightly enough that you could roll a coin from the pillow to the end of the bed, and clothes drawer contents had to be neatly folded—not just the top pieces, but the entire contents. In later years, once the incentive to win a cake was added, the cleanup requirement did not seem so bad. After the Saturday night movie at the Recreational Hall, the winners would be announced. Girls competed against other female dorms, and the boys competed against the other male dorms. The prize: a huge, double-layered cake. Yummm!

The Saturday afternoon free time from 1:00 to 4:45 p.m. was an opportunity to do whatever you wanted. Every second Saturday was allowance week. We each got $1.75. The allowance was actually two dollars, but twenty-five cents was taken for recreational costs, as the government's budget did not include the cost for movies. Some spent the entire afternoon playing cards in hopes of making more. On non-allowance weekends the card players gambled for cigarettes. For two and a half cents, you could buy one cigarette, but on the black market, one cigarette was worth five cents. Some guys who did not even smoke bought packs so they could sell them at black-market prices. The allowance might sound tiny, but a large pack cost fifty-five cents, and a small pack was worth forty-five cents. In Grise Fiord in 2011, one pack cost $20.85.

That allowance was my first lesson in looking after my money. I did not want to stay broke all the time. I learned to always have money put away for rainy days. On non-allowance weekends it paid off when I would have enough to give loans to those I trusted, and when the allowance days arrived, I had enough money to buy some things I wanted. In the first few weeks after our arrival at Fort Churchill, it was common to see students coming out of the commissary and the canteen with bags of junk food. Within two weeks, some of the same students were asking for loans so they could buy more. Every second Saturday, most of us would run to the canteen to indulge ourselves with junk food.

Saturday evenings were movie nights. Attendance wasn't mandatory, but it was encouraged. For guys who had girlfriends, it was a welcome event because they could sit at the back and make out. It was at one of these movie nights I first saw the original version of *The Fly* in black and white. The thriller sure was scary, but then, I was only a fourteen-year-old kid. During my first year I contracted a "movie bug" from one of the dormitory supervisors, Mr. Gideon. He was a movie buff who showed movies to students in his dorm once in a while. He was a short, balding man who had an analytical style when showing films. He would stop the reel every so often during the screenings to explain certain points. The style he used made an impression on me. My wife sometimes gets tired of me stopping the movies we are watching.

All the time I was a student at CVC, Sunday morning church services were mandatory. At least we could sleep in before the 11:00 services. We had to dress in our Sunday best, putting on our issued blue blazer, grey dress pants, ties, and our shop safety shoes that we called "elephant" shoes. Most complied with this regulation. We used to envy the Duke of Edinburgh and Hearne Hall students, who did not have such uniforms. The Sunday morning ritual was unchanged for the first six years of CVC's existence, with very few exceptions.

* * *

The first year was very tough for me. I was used to being the baby of my family as I was younger than my siblings by at least ten years. I had always been picked on a certain amount by my older siblings, but I always had my mother I could run to. I never had the opportunity to fight with siblings to give me hands-on knowledge. In other words, I had never learned to defend myself. When I got picked on at CVC, I was helpless. Students from certain communities, both from our region and Keewatin, were veterans when it came to gang-like groups. One student in particular, who was younger than I was, loved picking on me. He stole my money, took my comic book collections, and worst of all, took all my records, some of which I had never even listened to. I was helpless to do anything. Do you know what it is like to be helpless? Every time I confronted him, he always ran to the bigger guys in his group. He would get his goons to intimidate me. I felt like going to my supervisor about it would end up making things worse for me if they found out. I would cry myself to sleep with fear some nights.

I missed the next year because of him. When I went back, he did not steal my personal things anymore, as I had figured out how to hide things I valued. But what was worse, during the 1967–68 school year, he and his goons would hurt one of my best friends. The gang did not pick on just me, but also on other students they could beat. I'm not saying it was always violent at CVC; it's just that we avoided certain guys when they were in a bad mood.

In 2000, after more than thirty-five years, I got a surprise phone call from the individual who had instigated terrorizing me in our CVC years. He apologized. He explained he was now all alone in the world, with no parents. He wanted to say he was truly sorry for having behaved so badly when we were at CVC. I had actually forgotten all about him, but I was happy to hear his pleas for forgiveness, which I accepted. The head of this gang actually became a good guy in the last year of our CVC school years. It was sad to learn he had died under horrible circumstances during the mid-1970s.

I will never forget some students who protected me when I was being subjected to bullying. One student in particular who I will always be grateful to was David Kabloona. He was very big and strong, but he was a gentle giant. He wore thick eyeglasses that made his eyes look big. He never hurt anyone, nor did he look for trouble. He was from Baker Lake, and big brother of Eric and William. When he saw I was running from someone, he would get between me and them and say, "Hey, leave the little guy alone!" Students from Baker Lake and his siblings would tease him once in a while and he hated it, but he never hurt anybody. I also sometimes ran to my friend Sandy Tooma, who was from Kuujjuaq (*nakurmiik*, Sandy). During times of loneliness, I visited Akikulu Shappa and Jopee and Jayko Nutara when I longed to hear Pond Inlet–dialect Inuktitut being spoken. In later years more students from Pond Inlet and Arctic Bay attended CVC. Most of all, the one person whom I could confide in was a classmate from Baker Lake, Sally Seteetnaq. I would come to class late some days because I had been crying. She showed compassion and caring, and would offer condolences and give me words of encouragement. I will always be grateful to all of them.

Christmas was the loneliest and the coldest time of the year, although the supervisors did their best to make us feel at home. It was difficult not to think about the time of festivities after Midnight Mass and celebrating New Year's back home. We did not know that most Qallunaat spend quiet time over the holidays just being with their loved ones and reflecting on their good fortunes. In the Arctic, Christmas holidays are celebrated exclusively with square dancing and festivities until New Year's Day. The Christmas gifts we received in our dorm included cigarettes. Those who smoked thought this was wonderful.

Easter break was the time when school was out the longest. We could go to Akulliq and into town. I saw Tommy Berthe and Tommy Gordon again. Tommy Gordon was still quiet, and Tommy Berthe was still full of energy. I had stayed in Akulliq during my first hospital trip south, but it was only when I went to CVC that I realized Akulliq was located between CVC and the old Fort Churchill, where the grain elevators are. The train whistles I'd heard as a boy had actually been from the grain elevator area downtown. I also learned that at the old fort, there was a Dene village. That Easter, some guys purchased booze by giving money to Dene who were of age to buy it for them. The liquor store downtown was one place I never went to see.

In 1966, as first-year students, we were sent to Camp Nanook, a distance of more than fifteen kilometres away. It was a log cabin filled with a whole bunch of beds. It had originally been built for the military as part of their wilderness training facility. Our whole dorm was sent away to the camp for the duration of the Easter holidays. We had a supervisor, Mr. White, who was a two-pack-a-day smoker. He bought his cigarettes by the carton. He was also a Christian who was not ashamed to speak openly about his faith. He was the first Qallunaaq I had met who spoke about Christ like a minister, yet he was an ordinary man. You did not see non-Inuit preach except ministers in those days. Some students used to visit his room to ask him about Biblical things they wanted to know. His explanations made us want to know more. While at Camp Nanook, he read whole chapters of the Bible aloud in the evenings.

Every day we did a lot of hiking, just to kill the time and explore our surroundings. Some guys would catch ptarmigan and eat them on site. Those of us who hadn't seen any to catch would find ourselves drooling for fresh ptarmigan blood as the guys described how good the birds had tasted. We longed for fresh meat, but we dared not tell our supervisors.

Inside, the coziness of the cabin with the fireplace lit gave the atmosphere a touch of what it was like to be out on the land back home, even though it was not the inside of an iglu. We weren't used to being in the wilderness among trees. Since it was too far to walk back, we stuck it out at the camp until the bus finally arrived to take us back. Once we were back in a familiar environment, CVC did not seem so alien anymore, nor did we feel we were so far from our homes—a temporary relief.

Some teachers and supervisors went home during Christmas and Easter holidays. We would bombard them with questions to tell us about what was happening "in the world." The year 1965 has been considered by some historians as the beginning of the Flower Child generation, and when I watch historical films about the era, it makes me understand much better why some of the younger teachers and supervisors were less strict than the more mature ones we had known longer. In later years, it was more obvious to me why some of the younger ones had the tendency to be so vocal against the many rules we were subject to. One particular young supervisor was fired for speaking out against them.

After Easter break, we knew it was not long before we would be going home. In June, CVC students who lived in the most isolated settlements, from the Ungava region (Salluit, Kangiqsujuaq, Kangirsuk, and Killiniq) and the High Arctic, always left a few weeks before anyone else. Without regular commercial service, government charters were common. Those of us living in Grise Fiord, Arctic Bay, Iglulik, and Sanirajak were all taken to Sanirajak first to be picked up by Atlas Aviation. We waited for a whole week at the local transient centre. It was boring being young and restless, walking the beach day after day. Funny, I did not even make an attempt to befriend young people from the settlement. When we finally left, we flew direct to Arctic Bay. Three of us going back to Grise went for a walk while Weldy Phipps was refuelling the single Otter, waiting for people to come pick up Akikulu Shappa. Weldy had to shout to us to come back. It was the first time I had ever heard his voice and noticed how high-pitched it was for a man who looked so burly. Roger recalls, "We dropped off Akikulu Shappa and took off before anybody from Arctic Bay arrived to greet us. I could see a dog team coming on the ice, but it never arrived in time to see us."

When we arrived in Grise, after the aircraft's engines stopped and the pilot opened the door to let us out, none of us wanted to be first to get out. We were too shy. Tookashie was the brave one, getting out first.

Although I was often bullied during the first year, I have no regrets for having attended CVC. I learned many things. Being picked on and bullied was a horrible experience that I don't wish on anyone, but I endured and survived, and it helped me become a stronger person. Thinking back after forty years, I may have liked being at a place of "plenty," where there were regular meals, shelters with plenty of rooms instead of just one-room houses, and a selection of food that was just not seal meat, bannock, and tea. I could get Coca-Cola, ice cream, chocolate bars, popcorn, and comic books, among other things.

16

Living in Two Worlds

Once again, it was good to be home! It was so good to be where there was no such thing as rules to follow. No worry of having to get up in the morning! And most of all for me: no worry of getting bullied. I made up my mind to never ever go back to CVC! Everybody seemed extra friendly after being in a much bigger place.

My family still lived in the modified home my brother had reconstructed out of the two little houses we had back on Lindstrom Peninsula, but even though I had been gone only ten months, Grise Fiord seemed to have grown considerably. More children had been born; the co-op store had more goods to choose from. Like I had after my trips to Montreal in 1963 and Iqaluit in 1965, I had brought back some new things to share with my friends: comic books and records. As there was no Internet or television in those days, many boys of our generation read comic books. Sam Killiktee, who grew up in Elijah's care after Pauloosie passed away, was no exception when he was a teenager. There used to be advertisements for vitamin pills you could buy via mail order on the backs of the comic books. They usually featured bodybuilder Joe Weider saying something about how he had found success through the means offered in the ad. Elijah told me that Sam started ordering the pills. He would end up getting more in the mail before he was through the previous order. He wound up with so many extras that Elijah decided to try giving them to his dog team. Lo and behold, his dogs started to pull better!

Elijah was an industrious person. He was the first person to own a bicycle in Grise Fiord. Later, he was the first to have a little Bombardier dirt bike. While we still lived on Lindstrom Peninsula, he was the first to own a Winchester .30-06 calibre with a scope. Nobody from Lindstrom Peninsula had such rifles in those days.

Until Charlie left to go live in Resolute Bay in 1964, my circle of friends had increased threefold. When Tookashie and Martha left for CVC in 1966, Roger and I did not go with them. I was very nervous prior to their departure, thinking I was going to be forced to go. I did not know I did not have to go back if I did not want to.

It was the beginning of living in two worlds. I did not know I was starting to lose my true Inuk identity. I was missing hunting skills, traditional medicine, philosophy. It would be more than forty years before I would finally start meeting other former residential school students who felt the same way: a sense of something missing in your very core as a human being. I used to wonder why I was always so restless, why I had trouble identifying who I really was versus my Elders, who did not question who they were. They could not speak a word of English, nor could they read or write English, nor had they ever seen what it was like on the other side of the globe. Yet they knew who they were, they knew what they wanted, and most of all, they looked content. Their feet seemed firmly planted on the ground, snow, ice, they were standing on! They were proud of being Inuk!

The years 1966 and 1967 were a time when I gained tons of knowledge about my culture. Once the ice formed, I often went with Elijah when he went hunting for caribou and polar bear with his dog team, as well as seal hunts and fox trapping. His dogs were extraordinarily fast. They were trained to speed up as soon as their master got off the sled. It was a way of telling them to pick up the pace when they started to get sluggish. So every time I got off the sled to run to warm myself up, the dogs sped up. They didn't even get into a gallop, but I told Elijah I could not run long enough to get warm because the dogs sped up too fast for me and would have left me behind. He told me that this team was the second generation of dogs that had come from the female he had traded for with Maja. The first litter of seven, trained to be part of the team he had brought from Inujjuak, was even faster. When I guided big game sport hunters with my own dog team, he taught me some very important skills in how to get the best out of your dogs.

I have been travelling by dog team during the dark season since I can remember. Driving a dog team during constant dark has its own atmosphere that one learns to look forward to. Travelling in the starlit night, your eyes adjust, enabling you to see the trail up to a certain distance. When there are whiteout conditions, it becomes totally dark. In the daytime during whiteouts, the whiteness completely covers the sky and goes all the way to the ground. You have no point of reference for anything. You can't tell how far away things are, and nothing has a shadow. It's one of the most dangerous conditions for travelling in the Arctic as you can't see the trail or the horizon. Many tragedies have happened in these conditions. When it is dark in these conditions, everything becomes completely black. There is no starlight. You would stumble and fall if you did not have a flashlight. However, if the conditions are right and you are dressed properly for the cold, dark-season hunting is something you must try. During the dark season in Jones Sound, the weather can be mild when the open water in the middle of the sound hasn't quite frozen over yet. Being outdoors at that time can be quite pleasant.

The High Arctic can be a dangerous place even when there are not whiteout conditions. Elijah had almost drowned in 1960, and he had another close call in 1971. A strip of sea ice about three kilometres long would start to build up in front of Grise Fiord in late November each year. Elijah was one of the men who used the front-end loader to clear the snow once it was safe to do so. He had just finished doing work on the new ice strip. Daylight was short by then. He was coming back to shore, and at the edge where the grounded ice and the sea ice meet, the machine fell through. As the machine started to sink, he tried to get out of the cabin, but could not open the door. He had to wait for it fill up with water. It had fallen sideways, the lights still on. The way it was angled, he could see out the window above him as it sank about one hundred feet or more. He could see the opening where it had fallen through, and once it had stopped sinking, he sprang out and swam up to the surface. He had to walk half a mile or more soaking wet with seawater. When he got back, our stepbrother Tommy Aqiatushuk was the only one home. Everybody was at the weekend bingo game at the community hall. The incident made the national news. Prime Minister Pierre Elliott Trudeau wrote him a letter to commend his bravery and thank him for his dedication to his community.

* * *

Elijah and I had a trapline inside Starnes Fiord with Gamaliel and Seeglook. We used to camp about thirty-two kilometres from home at the mouth of the fiord, just past Lee Point. The father and son would arrive a couple of hours behind us, when we were already inside the newly constructed iglu. I enjoyed listening to their interactions. Seeglook was a very outgoing boy, and Gamaliel was a seal-hole hunting expert. Without fail, fresh meat and liver would be brought in half-frozen for our supper. Yummy—fresh liver and meat sure tasted good! Today, I love going out during the dark season to hunt seal, partly because of this experience.

I learned so much about my culture during the short time I missed school. It was like a catch-up period for me. I went with all of my brothers and brothers-in-law on various hunting trips that had a lasting impression I shall never forget. I had never really been outdoors for days on dog-team travel in the middle of winter. I learned to appreciate why our ancestors developed their survival skills in the harsh climate, without giving up, why the women learned to utilize animal hides for clothing as protection against extreme cold. Although I did not start school until I was twelve years old, I'd had no extensive training in winter hunting skills, which I would have learned by going with my big brothers. I used to envy my Lindstrom peers who went hunting.

Starting in mid-March or early April, we made plans to go on long-distance hunts. One particular hunt my brother and I went on was to look for caribou inland. We camped at the end of a fiord after a day of travel and an approximate distance of thirty kilometres. The next thirty kilometres snakes through the mountain valleys until you hit an ice cap. On the trail, you make a ninety-degree turn into a very narrow mountain valley. After another three kilometres, you'll find yourself in front of a glacier that seems to be blocking your way—but the ice cap is actually part of the trail. In 1967, it was about one thousand feet tall with a twenty-five- to thirty-degree gradual slope that you could ride the sled up. Once the dogs got into their rhythm of pulling, we could get to the top of the glacier easily. On the other side, there is a small lake with a disappearing ice cap that makes it look like twin lakes instead of a single one. We camped at the lake after the second day of travel. In later years, the ice cap that blocked the trail melted so much that rocks appeared and made the angle much steeper. In fact, it is outright dangerous to travel on ice caps in the Arctic today.

The next day, we resumed our travel. It was a quiet, pleasant day, and I enjoyed the change of scenery from the mountains I was used to seeing in the Grise Fiord area. It was inland, and flatter, without so many high, rolling mountains. There were many signs of animals; the tracks of Arctic hares, ptarmigan, muskoxen. Even with evening temperatures hovering around -40°C, I don't remember ever being cold. In March in the High Arctic, the sun is high enough that during the day, the light reflecting off the snow is a blinding, brilliant white. I love being outdoors when it's March, with bright light, yet cold. The light is beautiful when it starts coming back from January to March—a photographer's dream. Each season has its own qualities we welcome when it arrives.

At the end of our third day of travel, we set up a base camp and made plans to hunt caribou on foot the next morning. We hunted for two full days without success. On the third day, we decided to head for home. On our journey home, we didn't see any signs of caribou having crossed our old trail. Although we went home empty-handed, we had no regrets. Inuit hunters are taught from the time they start hunting to never reflect on an unsuccessful hunt. Our Elders told us that animals never stay in the same place for very long. One day, you'll see none, but on another day, you might see some. My uncle used to tell me to never give up hunting just because I come home empty-handed.

In early March of 1967, I went on my first polar bear hunting trip with Elijah, Joatamie, and Ikumak. We went by two dog teams. Since we left late in the afternoon, we camped only thirty kilometres from Grise Fiord. The second night, we camped just a few kilometres from Cape Hardy after crossing Jones Sound. The next campsite was past the present fishing lake in front of Cape Newman Point. Running low on dog food, we looked for signs of walrus on grounded icebergs between Cape Svarten and Nookap Island with no success. We turned back in front of Nookap Island just a few kilometres past Cape Svarten. On our way back, we camped in front of Truelove Inlet to hunt seal for dog food. The first day did not yield any seals, so we went to the land in hopes of finding muskoxen. Unfortunately, there was also nothing to kill on land. The next day, Joatamie and Elijah caught a seal each. With fresh meat, the dogs were revitalized. After giving them a chance to rest with full stomachs another day, we left for home. With lightened sled loads, Elijah and I were home before the daylight was even gone, travelling an approximate distance of eighty kilometres in six hours with his second-generation dog team.

Sometime around 1966, Simeonie Amagoalik, George Eckalook, and Ekaksak Amagoalik had arrived in Grise Fiord by snowmobile. A new way to travel on land and ice had arrived. It was an exciting time. After this introduction, most hunters started using snowmobiles to go hunting, although Elijah was still using his dog team. Some still went trapping, but more towards the area east of Grise Fiord. By 1969, the RCMP switched from using dog teams for patrols to using snowmobiles. Samwillie had purchased a second-hand Bombardier Ski-Doo from Simeonie, and he was using it to hunt all over Jones Sound, including north Devon Island. On the polar bear hunt, Elijah and I ran across his trail just a few kilometres past Cape Newman Point. Elijah noted that when hunters started using snowmobiles, polar bears that came across the tracks would suddenly turn and run in the opposite direction. However, it is normal when hunting that on some days you will not see any, but on other days you might. Although we did not get any polar bears, I learned much about what it was like to go on long-distance hunts.

* * *

While I was home in Grise Fiord, I was learning traditional skills. The rest of the world was hailing the Flower Child generation. Long hair was in style, people were experimenting with things like marijuana, LSD, speed, and MDMA. The Vietnam War and anti-establishment protests were happening. Our generation was preaching that the world should be run by peaceful means, without war. As the Bob Dylan song goes: the times, they are a-changin'! I was a naive teenager drinking it all in, caught up in the fashions of the period. Long hair, bell-bottom pants, flashy shirts, the whole bit. Each time I left Grise Fiord and came back, I would come home to a place that had remained virtually the same, as if caught in a time warp.

In the fall of 1967, I decided to go back to CVC. I was seventeen, and I missed being with other people of my generation. I was getting more exposure to the outside world through radio and television, and I wanted to experience things outside of Grise Fiord. Roger was going to finish his third year in order to graduate from CVC after missing one year. After graduation, he was to leave for Saskatoon to attend co-op management training. Tookashie Akpaliapik was on her way to graduate, having never missed a single year, and Martha was going for the first time. As always, it was difficult to tell my family of my decision to leave. Since I had started to go with him on his hunting trips, Elijah took it hard. I have always regretted having to compromise my family's feelings.

We landed for fuel at Truelove Inlet on Devon Island with a single Otter. I was horrified to see another single Otter belonging to Bradley Air Services at the end of the landing strip that had somehow ended up off the runway on the marshy ground. The next time we landed at the same landing airstrip, it was gone. For some reason, Roger, James Nashak, and I left a week later than the regular flights to CVC. Tookashie and Martha had left with the rest of the High Arctic students. In Iqaluit, our little group left with other stragglers for Kuujjuaq, but we could not land due to heavy fog. We were told the weather there was marginal, but the pilots wanted to have a look anyway. After that, they decided not to even make an approach, and we flew to Schefferville, Quebec.

We were escorted by one supervisor. It was one of the longest flights I had ever been on, besides the flights with the RCMP in 1958. We had been flying above an endless sea of fog and cloud since we had taken off from Iqlauit many hours earlier. The clouds were so high that we were just a few thousand feet above them. Descending was a long, slow process. When we finally got below the cloud cover, the trees were only a few hundred feet below us. After flying above the forest, we finally landed. Being young, we were not even concerned, except for being tired from flying all day. Nobody seemed concerned about running out of fuel. We were checked into a hotel. The supper at the hotel restaurant was so welcome after having had nothing to eat all day. Our room and meals were covered by the Department of Education.

Although we were anxious to get going, we enjoyed our short freedom in Schefferville. James Nashak seemed so knowledgeable about things like where to go for booze. He and Jimmy paid a local Cree person to buy them a case of beer. Of course, at sixteen, I was too scared to go to their room, so I went to a corner cafeteria for a Coca-Cola and to listen to some of the latest music on a jukebox. In 1967, The Monkees were popular. I played "I'm a Believer" so much that by the time we left Schefferville, I knew the lyrics by heart. Before we left, one of the older students bought shaving lotion, mixed it with water, and was drinking it. He offered me a sip—YUCK! Ooooh, ahhhh! UGH! It tasted bad enough that I did not try it again until many years later. It is so sad that people expose themselves to poison like methyl hydrate, turpentine, rubbing alcohol, mouthwash, and many other dangerous substances just to feel high. I know two people who went blind.

We were in Schefferville for three days and nights before we finally left. The pilots, not wanting to take unnecessary risks, waited until flying conditions were near perfect. When we finally arrived in Fort Churchill, I ended up bunking on the same floor as Jimmy. As a second-year student, I was very much older and more aware of my surroundings than I had been two years earlier. I was still subjected to being picked on on occasion, but it was not as frequent. The gangs from the "tough" communities were even bigger than in 1965–66, but I knew how to avoid them by then.

Although I did not pay much attention to the Resolute Bay students, it was the first time I met Allie Salluviniq. I didn't know at the time that his parents were Sarah and Daniel Salluviniq, who had been relocated to Resolute Bay. What struck me about Allie was the way he was dressed (in a black jean jacket) and his manner. He seemed so sure of himself, and I envied him. He took no pushing around, either; there was no sassing him. I still play a copy of one of his albums by The Five Americans, with their hit song "Western Union." The other album he had was by Petula Clark with her hit song "Downtown." I still have that album, too.

I don't know what year he first went to CVC, but he was always my senior. I never dared oppose him, plus he was from Resolute Bay. Resolute Bay students were always ahead compared to the rest of the High Arctic communities. It was quite modern in terms of southern ways. Every home I visited in Resolute seemed to have a grandfather clock that chimed at fifteen-, thirty-, and sixty-minute intervals. The Federal Day School in Resolute Bay was opened in 1958, four years before the school in Grise Fiord. When we passed through on our way south for school, we found that the students were way ahead of us in their grades. As far as being in-tune with cool things like the latest hit records, they seemed to have it all. Jimmy Naummialuk talked about things I had no conception of. He was miles ahead of me when it came to grades, and a million years ahead of me in terms of "this is where it's at, man." His record collection put sparkles in my eyes. You could not touch them except with the tips of your fingers. I also remember being impressed with Johnnie Eckalook's record collection, too. He had Simon & Garfunkel's album *Tom & Jerry*.

Jimmy and I remained good friends until he moved to Iqaluit to find a job. When he moved to Inujjuak in the mid-1970s, I lost track of him. He'd had a blood transfusion when he was shot in the stomach as a boy. Since the transfusion, he got cold easily, and I learned that sadly, he froze to death while lost out on the land.

Resolute was also the main hub of the region, with a lot of air traffic from Montreal, Winnipeg, Edmonton, and even Qaanaaq, Greenland. A great number of ships congregated there each summer. During the 1960s and '70s, the ship and air traffic in Resolute was greater than in Iqaluit. The air traffic was so heavy that in the mid-1970s, the territorial government was forced to move the Inuit community from its original site at the request of the Resolute Bay settlement council. The people were afraid one of the incoming aircraft could crash into the settlement. It was normal to see two or three aircraft on final approach coming to land, one aircraft behind another. During the peak period, filmmaker Douglas Wilkinson once commented in a documentary he produced that the local bar, Arctic Circle Club, had so many people from different countries pass through some nights, it looked like a bar from a Star Wars movie.

In my second year, I learned about dating girls. My first girlfriend at CVC was Eyuka Etidluie from Kinngait. We met the first Friday of the 1967 school year. For some reason our relationship did not last very long. Although our dates were nothing more than holding hands and kissing during free time, the thrill of having a girlfriend made it all worthwhile! It was drilled into us not to get a girl pregnant. Society frowned upon unwed parents so deeply. We whispered, not daring to speak out loud, when we heard about girls who had gotten pregnant. Any girl who did was automatically sent home. Some students who had met at CVC did get married after they left. Despite all of the risks we had to watch out for involved in dating, it was something we lived for during our CVC years.

* * *

Roger was a third-year senior, and he had special privileges I admired. The part-time pin-setting jobs the senior students got at the Knight Hall bowling alley was something I looked forward to. It paid a whole dollar an hour! I was also green with envy when he went to movies during weeknights. Regular students could only go on the weekends. One particular war movie he went to see had an "A" (for "Adult") rating. I was thinking, *Wow! Lucky guy!* Years later, I saw the same movie and noted there wasn't any adult content in it at all!

In the 1967–68 year, a record number of High Arctic and Baffin students attended CVC, many from Pangnirtung. At 9:00 each night, after free time, we gathered for a snack in the common room, where you could smoke. It was the biggest room in the dorms. There would be sandwiches and orange juice, and coffee shop orders were taken by a designated person who we could trust not to steal our money! Between paydays, those who were broke would be extra nice to those with money so they could "borrow" a few cents. Cigarettes were like gold for the heavy smokers. It was difficult not to share your precious pack. It was common to hear someone say, "After you?" meaning he wanted what remained of the cigarette you were smoking when you were done. Some guys would fight over "after you?"

Just before the school year was over, the tuberculosis returned, weakening my eye and causing the pain from my injury to come back. I was sent to Winnipeg's St. Boniface Hospital in the spring of 1968. I was put on strong medication. That was when I met the Souchan family. Mrs. Marie Souchan and her daughter, Diane, came to visit me one day not long after I had arrived. Mrs. Souchan worked for the government during the time Inuit were being sent to Winnipeg for school through the church system. She had been given the task to look after their wellbeing for many years as a volunteer. She had developed a special bond with Inuit, which continued until her death at ninety-three in the early 2000s.

From our first meeting on, the Souchan family became lifelong friends of my family. I enjoyed the drives they used to take me on to visit their home for meals, to go shopping, visit the zoo, visit the Red River Heritage Centre, and many other places. I never got tired of the long rides with the family. Mrs. Souchan had a way of keeping our attention with her narration of the history of Manitoba. She was a natural tour guide. I fell in love with Winnipeg because of them. Winnipeg will always have a special place in my heart.

While I was in Winnipeg, David Tulugak arrived from CVC for TB treatment, too. We hadn't really been friends at CVC, but in Winnipeg we got to know each other quite well. He was a born comic, sometimes imitating people we had interacted with during the day. One old Dene patient, Mr. Linklater, used to like visiting us even though he couldn't speak a word of English. He had that caring smile, and he obviously enjoyed our company. He would come into the room, put his elbows on the radiator, and visit for a while—never saying a single word, just smiling. After he left, David would pretend to be Mr. Linklater. He would come into the room, walk up to the radiator, and put his elbows on it, then smile and say nothing. We would burst out laughing. It was always good to see David again later in life. Sadly, he was killed in a small aircraft crash in Coral Harbour. I can still see his smiling face.

* * *

I was sent back to CVC after most of the students had left for home in late June. During the trip home that spring, I met Prime Minister Pierre Elliott Trudeau. By the time I arrived in Resolute Bay from CVC via Iqaluit, I was so homesick. To my horror, I was told I would not be going home for ten to fourteen days because there was no load to warrant a flight. The next day, the prime minister of Canada arrived—and he was scheduled to go to Grise Fiord the next day! I was too scared to ask for a ride on his charter. While I was visiting with Jimmy Naummialuk, he came in to shake hands with us. I had mixed feelings about meeting him, knowing he was going to Grise Fiord and I was not! My brother Elijah took 8mm movies of his visit to Grise Fiord.

Getting to Grise Fiord by plane also has other difficulties. Grise has some of the strongest winds in the Eastern Arctic. In July of 1968, an Atlas Aviation charter crash-landed in a windstorm. It was the famous CF-WWP ("WWP" for "Welland Wilfred Phipps"), known as "Whiskey Whiskey Papa." The pilot, Jan, made several passes before attempting to land. During a brief lull in the gusts of wind, he decided to approach from the west side of the airstrip. In those days, there was no VHF communication with pilots, nor were there any weather observers. Just as Jan was on final approach, the wind suddenly picked up, pushing his front wheel into the ground, where it broke off instantly. The aircraft was then thrown violently upwards into the air. Just as the pilot manoeuvred the aircraft downwards to regain balance, the wind pushed it back into the ground. The right wheel came off, the door opened, and mail came flying out! The third time the wind picked him up, it slammed him down so hard his left wingtip bent. The plane slid across the runway and off of it, heading straight towards the cliff at the end. For a few long seconds, those of us watching the whole scary incident thought for sure it was going to plunge off the cliff. If the wheel hadn't come off, creating a brake, it would have fallen into the river some one hundred feet down. Watching this happen was a harrowing experience. When the badly damaged CF-WWP stopped, you could hear shouting inside. When the passengers and crew emerged, they ran as far away from the plane as they could. Luckily, there was no fire. Hanna Quaraq, one of the witnesses, was crying hysterically for a while.

A few hours later, Weldy Phipps and Markoosie Patsauq came in from Eureka to pick up the crew of the damaged aircraft. It was the first time I had ever seen a Twin Otter land on a strip shorter than four hundred feet. With the wind still blowing in strong from the valley, it was like watching a seagull flying on a windy day. Markoosie has told me about his experience that day. "We made a pass over the Grise Fiord runway a couple of times," he said. "On one pass, the wind suddenly picked up, taking us along with it, heading straight towards a mountain! We had no control of the aircraft. We could only watch helplessly as we headed towards it." Thankfully, the updraft carried them over the mountain, but it was a very close call.

Graduation

My final year at CVC in 1968–69 is one of the most memorable for me. I started to date girls more than the previous school year. It seemed my being here on earth had a purpose at last. It was a whole new world; a cycle of boy meets girl, falls in love, has a broken heart after the break-up. The world seems perfect when one is in love. It was also the most miserable place when one broke up with his girl. My heart lived on cloud nine at least three times. I was also sent to a world where I received "Dear John" letters ("Dear Larry," in this case) three times.

My first girlfriend in 1967 from Kinngait had sent me soaring into the romantic clouds, then sent me crashing back to earth without a parachute! In the first week of my third year, Eyuka and I got back together again, and once again I was sent soaring into the clouds. Yet once more, I came crashing down to earth just as quickly, in less than a month. My heart was shattered!

My second girlfriend was Leetia Kov, and she dumped me just as fast as Eyuka. At least she told me why: I was simply too naive, an immature seventeen-year-old. My heart was so broken, I thought it would never stop bleeding.

I dated two different Louisas before I met Annie. She was from Salluit. I fell deeply in love for the very first time. She became my steady girlfriend. We saw each other at every opportunity. I looked forward to our weekend dates. Then, the week before our graduation, I made the mistake of taking someone else's pain medication, thinking it would get me high during our date. Instead of getting high, I lost my sensible behaviour. Of course, she dumped me in embarrassment. I could not blame her, nor could I get her back. I was so deeply broken-hearted; I did not date another girl for the next two whole years. I never saw her again. I have always wanted to see her again to explain what happened.

The lessons I learned taught me to expect what it was like to be heartbroken. Just like the Sonny James song: "Young love, first love, is filled with true devotion / Young love, first love, we share with deep emotion." How true those words are. Good thing we had school counsellors and supervisors who told us the pain would eventually go away.

I broke someone's heart too, while I was going to school in Ottawa in 1970–71. I broke her heart so badly, she did not date again for a year. The reason I left her was out of principle. Being a "perfect" gentleman, I wrote her to tell her I was too much into drugs and booze and that continuing our relationship would cause her too much pain. At the time, my reasons seemed to justify it, but I wondered for a long time if I had done the right thing. Do you think my reasons made sense? You be the judge.

* * *

My last year of CVC is full of wonderful memories. It was great to be a senior student at last. I was involved in many CVC activities. I became good friends with Allie Salluviniq and Isaac Kalluk, who was also from Resolute Bay. We formed an acoustic guitar group, with Allie as our lead singer. We couldn't afford electric guitars or drums. If there ever was a perfectionist, Allie was it. I learned a lot about the importance of pre-performance preparations. Isaac and I used to get corrected when we made a mistake during rehearsals days before the concert. We had to take the discipline in order to stay in the band. We once performed before a live audience at the Christmas concert at the Garrison Theatre. Boy, it was nerve-wracking. I was so scared that I stood sideways, not able to face the audience. We played our songs flawlessly. As I said, our leader, Allie, was a perfectionist. Allie formed a group in Resolute Bay during summer break with Paul Amagoalik on drums, Isaac on electric rhythm guitar, John Amagoalik on bass, and himself on lead guitar and vocals. It was really good. I played a few gigs with them. There is nothing like playing before a live audience.

While at CVC, I met many students from all over the Eastern Arctic. The high school students were receiving a more advanced education than those of us at CVC, and they also seemed so senior to us when it came to keeping up with new styles, including new music. The CBC played top hits on the radio, and we would look for them on the 45 rpm records at the commissary. It was during my last year at CVC that I first met Sheila Watt-Cloutier. Her hair was so blonde, it was white. I had never seen an Inuk with hair that colour. At twelve years of age, she acted so mature she could've passed for fifteen or sixteen. Carrying her radio while we were hanging around with the other high school seniors, she looked so "with it." When the song "Crimson and Clover" by Tommy James and the Shondells started, she turned up the radio volume to full blast, saying, "I like this new song so much!"

Later, the CVC students were invited to The Guess Who's jam session at the Garrison Theatre. They played their new song, "No Time," for us. Every time I hear that song, it reminds me of the time we got to watch them rehearse. None of us could afford to attend their regular concert, but the jam session was good enough for us. I sure was proud to have been in the same room with the first Canadian supergroup. I was having a pop at the Snack Bar when I saw Sheila walk in with them and The Harpoons. Sheila was one of the Go-Go girls for our very own CVC band. They were playing pool by the time I finished drinking my pop. I was thinking how cool that was. I realized Inuit can make good impressions among rock stars too!

* * *

During the Easter holidays of my last year, Allie Tulugak's big brother, Zebedee Nungak, came to CVC to visit his "kid" brother. Zebedee was my cousin, although I didn't realize it at the time. He was unusually mature, even though he looked quite young. He did not hesitate to say whatever was on his mind to anyone, including the authorities. I was captivated by his outgoing nature. Straight away, from the day we met, I made sure I was on his good side. I went to great lengths to make an impression on him. One thing that fascinated me about Zebedee was his knack for making his stories come alive. He was a master story-teller. In fact, he seemed to be master of whatever was around him. Atachie Goo from Kinngait quickly collided with him.

Graduation

Atachie Goo was one of the biggest students at CVC. Only two people could ever beat him in a fight: Phillip Nungak from Resolute Bay and Davidee Naluktuq from Inujjuak. He had matured by our third year, and he more or less defended our dorm. Yet we still never dared to make him angry. He knew his own strength, and he was not afraid of anyone. He was part of the CVC basketball, volleyball, track, and hockey teams. He was an all-around athletic student.

It so happened that there was a pair of boxing gloves in our dorm that students would occasionally put on to practice boxing skills, which were more just loafing around matches. Our supervisor had warned us about the dangers of boxing that could result in a permanent head injury, so we did not use them often. Atachie liked to test new guys, and it was obvious that he and Zebedee were fast approaching a boiling point. Something needed to be done. Someone got the idea of holding a boxing match to end the feud. When the match date arrived, everyone in our dorm gathered at the common room. Our supervisor was designated as the referee. In the opening round, it was obvious neither man was not going to stop until one of them went down. Atachie was determined to put down this short kid, but Zebedee was too fast on his feet. After they hit each other a few times, Atachie started to swing hard, determined to hit Zebedee with a knockout blow, but he could not. Then, Zebedee's right-arm hook hit: *SLURWHUPP!* Down goes Atachie. As soon as his head hit the floor, he gave out a strange wheezing sound, his lips puckered, and his body suddenly started shaking all over. When I watched the movie *Atanarjuat: The Fast Runner*, the scene where Natar Ungalaaq knocks out his opponent reminded me of what happened between Zebedee and Atachie in 1969. Atachie went silent, and the supervisor woke him up by slapping him on his cheeks. He got up smiling, his grin wider than any smile I have ever seen. "What happened?" he said. He looked so funny. Zebedee shook his defeated opponent's hand. The two became friends, and Atachie never tried to bully Zebedee again. After that fight, until we left for home, Atachie seemed to become timid as a kitten.

Something else happened during the Easter break of my last year, but it was something that makes me sad to remember. One of my three roommates that year was Paul Meeko from Kuujjuarapik. Paul was a very popular guy. Everyone loved him. On the weekends after morning cleanup until 5 p.m., we usually had the freedom to go anywhere (after notifying our supervisors), including downtown Churchill. Often, we would simply walk around. One day during the break, Paul apparently decided to go for a walk in the area with David Mikijuk and another boy from his community. They were walking along the outskirts of Churchill when they came across polar bear tracks. They tracked the bear along the edge of town. They were behind the bowling alley, in between the building and the trees behind it, when they suddenly came across the sleeping polar bear. Polar bears' natural instinct is to repel anyone they see as intruders, and the three boys had just disturbed its sleep. David and the other boy ran off. Paul tried to get out of the way, but the bear had already cornered him. It bit into his neck, letting go when Paul went limp. The boys ran to the nearby hospital. Help arrived quickly to bring him in, but he was pronounced dead on arrival. As soon as the news reached CVC, everyone was called into their respective recreation halls, and it was announced what had happened. It was a sad day for all. I could not sleep for a long time after that. I could not grieve. Finally, on one of the trips I took to Ottawa when the relocatees were lobbying for a formal apology during the '80s and '90s, I met the minister who had been in Churchill at the time of Paul's death, and I was able to grieve properly.

* * *

The work experience before graduation was an eye-opener for me. Various work-places in Churchill were given two students per week. It was meant to give us an idea of what a workplace feels like. I spent a week at the grain elevator near the historic fort downtown with another student. The elevator is a huge structure, full of grain ready for shipping to anywhere in the world. I did not enjoy working there; it was too slow and too mundane. My work partner was on a different floor. All seven floors were full of grain, nothing else. You could have gone to any floor and slept all day and nobody would have known.

My time at the Department of Public Works was just as boring. My two supervisors, who were supposed to give me work experience, took long coffee breaks and basically just drove around Churchill. One time we went to the dump so they could shoot at the seagulls from the car with the windows rolled down. One was sitting on top of a rock surrounded by water. Those two guys could not have hit a barn if it was in front of them. I was given the .22 long rifle. Even with my bad eyesight, I shot the bird dead centre. I could have been the one teaching them how to shoot. It went into the water, mortally wounded. Seeing the wounded bird, we sped off, not wanting to get caught! I'm sure the bones of the seagull I shot illegally were never found. So much for my work experience.

I also worked with an old gentleman inspecting building pipes below the former military barracks, which I enjoyed. He had a hunchback from an injury he never went to see a doctor for. He told me to look after my body and always report any injuries right away. He was very good at explaining everything as we went around to each pump station. He oiled every moving part and explained why it was necessary to do so.

What I liked most was working at the sheet metal shop. My supervisors were Second World War veterans. I asked them about their wartime service. Being just eighteen, I was ignorant about showing respect for something they would rather forget, but the way they explained the futility of war had a deep impact on my young life.

* * *

Leaving CVC after three years made me become reflective. In the days before we left, we would go to the storage room at night to be together without disturbing those who were asleep in the dorms. Even some old enemies became friends. One night in particular stands out. Isaac Kalluk, David Partridge, Atachie Goo, myself, and a few others were there. We were talking about our future plans. As youngsters, there were standards we had adopted when it came to which jobs we wanted and which ones we would never want to have. One job in particular none of us wanted was to become a sanitary engineer, or garbage collector. In the mid-1980s while I was passing through Resolute Bay, I saw Allie and Isaac. It was obvious they were working together. I asked them what kind of a job they had. Both replied, "Garbage collectors!" almost in unison.

During the graduation ceremonies, students with the best marks were announced. I thought, *How do they make school seem so easy?* The top students in my year included Monica Ittusardjuat from Iglulik, Betsy Anahattaq, Carmen Levi, and Sam Willy. Betsy and Sam had made a trip to Ottawa as part of their scholarship earlier in the year. I wished I was as smart as they were. Still, although grades were important, they were not a huge factor at CVC. You would be considered graduated if you had made it through all three years. I came close many times to giving up at CVC, especially when I still got picked on, but I'm glad I endured. There was a sense of accomplishment from having gotten through those years.

18

Winnipeg

When I arrived home from CVC in 1969, the special constables had moved into three-bedroom, low-rental units, and the duplex apartment they had lived in had been turned into a co-op store. Roger Killiktee was working at the store as a general manager. Gunther Lobe was the power plant operator. Samwillie and Ookookoo were the Department of Public Works (DPW) Inuit staff, and Gunther was their supervisor. My brothers had upgraded to more modern snowmobiles, so I was given one of their old ones. I spent a lot of time on it, using it to go on hunts.

Roger told me he was going to ask for a raise, saying he was entitled to a job review every six months. His plan was to quit and go back to school if he did not get his raise. When September 1969 arrived, I left for Winnipeg. I was going to upgrade my education and get my grade ten. Just before I left Resolute Bay, Roger arrived from Grise Fiord just as he had planned, explaining that his request for a raise had been turned down. He was on his way to Ottawa to attend Algonquin College. We left Resolute Bay with some former CVC students, including Allie. We spent one night in Montreal, in the Dorval area, at a hotel with a swimming pool. Being typical teenagers, we weren't tired, even though we had flown more than five and a half hours with a one-hour layover in Iqaluit. Most of us didn't even know how to swim. Allie hit his head on the bottom of the pool. Luckily, he did not injure himself. I dove and scraped the bottom, scratching my left nipple and causing it to bleed. I still have the scar today.

The legal drinking age was twenty-one in Montreal back in 1969, but that did not stop us from going to the hotel bar. My plan was to drink as much as I could and have a good time. I figured I could just sleep it off on our way to Ottawa. What I didn't know was that the flight only takes twenty minutes! It was a lesson learned the hard way!

After Roger was picked up at the airport by the Indian Affairs supervisor for Ottawa students, Allie and I found out we didn't have a ticket to continue our flight to Winnipeg, so we decided to book our own flight. The government contact was late to meet us for the connecting flight. He promptly cancelled our tickets and put us on a direct flight on another Air Canada flight. Air Canada was still owned by the federal government in those days. Everyone who had flown with us from Resolute Bay down to Montreal got off in Ottawa, so it was just me and Allie on the flight to Winnipeg from Montreal. When we arrived in Winnipeg, Dale from Indian Affairs met us at the airport to take us to our billets.

We billeted with Neil and Mona Kliewer. They had four children: Brenda, Linda (who was a baby at the time), Brian, and Bruce. Their house was within walking distance of downtown. The brothers each had their own place elsewhere in the city. Sam Willy from Arctic Bay, Timothy Kayak from Pond Inlet, and Noah Kumak from Salluit were the other students we shared the house with. Allie and I were roommates on the second floor. The three other boys were roommates living in the attic. We were given a very warm welcome by the family. Neil was very frank about what rules we were to follow. He told us he would treat us as adults, but he said he expected certain behaviour from us. He told us alcohol consumption would be tolerated only if we were of legal age. The only exception was if he gave us a drink, and that would only be at the house. He said that was perfectly legal, and we could only drink on special occasions. In fact, the only times we drank with them was the on the balcony the first day we arrived, since it was such a hot day, and on New Year's.

One thing we were told never to do was venture into the downtown main street of Winnipeg at night—and that is exactly where we went on allowance weekends. We were told the bars could get very rough, with fights often breaking out. We were cautioned to be careful around Dene. But as it turned out, my first girlfriend in Winnipeg was Dene!

Communication from home was via air mail, just like it had been while I was in Fort Churchill. The living allowance we received every two weeks from the government was substantially larger than the $1.75 we got while attending CVC, but the few dollars I received from my sister Minnie were always welcome. I bought my first electric guitar not long after our arrival. Sam Willy and Allie bought theirs later. Sam learned to sing and play rock 'n' roll music. He ended up having his own band in Arctic Bay not long after he was in Winnipeg.

Martha Martee, Percy Quvitsatsiaq, Allie, and I attended an adult education school that was held in an old army barracks called Fort Osborne Barracks. It had adult students of all sorts. It was the first time I realized even Qallunaat went back to school. I also learned that waiting for a bus at 8:30 in the morning can get pretty cold in the middle of winter in Winnipeg.

Our administrator, Mr. Rod Evans, was like a father to us. He made sure we were comfortable in our homes, often making visits to check up on us. He hand-delivered the living allowance to the Kliewer family and to us. He would invite all of the Inuit students under his care to his home at least once a month, although sometimes our weekend parties were held at the Souchan home. Even though some students were of legal drinking age, no alcohol was ever served. But just because there was no booze did not mean it was not a party!

* * *

I was very happy to see the Souchans again. Mrs. Souchan showed me what being a person of faith without being preachy or judgemental was like. The way she lived and what she taught was in line with the lessons my mother taught me growing up. The Souchans introduced me to Canon Jim Slater, the minister at the St. Margaret Anglican Church just down the road from the Kliewers'. I enjoyed attending the Sunday services there and participating in church events, like when they organized a canoe ride down the Assiniboine River. I was confirmed by Canon Slater through the Diocese of Rupert's Land.

Mrs. Souchan and I continued to correspond on a regular basis for many years. She often sent my young family care packages, which we always enjoyed opening as if they were Christmas presents. I know she is now resting with the Lord, who gave her so much guidance in making Inuit feel welcome in Winnipeg. Diane once told me how amazed she was that her mother knew almost every Anglican minister in the Arctic by name, even though she never met many of them.

During my stay with the Kliewers, I also met a young Pentecostal priest at a Salvation Army church near downtown who said he was a born-again Christian. The way he explained the importance of being "born again" made so much sense. We uttered the sinner's prayer together, and then he said I was born again. I did not feel anything different, but I was struck by his kindness. Of course, I explained what happened to Mrs. Kliewer. She warned me about people like that, saying that they know how to play with your emotions and make you feel guilty. I saw the same man a couple more times at the Salvation Army church service. Sure enough, when I noticed how persuasive they were, trying to make the churchgoers walk up to the altar, I remembered what Mrs. Kliewer had said. I stopped going to that church soon after. I have grown to think quite differently since that time, though.

Sometime before Christmas, Noah Kumak introduced me to Al Lewis, a former Hudson's Bay Company manager from Salluit and a Second World War veteran. He was so fluent in Inuktitut, he even knew Inuktitut words that were no longer in use. He hardly had an accent. It was fascinating to listen to him tell stories of his time in Salluit. Noah and I used to enjoy Al's company, as he spoke Inuktitut most of the time even though he was a Qallunaaq. It is always good to hear Inuktitut being spoken when you've been away from home for a while.

When I last saw Al Lewis, he had moved to a war veterans' hospital. He told me he had become a born-again Christian and said he no longer drank. He said he used to have to drink a fifth of whisky on a daily basis or else he would get awful headaches. He warned me once to never get hooked on booze. He said to me, "Larry, don't drink!" It was a short statement, but I have never forgotten it. He was a good example of the fact that people can change, if you believe in that. Not only had he stopped drinking, he had started having regular prayer meetings with friends, and he no longer used foul language every second sentence. When we parted for the last time, he wanted to have a prayer together. Out of respect for him I complied, even though I was very nervous with Mrs. Kliewer's words still in my memory: "They play with your emotions." Many years later, I heard from Noah that Al had gone back to Salluit for a visit, since that was what he used to wish for. He had worked at Deception Bay, and he hired a local person to take him to see it. Sadly, their snowmobile broke down, and he died of hypothermia before they were able to be rescued. He was already well past sixty years of age when I met him in 1969.

Over Christmas, I was pleasantly surprised to get a long-distance phone call from Roger, who was in Ottawa. We chatted for a while, catching up on the news from home. After the phone call, home didn't seem so far away. It's so easy today to call home from anywhere in the world. Mary Panigusiq's statement from back in 1961 has truly come to pass: the world is indeed very much smaller!

On New Year's Eve, just as Mr. Kliewer had promised, we were given alcohol to celebrate the arrival of 1970. We sure felt grown up! It was snowing outside, and it was funny to see Noah Kumak get so excited—he wanted to go build an iglu! Mrs. Kliewer thought it was hilarious. She just about started rolling on the floor in laughter!

* * *

The Kliewers would sometimes host students who were passing through Winnipeg for a short time. One student who came to stay with us in early 1970 was on his way to Brandon, Manitoba, to take a plumbing course. He was twenty-one, and we wished we could go to a bar like he could. Sure enough, a few days before he was to leave for Brandon, the Kliewers received a phone call from a bar on Wellington Avenue. Mr. Kliewer asked if we wanted to go with him, so two other boys and I went along. It was snowing heavily when we saw him. He fell down in the middle of the street. Looking back, I think this was Mr. Kliewer's way of teaching us a lesson without saying anything. That was probably why he had asked us to go along in the first place.

Just before the end of the year, it was announced that Manitoba's drinking age was being lowered to eighteen on April 1, 1970. I could not wait for April to arrive. Not long after the New Year, Allie told me he knew a place down on the main street, a Chinese restaurant where he went on paydays to eat and drink Cracklin' Rosie wine. He said they never checked his ID. *Hmmm, interesting,* I thought. One payday, we decided to go together. He ordered his usual meal and a bottle of Cracklin' Rosie with two glasses. I felt so grown up! We became payday regulars. I was never asked to produce ID. Sometimes I struggled to act sober when we were leaving after our meal, but the Kliewers never suspected that we had just come back from a licensed establishment. I looked forward to payday weekends.

One weekend, Allie was away, so I went to the restaurant alone. I ordered my usual meal and a bottle of Cracklin' Rosie. I ate my food and drank the whole bottle by myself. As soon as I got up to leave and my body started to move, the alcohol took effect. I fought to keep my balance and composure. The manager, a Chinese woman, was bowing in a gesture of gratitude as I passed by. I smiled back, saying "thank you" as I walked out. When I opened the door, I inhaled a whiff of cold air that hit my lungs like a shotgun blast. My head started to spin, and I struggled to walk in a straight line. I had never fought so hard to concentrate. As it was the middle of winter, I realized I was not going to be able to walk all the way home in my condition. I knew I was in danger of passing out in the cold. I came very close to falling asleep outside. I have been grateful that I did not. My last clear memory is of making the decision to look for a taxi, even though I knew I didn't have enough money. The recollections I have of that scary night are like movie clips with blank spaces between scenes. Before finding a taxi, I seem to have a memory of going into someone's house, yet it seems like a dream. I can't be too sure of anything until I got home. I know I stopped briefly to warm up somewhere after I passed the corner of Main Street and Portage Avenue; it's famous for being one of the coldest spots in Winnipeg. I remember being relieved to get into a taxi. I was so cold by then I did not care that I couldn't afford the taxi ride home. I wasn't going back out again until I got home. The ride home is a blur. I vaguely remember negotiating with the taxi driver about terms of payment and him accepting. When we arrived outside the Kliewers' front yard, I gave the driver my shoes. When I stepped out and my left foot hit the soft, cold snow—*brrrr!* So cold! Thank God I had socks on! Leaving the taxicab and going out into the cold air helped to sober me up. The space between the street and the door to the house seemed ten miles long with the ground being so cold. I walked up to the house as quietly as I could, like a cat stalking a mouse. When I entered, I was relieved to find that nobody was awake—or so I thought. I found out the following morning that in fact, someone had been awake in the kitchen. We didn't know until we were about to leave for home at the end of our stay with them that the Kliewers never went to bed on the weekends until we were all safely home.

The next morning, Mr. Kliewer came to my room to give me a talk about the importance of avoiding getting too intoxicated lest I suffer the consequences. He said alcohol abuse had a way of getting back at you. It could make you fight, or say things that are deep within yourself that you ordinarily would not talk about. That talk he gave me struck a chord so deep within me that I never passed out or lost control of my drinking again, at least not in my first twenty years of drinking.

Linda Guimond was a Dene woman from a small town north of Winnipeg, and she was a student at the Fort Osborne Barracks. She was billeting at a private home. She introduced me to the bars along the main street. Most Dene knew her and respected her. She had been a bartender before, and she was highly respected by some of her former customers. Not knowing how to pace beer drinking, I drank as if I were having pop. My companion tried to warn me about the consequences of drinking too fast lest I get sick. Of course, once the bitter taste went away after the first sip, and I felt euphoria sweep over my head almost instantly, I paid no mind to her warnings. By the third beer, I started feeling nauseous and had an awful urge to pee and vomit at the same time. As I entered the toilet, all that I had drunk came rushing out. Man, I was never so sick! Not only was I sick, I suddenly started to sob.

After we left the bar, she told me not to drink so fast next time. After I met Linda, I learned to pace my drinks. Mr. Kliewer's words about the importance of respecting alcohol, controlling it instead of it controlling you, would come back to haunt me. Later in life, I became addicted to alcohol, something I regret. I misused Al's advice. Instead of not drinking at all, I made sure not to drink so much that I passed out after what had happened that night after I left the restaurant. Being eighteen or nineteen, starting out into adulthood, I felt so sure of myself. I felt like there was no mountain I could not climb. When I was in school in Fort Churchill, we were taught to be responsible for our actions, so I learned to make sure I got up the next morning when I had to, whether I was hungover or not. I think that if Mr. Kliewer had not spoken to me about it the day I sold my shoes, I would still be trying to find out everything that alcohol can do to you if you abuse it.

19

Old World

*I*n the spring of 1970, I borrowed an old 8mm movie camera from the Kliewers and took a roll of film. I was so impressed with the film I had made, I decided to buy a movie camera. I purchased a Super 8 movie camera and started to experiment with making movies. Many years later, I graduated to Beta and VHS-C video recorders, but I have continued to film ever since. My brother Elijah already owned a hand-wound Bell & Howell movie camera that he had bought from Joatamie, who in turn had bought it from Bob Pilot. I started filming everywhere I went, including bus rides. My earliest footage is of bus rides to downtown Winnipeg, and later, visits to the park and the zoo, and of young people jumping off a bridge. I have a few clips of me dressed in hippie-style clothes, barefoot, on warm summer days.

The weather in Winnipeg was getting unbearably hot when I left to go home after finishing the school year in the summer of 1970. In my Super 8 movies, you can see how green Winnipeg looked. I took footage of the entire trip home from Winnipeg. Our pilot was Jack Austin, who had flown for the RCMP during the time I first left home in 1958, and the other passengers were the family of Josephie Koonoo. In Resolute Bay, I met Martha, who was coming back from CVC for the summer. My Super 8 movies show the water puddles on top of the ice getting deeper when we landed in the third week of June. You can see us waiting for the people to come meet us from the settlement. Once again, I was experiencing the back-and-forth of living in two worlds.

When I got home, I saw that the community had gone through a few changes. The settlement council now had the water/ice and sewage delivery contracts for the community. A few years prior, the community's garbage disposal was on the ice. The idea was to let nature take care of the debris when the ice melted, and it disappeared underwater. And indeed, the garbage disappeared nicely each spring. At that time, people did not take the environmental hazards into consideration. Later, the garbage was thrown into different places east of the community. Before the present site was finally selected, three areas east of the hamlet were used as dumping sites. The old dump sites are eyesores you wouldn't care to see.

Tookilkee Kiguktak and Paulassie were the water/ice delivery workers. In the winter, a Bombardier with continuous tracks (like the kind you would see on tanks) and snowmobiles with sleds would be used to haul ice. In the summer, the Bombardier was used to deliver water. Tookilkee and Paulassie were responsible for the delivery for many years. In 1974, Jimmy Nowra joined the two men in the responsibility right up until he died. Paulassie was later hired to work as a janitor for the school. Tookilkee was told to retire when he turned sixty-five, but did not realize he did not necessarily have to.

Up until he was forced to retire due to poor health, Josephie Flaherty was responsible for the honey bucket disposal, with a separate driver as his helper. Until sewage trucks were used, a front-end loader was the only vehicle available, which Jopee Kiguktak drove. The co-op had the gas and diesel fuel delivery contract.

During that time, I met Bezal Jesudason, who had replaced Gunther Lobe as the DPW power plant operator and foreman, although it was obvious that he did not like the DPW's chain-of-command structure. He was also the Kenting Atlas Aviation agent, the postmaster, and the first non-Inuk to get married in Grise Fiord. Bezal was from India and fascinated by Inuit culture. I noticed he bought carvings at extremely low prices, yet the people who were selling them did not complain or seem to care. I sometimes interpreted for him when he made his transactions, and I did not hesitate to tell him what I thought about his shrewd-ness. He told me how spoiled and well-off he thought Inuit were, taking things for granted and even complaining about low wages. He explained that where he came from in India, people struggled just to make ends meet. He told me he sent half of any money he made to his family in India. Still, no matter how many times I tried explaining to the carvers how little he was paying them, it did no good. In time, when I got to know Bezal, I saw why the carvers never considered taking more money from him. He was kind, considerate, and good at explaining things with clarity. By the time he was finished explaining why it was necessary for him to pay you very little, you were ready to give him all your money. He is the only person I have ever met who people enjoyed giving money to. He was also the first non-Inuk to openly speak out against the territorial government. He said the Government of the Northwest Territories had way too many regulations, and called it "wishy-washy" when bureaucrats behaved like they did not have common sense. He lived in Grise Fiord for almost ten years.

* * *

Another change took place that summer: Abraham Okpik was given a Government of the Northwest Territories contract to travel all over the Eastern Arctic and replace the E-numbers with last names for all Inuit. He spent a week in Grise Fiord. It was an opportunity to choose any name you wanted.

I introduced Abraham to my relatives and helped him explain what he was doing. He said that most people around the world used the last name of the head of the household, but he stressed that this was a chance to take any name. I had never liked being Aqiatushuk, for it sometimes subjected me to being called "fat." From what I know, Qallunaat would differentiate between Inuit with the same first name with a physical description. If there were multiple Larrys, perhaps there would be "tall Larry," "short Larry," and "thin Larry." There was probably another Inuk with the first name "Isa," so Qallunaat would call my father "big Isa" or "chubby Isa" to distinguish him from the other Isa. At some point, someone must have translated "fatty" into Inuktitut, and "Aqiatushuk" made its way into the official documents. I changed my last name to Audlalook, and later became Larry Aqiatushuk Audlaluk. Audlaluk was my born name. I was named after a prominent, colourful figure from the old days who had made his way into legend. Audlalualuk (as was the original spelling) was someone people remembered from way back. There's a song about him. He was a great hunter and probably a person of some controversy. When you become a very great hunter, you become an easy target.

My uncle chose his father's last name, Novalinga. His son Paulassie took his namesake at birth, Nungaq. Samwillie E9-913 became Samwillie Kasudluak at first, but later took his father's name, Elijasialuk. Elijah E9-912 decided to become Elijah Nutara. "Nutara" was his childhood lullaby name. My mother, Mary E9-909, became Mary Aupaluk Aqiatushuk. It was a chance for my brother Josephie to take Robert Flaherty's name. He was proud to become Josephie Flaherty. Some families kept the names they already had and just adopted their baptismal names as legal first names. For example, everybody always knew Akpaliapik as Akpaliapik, so he became Simon Akpaliapik. Even though my sister Minnie E9-914 never technically married Pauloosie E5-705, he was still considered her common-law spouse, so she became Minnie Killiktee.

* * *

When I was home that summer, I was back in my old world. When I got home, I learned that hunters in Grise Fiord had been told the Vancouver Aquarium was looking to live-capture a baby narwhal and had offered a financial reward for anyone who managed to complete the task. They had been attempting to do this for quite some time. In fact, when I got back, Elijah had already constructed a noose device, much like dog-collaring equipment. Live-capturing narwhals is not impossible; however, they don't live long in captivity. The aquarium's most recent catch had been from Pond Inlet, but it had died.

As I mentioned before, narwhals did not always come to the south end of Ellesmere Island, but in the summer of 1970, they came. Day or night, if whales come, hunters will run to their boats. I was enjoying being up all night when a pod of narwhals passed by. I ran home to wake my brother. He still had the wooden boat fitted with a 25-horsepower outboard motor, and he brought his whale-capture noose with him. We quickly took off, as did the other hunters. We came across Corporal Al Kirbyson, Bezal Jesudason, and Abraham Pijamini in an RCMP canoe. It was on a weekend, and the men's breath smelled of a whisky distillery, but none of them looked too intoxicated. We asked which way the narwhals went. We were told there were narwhals everywhere, and to just wait for them to come up.

Sure enough, we saw a good-sized group and gave chase. My brother spotted a mother narwhal with a young one, and we concentrated on separating them from the main group. Right in front of the community, Elijah told me to take the outboard tiller. He picked up his lasso and went to the front of the boat. He tried several times to lasso the young whale without success. All the while, the mother was never far from her baby. My brother decided to get on top of the front platform of the boat. I was not a good driver on the tiller. I was scared I would make a sudden turn and drop him into the water, so I slowed down considerably. The animals started to get farther away, and he shouted for me to go faster. I had no choice but to comply, but to my astonishment, he never fell off! We chased the creatures into water that was so shallow they grounded, much to our relief. As we drove behind the animals, Elijah kept trying to lasso the young whale without success. When he saw he could not lasso the young narwhal from where he was standing, he jumped into the water in a desperate attempt to get the noose around the whale.

You could've thrown a basketball into my wide-open mouth and I probably wouldn't have noticed, I was so surprised to see him jump into the water! He was wearing hip waders and a parka without a cover. When he jumped in, he shouted at me to stop the engine. The whales were splashing water all over the place; it felt like we were being rained on. I watched this entire spectacle in astonishment and silence, the whales thrashing around, and my brother in the middle of it all! It was a wild struggle, as if he were in the water trying to tame a wild horse. Eventually, he succeeded—we had successfully live-captured a young narwhal!

Nobody could give us assistance right away as they were busy hunting another group of narwhals, but a few hours later, some hunters came to help us out. As the tide was still going out, the mother was given a helping hand to get into deeper water. The young narwhal was kept in the local pond at first, but the pond is not saltwater. The animal was a saltwater creature and needed to be in its natural environment, so a couple of days later, it was moved to the water in front of the RCMP detachment, with a rope attached to its tail to keep it from escaping. A piece of soft linen was wrapped around the tail to prevent the rope from cutting the skin. Jamie Flaherty was hired to fish for sculpin using the RCMP canoe. The animal was fed every day for two weeks while we waited for the Vancouver Aquarium charter to arrive.

When the plane arrived, it was piloted by Jack and Jan of Atlas Aviation. One man from the aquarium came to prepare the whale for transport. It was the first time we had ever seen a man wearing a wetsuit in real life. The whole community went down to the beach where the whale was to watch it being prepared for the long flight south. I shot the whole episode on my Super 8 camera, and you can see that almost everyone in Grise Fiord went to watch. Looking at the footage, it makes me realize how good life was in Grise Fiord. The animal was put in a padded sling used to move marine animals, and then it was put into a wagon pulled by front-end loader. You can see people walking up the airstrip behind the whale to watch it being loaded onto the aircraft.

Sadly, we heard that not long after it arrived at the aquarium, it died. There had been nothing wrong with it physically. I'm certain it was from loneliness for its mother. Inuit Elders know young whales have been known to die of fear, too. Maybe the Elders were right; it may have died of fright. After all, it had been captured from the wild. I didn't know better at the time. If I were offered the same chance today, I wouldn't do it.

* * *

That same summer, I went on a camping trip with Paulassie and Tookilkee Kiguktak to the Skerries sometime before the ice left Jones Sound. In the evening the first night we were there, Paulassie and I were talking in his tent. He started to tell stories about mythical creatures of the sea. My imagination took hold, and I could not go back to my tent until long after he was finished his stories. It was broad daylight, with the sun high in the sky, yet I was petrified!

Although I have never seen any ghosts, I believe in the existence of unseen forces. The Inuit world is full of spiritual stories, most of which can't be explained by things in the physical world. Like other people around the world, Inuit have many stories of various beings. I have always been fascinated by the legends my parents and Elders told me about when I was growing up on Lindstrom Peninsula and in Grise Fiord—the difference between our Elders and non-Inuk storytellers is that some of our Elders truly believed in what they were telling us.

My mother used to say that animals turned into humans frequently in the olden days. She believed that *tarriaksuit,* shadow people who look like humans, existed. In Nunavik, people call them *tuurngat,* ghosts. Tuurngat appear and behave just the same as tarriaksuit. The only difference is that their eyes are slanted sideways. Tarriaksuit and tuurngat are no threat to anyone who encounters them. In fact, they have been known to live just like Inuit. There are two big differences between them and us. One: when they chew solid food and swallow it, the food will come out the windpipe. Two: when startled, they disappear. Some tarriaksuit have kept up with the changing times, like Inuit, but in the majority of sightings and encounters with them, they are dressed in traditional clothes. My mother told me of a time when she was still living at their traditional home, Uugaqsiuvik. She saw my father coming back from a seal hunt, so she put the teakettle on. But the dog team never arrived—it was probably a tuurngat dog team that she saw.

A respected Elder from Resolute once told me about a family that lived alone in a traditional home on Baffin Island. When her husband was away hunting, the wife would do chores outside their peat house. Once in a while, she could swear she saw someone out of the corner of her eye, yet when she turned to look, there was nobody there. Pretty soon, she was convinced she was not alone. After trying to figure out how to see the elusive figure, she got an idea.

The next time she saw someone at the edge of her vision, she did not turn her head. Instead, she looked at the person out of the corner of her eye and walked sideways towards them until she bumped into them. As soon as that happened, the elusive person appeared! It turned out the Inuit family was living side by side with a tarriaksuit family. She started visiting them every day. They lived just like modern Inuit, with the same frailties. One of their children was ill and soon died.

Unlike tarriaksuit, sightings of strange women wearing *amautit* with no infant on the back is not good. These women have been known to take newborn babies while the parents are asleep. An attempted kidnapping of a newborn is said to have happened during the early 1980s in Nunavut. The mother was asleep with her newborn during the day when she suddenly awoke to a strange woman slowly heading towards her son.

"Who are you? What are you doing? What do you want?" she asked. The woman did not answer and quickly backed out. The mother followed her out, but the stranger was nowhere to be seen. The strangest thing about the whole story is that the mother did not tell anyone about it for eight years! It was as if she was made to forget about the whole incident for a long period of time.

The Inuit world is full of strange stories involving shape-shifting creatures. They look like ordinary animals, yet when you look at them closely, you can see they are stunted versions of the real thing. Caribou, polar bears, and other four-legged creatures with short legs; foxes that turn into wolves or Arctic hares; that kind of thing. Hunters have been known to pursue these animals, but to no end, as they could not get close.

A friend told me about a time his father went on a hunting trip for caribou with couple of other men on Baffin Island. The men sighted a herd of four animals and pursued them for a long time but could not get close. After each time the animals went behind a hill, they were twice the distance away when the hunters saw them again. Realizing they were wasting time, the hunters stopped chasing the caribou and turned back. When they reached the place they had started from, they found they had travelled in a single day a distance that should have taken four! In other words, the caribou led them on a wild goose chase. There is an Inuit belief that the land can become reactive. I have heard stories of people trying to make it home, but the journey is taking two, four, five times as long as it should. To make it stop, Inuit will take a knife or *ulu* and cut a line into the path in front of them. Past the line, they are able to travel normally.

Stories about meeting "little people," who we call *inugagulliit,* involve tales of survival. Inuit are filled with fear when they see evidence of their presence. Inugagulliit are very strong physically and can suddenly grow very tall when threatened. They dress in traditional clothes, use bows and arrows, and walk instead of using dog teams for transportation, as they have always done for centuries. They stay well hidden from the world, but Inuit don't doubt the existence of these elusive people.

One Elder used to tell a story about a hunter who came across a family while hunting seal. As it was custom to use dogs to sniff out agluit in April when the snow was too deep to spot them, the hunter had two of his dogs with him. He unexpectedly came across a tiny iglu with two huge caribou buttocks leaning against it towards the sun to thaw. An inugagulliq came out of the iglu and started to run towards him. Before the hunter could react, the inugagulliq jumped up towards his head. This tactic is how inugagulliit suffocate their opponents—they will cover the Inuk's nostrils and mouth to asphyxiate them. The hunter found himself in a dangerous situation. Since his two dogs were barking violently in protection of their master, he fell towards them. The dogs tore the inugagulliq into little bits and pieces. But a strange thing happened. The inugagulliq's little heart, still beating, bounced around all over the ice for a few minutes before it stopped. After recovering from the attack, the hunter heard someone crying from inside the iglu. He looked inside through the ventilation hole and saw a woman and child crying in grief. The hunter tried to console them, saying he was going home to get help, and telling them not to go anywhere.

The next day, when he came back to the camp, the caribou buttocks were gone, along with the woman and child. The tracks indicated that they had carried the meat on their backs! The footprints were going in the direction of the mainland. The Inuit tracked them all day without catching up, eventually giving up when the tracks led into very rough, rocky terrain.

Another hunter in more "modern" times ("modern" meaning after the arrival of the Hudson's Bay Company) had an encounter with an inugagulliq while checking his traps. The hunter had just removed a fox and was covering the trap with snow when an inugagulliq arrived. Seeing the dead fox, the inugagulliq demanded to be given half of the animal. He explained to the hunter that it was a prize fox that he had tracked all day. The hunter did not hesitate to give him the other half. The inugagulliq left as soon as he got his portion.

The most recent encounter took place in 2009. A hunter was travelling on the land with his ATV when he suddenly found himself face-to-face with an inugagulliq—like the two of them were in a standoff. The inugagulliq was cornered by the Inuk, who carried a rifle slung over his shoulder. The hunter reached out his arm, telling the inugagulliq to come home with him. The inugagulliq took out his bow and an arrow and aimed at the hunter in defiance. The hunter noticed many bones scattered all around, an indication of harvest remains. When the inugagulliq ran, the hunter gave chase on his ATV. After quite a distance, they hit a rocky area, and he lost the inugagulliq. As is common with such encounters, the hunter did not tell his story for some time. He had forgotten about it when he got home. When he finally remembered the incident, he went back to look for the site of his encounter with the inugagulliq, yet he could not remember any of the details.

There are also tales of *nunaup inungit*, very tall, hairy creatures that walk upright, and of *ijirat*. Ijirat look like ordinary people, but their main purpose is to make Inuit hunters lose their way back home. Disappearances of people without explanation have been attributed to them. You don't want to be deceived by ijirat.

A few years ago, my wife's nephew and his family were camping at Anstead Point. He had brought along an ATV, and one of his daughters went exploring on it with her cousin. The girls came across what appeared to be the grave of a young child. One of the girls, Sarah, picked up a piece of the child's jawbone to take back to their camp. As soon as she touched it, both girls heard a loud whisper in Inuktitut: "Don't disturb that!" But they did not tell each other. Now scared, neither of them knowing the other had heard the whisper, they quickly decided to leave. The jawbone was in Sarah's pocket when they left. As they drove, they could hear someone running after them, whispering, "Leave it alone!" No matter how fast they drove, the voice kept up with them. Only when Sarah threw the bone from her pocket did the ghost stop chasing them. Back at the camp, they related the story in tears, for they were so badly shaken.

Tookilkee Kiguktak and Abraham Pijamini told the story of Kiviuq, one of the most important figures in Inuit mythology, in such minute detail that it was hard to listen to other versions for a while. The other stories the two men told were equally interesting. Like most Inuit storytellers of their generation, both men told legends in meticulous detail, captivating their audience in a spell that can only be described as magic.

* * *

Unlike Tookilkee and Abraham, my uncle Philipoosie did not like those kinds of stories. He did not like it when I started to tell the saga of Qidlarsuaq over the local FM radio. In fact, he was against any kind of storytelling, saying it was against the word of God.

When Christianity began to be integrated into Inuit culture, one of the most misunderstood messages our Elders heard from the Christian missionaries was "repent and turn from your evil ways." In Nunavik especially, most of them thought it meant they were to forget about absolutely everything, including their legends, habits, and survival skills—to completely stop telling stories about anything from the past, and to abandon all their traditional ways of doing things. But what the message meant was to stop coveting, lying, murdering, practicing black magic. The Gospel says instead to love thy neighbour, do good to others, believe in only one God.

From the first day of contact with Christopher Columbus, traditional spiritual beliefs were a target in the missionaries' battle plans. The missionaries knew exactly what they were doing when they forced the first peoples to give up their beliefs, practices, legends, and stories. As a consequence, many of my Elders from Nunavik forgot many of their traditional stories, with few exceptions. When you lose your most sacred rituals, you lose the foundation of your culture, whatever race or creed you are. Forcing conquered people to live without their foundational beliefs will eventually destroy them. In the beginning, our people embraced the new ways, but time has proven them wrong. Today, young Inuit feel hollow, helpless, and without identity. With the high rate of suicide, our Elders are trying to grasp why so many are taking their own lives. Nobody knows why some people kill themselves—some have reasons fuelled by substances or by fear. The deaths with no apparent reason attached to them are the most puzzling, yet one can't help but think some of it stems from feeling like nobody, feeling worthless.

I've asked some Elders why they gave in to the European ways so easily. The most common answer I've been given was the technology the Qallunaat brought with them, like guns, wooden boats, wooden houses, ships, metal. Our skin boats, little kayaks, houses made of snow, bows and arrows, and our skin clothes that needed replacing often seemed puny in comparison. One Elder said, "We just felt inferior." When the missionaries preached their doctrine, Inuit and other Indigenous peoples felt they had to obey, lest the goods they had become dependent upon be taken away.

In the Arctic, the whalers, prospectors, independent trappers, and foreign explorers were of concern to the Canadian authorities and the missionaries. Churches from Belgium and England started to send ministers on the whaling ships specifically to minister to Inuit and Qallunaat spiritual needs. Reverend Edmund Peck was one of the very first Anglican ministers to preach to Inuit of the Cumberland Sound area. He was determined to eradicate the demons from the shamans. Stories are still remembered about his fights with some of the most powerful shamans in the early years of his ministry in South Baffin. An Elder said that shamans thought they were going to work alongside the European preachers. Instead, the preachers rudely told them they were godless people, heading straight to hell, and that they were serving Satan.

Some of the priests labelled Inuit "heathens" without bothering to find out the foundations of our beliefs. If they had bothered to study our spiritual beliefs, they would have been surprised how many similarities there were between the Old Testament and Inuit laws. They would have seen that we believed in good and evil. I am not trying to say we could do no wrong. Human behaviour is the same everywhere when it comes to personal desires, and Inuit were no different than Qallunaat when it came to frailties. We coveted others' wives, property, skills, and popularity, plotted to gain the upper hand, that kind of thing. Family feuds were not unknown in Inuit society. Sometimes they even involved murder. Clan grievances could last for generations. I am simply pointing out that Inuit knew the difference between right and wrong. We were not the godless heathens the early missionaries reported us to be.

20

Steppenwolf and Robert Janes

*W*hen I left for Ottawa in September of 1970, I was headed to Ethel Gould Business College. I wanted to learn basic office procedures and just be more up-to-date. At the start of the school year, there were only three Inuit in my class. One of them, Adamie Kalingo, was an exceptionally great student and passed at the end of the year with flying colours. A month later Willie Watt from Kuujjuaq arrived. Roger was going back for his second year at Algonquin College. When I think about my "should haves," that is where I should've gone instead. It offered a broader education than Ethel Gould, and I would have been able to learn different kinds of things. Once more, Allie Salluviniq and I were roommates and attending the same school. We were billeting with Mr. and Mrs. Jim Taylor and their three children in Ottawa's west end. When my cousin Peter Inukpuk came south from Inujjuak, I got to meet a cousin I had never known before, whom I had left behind in 1953. He started out living in the basement, but he soon found it too cold, and we switched places until we left for home.

I had more money than I had ever had in my entire life after my brother and I got paid for capturing the baby narwhal—more than $2,000 each! I knew if I looked after it, I would have money for quite a while. Of course, the money did not last, but at least I bought the quality guitar I had always wanted.

Now that I was over nineteen, Allie and I spent our weekends at a couple of bars downtown in the Bank and Sparks area. It was the first time I'd ever entered a bar where people were so quiet they didn't seem to be drinking. The bars in Winnipeg's north end were full of noisy customers, and I had thought that was generally how it was supposed to be. When it came to drinking, Indigenous people had adopted Qallunaat behaviour, thinking that was how it should be. Even the first "cowboys and Indians" movies had drinking scenes complete with bar fights. The first Europeans—the Hudson's Bay Company, the RCMP, free traders, and civil servants, including some teachers—brought alcohol to the North with them to alleviate their loneliness for "civilization." When the military started coming up after the Second World War, the soldiers' regulation requirement to have a shot of rum each day did not go unnoticed. I was confused for a while when I saw with my own eyes people just sitting quietly all night, drinking booze and not showing any sign of intoxication at all!

Roger, Allie, and I eventually started going to different places at night in Ottawa on the weekends. Allie and I found out from Roger that Quebec liquor laws were quite different from Ontario's. After the establishments closed in Ottawa, we'd cross to Hull, Quebec, to continue our Friday- and Saturday-night bar hopping.

One weekend, Peter Ittinuar, the first Inuk Member of Parliament for the Northwest Territories, invited us to a gathering in downtown Ottawa. He is the grandson of the famous literary adventurer Peter Freuchen of Denmark. Peter's legacy contributed to great positive changes in Inuit politics, pioneering Inuit's entrance into the Canadian Parliament and paving the way for the creation of Nunavut—the stuff of legend. He was working for Inuit Tapirisat of Canada (now Inuit Tapiriit Kanatami) by the time I was in Ottawa. I was proud to have met him at that time.

I enjoyed taking long walks with our neighbour Mark Gordon to the local YMCA. I had first met Mark at CVC when he was a high school student. The walk took more than half an hour, yet it never seemed to take that long. Mark was a natural storyteller who had a way of making his subjects come alive. He'd tell me all about what they were learning at the university he was attending. He told me how paramedics dealt with traumatic situations in the field. His descriptions of the film footage they were shown in class horrified me, but it was his description of how substances like tobacco, alcohol, and drugs affect the human body that had a lasting impression. The consequences of long-term use of LSD, amphetamines, cannabis, and other mind-altering substances were not known at the end of the 1960s and early 1970s.

Mark and I became much closer friends after the Christmas holidays. I met a lot of his friends and colleagues from school. I felt privileged to be included in his circle of friends; it gave me a glimpse into what some young people in a city were into. I experimented with different substances. I took an occasional "trip" and listened to Led Zeppelin, Jimi Hendrix, and Cat Stevens, among others. I met The Byrds' Mr. Tambourine Man, took a ride on Steppenwolf's magic carpet, and visited Jimi Hendrix's castle in "All Along the Watchtower." When I tried MDMA, I was so blown away, I was ready to go to Washington and help bring about the end of the Vietnam war. Mark and I would go to the country, not necessarily to go fishing or hunting. On one such "camping trip," a friend's dad had agreed to pick us up after the weekend. He asked his son, "Are you boys doing pot?" After a few seconds of total silence, we all stammered, "…Uh, no," almost in unison.

One night after midnight, we were driving home from an evening of hanging out at a friend's house when the police stopped us. We were driving an old white van. The police told us to form a line facing them so they could conduct a search for any illegal substances we might be carrying. Mark and I were the last ones in line. When it was his turn, Mark told the police that we were Inuit, Eskimos from the Far North. Halfway through their search, they stopped. I was so relieved to be spared the humiliation that my friends had gone through. Had I returned to Ottawa the following fall to go back to school, I would most likely have been subject to many temptations I would not have been able to get away from.

A few months before summer break, Mark said he was leaving. Charlie Watt, who had accompanied me on my hospital trip when I was eight years old, was working with the Northern Quebec Inuit Association. He had offered Mark a job as a negotiator for their land claim negotiations. I was saddened to see him leave.

At the end of June, when the school year was done, I decided I'd had enough of getting up in the morning. Besides, I did not pass the typing course at Ethel Gould. So, I gave up school. The Northern Affairs administrator told me I could attend Algonquin College in September, but I declined. On the way back from Ottawa, Allie and I spent a week in Iqaluit to see if we could find work with the Government of the Northwest Territories.

After Allie and I were checked in to the new Frobisher Inn hotel, I went for a walk. I ran into Parnee Noah, who had been one of the interpreters on the ship in 1963 when I was on my way to Montreal. She was with this gorgeous young woman, who I learned was Annie Manomie. I thought I was meeting her for the first time, but it turned out that she remembers me kissing her on the cheek in 1965 around the time of the Toonik Tyme festival. She says my kiss caused her to get a rash! And I don't remember any of it. What a powerful kiss it must have been to have prevented her from meeting anyone else until 1971! She tells me when she met me for the second time, it was love at "first" sight. We had a connection immediately. I have been with Annie ever since.

I ended up being hired by Naomi Griffin from the Economic Development department as an interpreter/translator. I was given an apartment on the second floor of the high-rise in Iqaluit, connected to the new hotel. Before I started work, I went home for two weeks. Since 1969, Nordair, an airline company, had run a jet service from Montreal to Kuujjuaq, Iqaluit, and Resolute Bay with a fleet of Boeing 737s. Oil, mineral, and geological explorations were creating so much traffic from the south, airline companies could afford to use jet services. It was a giant leap from the days of using the noisy, slow, transcontinental aircraft. Service out of Winnipeg to Resolute Bay by Transair airlines started later. The Pacific Western Airlines out of Edmonton switched over to jets as well. The jet service traffic to Resolute Bay had a positive impact on the Twin Otter service to Grise Fiord, as it was no longer necessary to spend time in Resolute Bay to wait for enough traffic for a flight to accumulate.

After spending two weeks at home, I moved to Iqaluit to start work. The job required travelling to the co-ops in our region to promote government-assisted crafting and carving. The first place I travelled to was Kimmirut on Nordair's single Beaver on floats. In Kimmirut we stayed at the local transient centre; there were no hotels in those days. Naomi and I were scheduled to be in Kimmirut for a week because the Nordair service was weekly, even though we only had two days of work. In the middle of the week, a twin-engine Beechcraft floatplane, an

Austin Airways charter, arrived from Salluit in northern Quebec. Naomi made arrangements to charter, it and we went home early. I was never so glad to be home. I missed Annie so much already.

We visited most communities for work. After New Year's, we went to Sanirajak. It was the first time I had ever been in a bar named after a walrus penis: Usuaq Bar, at the former DEW line station. One particular trip I remember well was to Pond Inlet. When we arrived, the transient centre was empty, so we had the place to ourselves. Sometimes the centres would be so full, we'd have to billet in someone's home. In the middle of the week, a DPW charter arrived, complete with senior managers to do an annual inspection of all the government buildings, the power plant, government vehicles, and heavy equipment. A fire marshal, mechanic, linesman, and carpenter came. Naomi and I suddenly found ourselves living in a circuslike atmosphere! We ended up with a roommate, a power-plant linesman who had come to work on the electrical wiring. Of course, in keeping with Qallunaat tradition, there was a party at the transient centre after supper. Unbeknownst to me, in the middle of the night, the furnace had stopped working. The only furnace mechanic there that night was Olaf Christiansen, who was now my brother-in-law. It had been eight years since Pauloosie's death, and Minnie and Olaf were now common-law. Of course, Olaf was drunk when he found himself to be the only person there qualified to fix it. He did fix it, but not before he almost electrocuted himself to death. The shock shook him so badly he had to lie down for a while before he recovered fully.

I liked working with Naomi Griffin, but it was difficult to deal with the rest of the staff's reluctance to make me feel part of the team. When I attended work functions, I spoke my mind, and in the end, I was demoted to a manager trainee position at the airport co-op store.

When I was offered a job as a Government Liaison Officer trainee in Grise Fiord in the mid-1970s, I flatly refused, knowing the attitude of the non-Inuit towards Inuit. When I thought about what I had done many years later, I could've been less direct. After what the government had done to the Inujjuarmiut, my attitude towards them was not favourable, but I truly regretted my refusals later when I realized the benefits I could have gained for my family.

* * *

While I was living in Iqaluit, Annie and I used to enjoy visiting my stepsister Leetia, brother-in-law Charlie, and their three children, Tommy, Lizzie, and Martha. We would go with them to Sylvia Grinnell River to fish for Arctic char. I had stayed with the family when I first went to Iqaluit in 1958. I remember that Tommy was learning to walk at the time.

Leetia's father was Elijasie, my father's youngest brother. My father had taken Leetia and Josephie as his own when Elijasie died. Charlie was originally from Inujjuak. I don't know when Leetia and Charlie got married, but it was probably in the early 1950s. In the late 1950s, the Canadian government moved many Inuit families from the Eastern Arctic communities, some as far away as Coral Harbour, to Apex Hill and Iqaluit to be near a hospital. Because Leetia had been stricken with polio when she was a young girl, they qualified to be moved. In May the year I moved to Iqaluit, Leetia went to Grise Fiord to visit my family. It was the first time she had seen them since they had left Inujjuak in 1953.

At the time, like many Inuit families, they did not drink, although alcohol was readily available. And as most families did, they all went to church on Sundays. Charlie was a good husband and father. He was a very quiet person. He had been born in a time when Inuit could live off the land without a rifle or any other modern conveniences to hunt with and was capable of surviving in the harshest conditions. In midsummer, Charlie went on a long weekend boat trip with his companion Nujalia. The hunters took Charlie's boat. When the hunters' return was overdue, a search was launched. It ended with the grim discovery of Nujalia's dead body in the front of the canoe. Charlie was nowhere to be found, although his hunting equipment was still there. It was so sad to see my sister lose her husband, especially with three young children. Nobody helped her look after her estate after Charlie was gone. I felt helpless seeing my ningauk's hunting equipment being sold at a fraction of the value. Today, I feel like I should have done more to help her through that time.

* * *

Like my boyhood friend Allie, after his companion died, Charlie may have been scared to come home, afraid of the authorities. We will never really know what happened to either of them, but they are far from being the only Inuit to have feared Qallunaat law.

Many stories are told about the first clashes between Inuit and the Qallunaat legal system. One of these is the story of Robert Janes. Robert Janes was a free trader who came to the Pond Inlet area from Newfoundland in the early 1900s with plans to get rich buying and selling furs. When his plans to get passage home did not work out, he found himself stranded, with no way to get home by ship. He decided to hire dog teams to take him as far as Churchill, Manitoba. Apparently, he had an aggressive style of trading that some Inuit never forgot. On the way, he encountered an old rival, Nuqallaq. His behaviour became irrational, and it was decided that Robert Janes was a dangerous man and must be put to death.

People still talk about the trial of Nuqallaq and his companions in the murder of Robert Janes under the Canadian legal system. Ululijarnaaq, one of the accused, was sentenced to two years of imprisonment with hard labour, which he served in Pond Inlet. Nuqallaq, Ululijarnaaq's partner in the killing of the Qallunaaq, was sent to the Stony Mountain Penitentiary in Manitoba to serve hard labour. He came back a broken man and ill with TB. He had contracted the dreaded disease from being in a damp prison cell. To be imprisoned in any Canadian penal system was horrible during the 1920s. It was probably worse for Indigenous inmates during that time.

Sometime in 1972 or 1973, Ningyou Killiktee told me about two RCMP graves at Dundas Harbour. I don't remember how the conversation started, but I am sure I initiated it. I knew Ningyou had worked there in the late 1940s and early '50s. I had read that the official cause of death of the two police officers was suicide. I shared this information with him. Ningyou had met many Inughuit hunters from Siorapaluk and Qaanaaq over the years, and he told me their official cause of death was different than what the Inughuit had told him. He was told it may have been murder. Not long after I got home, while it was fresh in my mind, I wrote his story in my journal. That was that.

In the mid-1980s, two people from Qaanaaq moved to Resolute Bay and got married. One of them, Martha Aronsen, told me she used to work at an Elders' centre. There was a former RCMP special constable who was a resident there. I knew of the man. I had met him the first time we went to Qaanaaq by airplane in 1973. His name was Kisuk. Martha said, "Kisuk told me on more than one occasion that he once shot a policeman while working in Canada." Of course, I did not believe this. After all, he was an old man, perhaps senile by that point. At the time, I dismissed the story.

Later, I read a book on the murder of Robert Janes and the trial of the accused. In it, the author wrote about the two graves at Dundas Harbour. She said the officials ruled the cause of death as suicide in order to save face—it would have looked bad for the RCMP. The two stories that were told to me were told at least ten years apart by two different people in two different places. Today, I do not doubt that the perpetrators told the investigators exactly what happened, and that the "official" story was something else entirely.

When the RCMP started to open detachments in northern Canada, they told Inuit they would not be exempt from Canadian law. When Inuit were found guilty, the judge and jury made no exceptions when it came to killing Qallunaat. The white man's law instilled great fear among some Inuit. Even my uncle Philipoosie once told me to be careful about how I dealt with Qallunaat because they make notes of everything that is said and done. He said they can slowly drain away my life, *inuusikillisaisuut*.

For many centuries, Inuit had a system not unlike other cultures around the world—an eye for an eye, so to speak. The RCMP told them to stop this way of life when dealing with grievances. When Knud Rasmussen first went to the Thule district, he was very disturbed when Uiasakasak was murdered by Sigluki during a narwhal hunt. He held a special meeting of the Thule tribe to explain to them the senselessness of the act. He told the people how it affected everyone in the tribe when it came to the responsibility of the widow. He asked who was going to take care of the children. The gathering had a profound effect on the group.

Some tribes would deal with injustices in group sessions. The person in question would be invited to a feast. After the meal, the Elders would confront the offender about the offence committed and consider it a first warning. After such counselling sessions, most offenders never repeated their actions against society. On rare occasions, more drastic measures were taken, such as banning the offender, the most humiliating sentence.

Young Husband, Young Hunter

My wife, Annie, was born Annie Manomie to Oloosie and Manomie Sarquq at their traditional home, Nuvutjuaq, over 150 kilometres west of Kinngait, on January 13, 1953. Her original birth certificate is written as December 31, 1952. Oloosie was Manomie's second wife. His first wife was Elisapee, with whom he'd had four children: Towataga, Qaivaluaqtuq, Tapaani, and Enuk. Manomie was a true Inuk hunter, travelling as far north as Natsiliq Lake to harvest game. Annie says her father loved hunting different types of birds—snow geese, Canada geese, eider ducks, merganser ducks, loons, and many other smaller birds. She remembers seeing him far in the distance coming home from hunting, his body draped in white with the birds he was carrying.

Manomie and Oloosie had two daughters, Annie and Sitaa. Sadly, Oloosie died from tuberculosis at Nuvutjuaq when Annie was just an infant. Her older sister Qaivaluaqtuq raised her as her own. After he lost his wife, Manomie moved the family east to Iqaluit to start a new life. Every time I fly over Nettilling Lake on Baffin Island, part of Manomie's old hunting territory, I think about him and reflect on how different life must have been when our parents lived mostly off the natural resources of the land and the sea.

Annie's first recollections are of hunting life, being on the land. She missed schooling when she was young, but she knew more about the land than I did when we started to go hunting together. In the early years of our life together, we went hunting almost every day from April until the dark season started, as she loved the outdoors so much.

The injury to my right eye forced me to shoot left-handed. Annie's eyesight has always fascinated me. Like Elijah, her vision was extraordinary. I was flabbergasted one day when she asked me if I could also see the earth's curvature on clear days. She described how scary it was to see the edge, saying it gave her shudders when she thought, *We could fall over the horizon!*

Mary Oloosie Christine Audlaluk was born April 9, 1972, at the Frobisher Bay General Hospital. She was premature, weighing only four pounds. Since our apartment was just a one-room, we could not fit a crib, so we used a dresser drawer.

Three months prior to my daughter's birth, my brother Samwillie came down during the winter for medical attention. He had a metal fragment in his finger, which had gotten infected. He had to stay with us longer than he planned when his finger was reinjured and ended up having to be removed. I had started to drink heavily, sometimes going into weekend drinking binges. Samwillie wanted me to move back to Grise Fiord with Annie, although her brother Towataga was against it. He felt we hadn't been together long enough. Samwillie, who was fifteen years older than me and had been like a father to me, was thinking about his own experience trying to find a wife. He'd had a difficult time and didn't want me to go through the same thing. And then, in May, I received an urgent phone call that my mother had been very ill, but had recovered.

Mom was no longer herself due to the difficult life that came with the relocation experience. One of the things that contributed to the early deterioration of her health was the physical work she endured collecting heather for so long back in the first few years after the relocation. By 1969, the trauma of the forced move had started taking its toll on her. She had developed the worst case of arthritis; it became so bad that it was necessary to physically move her in order for her to get into a comfortable position in bed. She also had Parkinson's disease. It was difficult to see her deteriorate from a very active person to a helpless, senile, bed-ridden invalid.

Mom's health prompted our decision to leave Iqaluit. Combined with my job difficulties, it was a good time to make travel plans. In early June of 1972, we left Iqaluit with a two-month-old baby. The ice strip we landed on was close to the mouth of the fiord that year. It was a beautiful June day when we arrived. The seagulls were out in full force, and seals could be seen far out in front of Grise Fiord when the sun was high. Annie recalls how much of a "time warp" she experienced when we arrived. The tiny village reminded her of her days as a young girl back in Kinngait, with home-cooked meals and country food. Being naive, I remember none of what she remembers about arriving.

When Annie and I moved back to Grise Fiord, Mom still enjoyed making sealskin mittens. It was all she could do by 1972. I was saddened, remembering a time when she sewed all of our kamiit, mittens, caribou parkas, pants, and mannguat.

* * *

Within a matter of days of our arrival I was hired as an assistant co-op manager. Before I started, I got a call from Paulassie saying he was going fishing at Pirlirarvirjuaq Lake the next day, and we jumped at the chance to go with him. We gave our baby to Elisapee, Elijah's wife, to take care of. It seemed like a simple solution. I hadn't been to the lake since the dog-team days. I had never gone by snowmobile and had no sense of how long it would take. All I knew was that snowmobiles were a lot faster than dogs. Paulassie's average travel speed rarely exceeded 25 km/h. When the trail was good, it would take five to six hours to reach the lake. He admitted that he kept to a slower pace because he didn't want the engine to burn out—he didn't trust the machine as much as he had trusted the dogs.

"I kept asking Larry how much farther it was to the lake, and he'd just say, 'Oh, not far,'" Annie remembers. "I'd further ask, 'Over the hill?' And he'd answer half-heartedly, 'Yeah,' until we eventually camped even before arriving!" I had no idea how far away the lake was.

When the weekend was coming to an end, Paulassie wanted to do more fishing, and I decided to head for home alone with my young wife-to-be. I had promised to start work as soon as possible, and we were worried about our baby.

Thinking back, I don't know how we got over the big hills a few kilometres above the lake by ourselves. One hill in particular sometimes requires two snowmobiles to get the sled over it.

When we were still fifteen kilometres from home the snowmobile engine started backfiring. I was using Samwillie's 20-horsepower machine, and I had no clue about carburetors. All I knew was that one screw was for fuel and the other was for air. I fiddled around with the screws, then started the engine, and presto! It didn't backfire anymore! Shows you I should've paid attention to our small-engine mechanic teacher back in 1968 instead of making him tell war stories!

Annie says, "By the time we got home, I had a splitting headache. My husband had no clue how to pack a sled properly. He had put me in the front like a dog-team driver. In the front is where all the bumps are!"

I didn't know the difference between a dog-team sled and a snowmobile sled other than that the latter will travel a heck of a lot faster than the one being pulled by dogs. The passenger is guaranteed a constant up-and-down motion with bumps that will quickly get annoying. I subjected my beautiful young wife to this torture without knowing it until she told me much later.

We got married on November 11 that year. The minister from Pond Inlet was in Grise Fiord at the time for a short stay, and we decided to take advantage of his visit while we could. When Annie and I think back on our first years as a married couple, we know we were young and inexperienced. We didn't know what we were doing. When we see young couples today, some of them remind us of ourselves, and we look at each other and smile.

* * *

The RCMP was responsible for managing the co-op's books, a carryover from the old trading store days. In 1953, when we arrived from Inujjuak, the government was not allowed to run any for-profit stores, so it was necessary to create a private store. None of the RCMP staff or their families were allowed to run their own business, so they named the trading store after my father and ran it that way, essentially using his name as window dressing.

Corporal Hank E. Johnson was the manager and Seeglook Akeeagok was my assistant. I worked at the co-op for over three years until I moved to the settlement council to work for the Arctic Airports program. I enjoyed working with Seeglook, managing the daily activity of the store. The money was not the greatest, but it was a living. We would purchase sealskins, carvings, and handicrafts daily. It wasn't until 1970 that we started to see cash used in the community. Only a few Inuit had full-time jobs. In 1972, most people still did not use cash to purchase goods. We would see it on occasion, but for the most part, they still used sealskins and fox pelts, even though hunters had stopped using the long-distance fox traplines to Cape Storm after we moved from Lindstrom Peninsula. Only when the fur market crashed due to the anti-sealing campaign, spearheaded by French actress Brigitte Bardot, did we start using cash more frequently.

At the end of June each year, we packed up all of the furs to be shipped to Vancouver for auction. It was hard work laying out all the furs and skins outside the warehouses, setting aside the ones that needed washing, then packing them into the pre-addressed bags supplied by the auctioneer. The skins and furs hadn't been seen since they were bought, and as a result, some required cleaning. We would hire some women for the job of cleaning them. For the annual inventory, Arctic Co-ops Limited would send an economic development officer to assist us. During the week, Seeglook and I often worked at the store in the evenings after supper to restock. With no vehicles to carry large items from the warehouses, we often used our own snowmobiles in the winter and spring. One time, Seeglook was transporting a load of sugar when one of the bags sprung a leak. His snowmobile carburetor sucked sugar into his engine, causing it to seize. Gamaliel, Seeglook's father, had been given a Ski-Whiz Polaris snowmobile after working for an oceanographer. The muffler on it did not quite muffle the engine noise, but one day Seeglook came to work with his father's Ski-Whiz, and you could hardly hear the engine. He had attached another Bombardier muffler to the engine. He should have patented his invention. I enjoyed working with Seeglook; we had some fun working at the co-op store. ·

* * *

After I returned home in 1972, I had to cope with humiliation in my early years as a young hunter. I was not as skilful as my peers due to the combination of my bad eye and having been away in the south for medical attention and then for school. Do you know what it's like not knowing how to hunt seals through an aglu during the dark season or how to skin a polar bear after you kill it and being criticized for not knowing how to live off the land? Not knowing anything about the "old ways"? My uncle Philipoosie ridiculed my shortcomings, which was very painful. My father had died before really having had the chance to be a father to me, and I felt robbed of a father-son relationship. Sometimes I would get envious of some of my boyhood friends when they got attention from their fathers. Instead, my primary father figure was my uncle, but I did not always like going to see him. He often criticized me when I made mistakes.

But I never gave up. Instead of giving up and leaving for the south or fighting back, I resolved to stick it out. And although I've had many mixed feelings about having stayed home to learn about my culture, I'm glad I did. And although he was critical, what my uncle taught me about hunting is something I'm happy about. I'm glad he was there when I sometimes came home from a hunt empty-handed. He would tell me to never give up. He said animals never stay away long. He taught me the importance of continuing to go to the same area to hunt. Sure enough, some days I would do as he advised, and get a seal at a place I had not seen any the day before.

When my brother Samwillie saw how rough my uncle was and how I was being taught to be confrontational, I think he felt obligated to say something. He started to teach me morals like "turning the other cheek." His approach was refreshing compared to my uncle's rough style; I don't think he liked my uncle's eye-for-an-eye attitude. Philipoosie used to tell me that if I was attacked, I was not to take it lying down. Samwillie would say the opposite, as if he were erasing everything else I was being taught. My brother would tell me it was better to take a beating than to fight back. I liked my brother's philosophical concepts. I have no regrets having listened to Samwillie Elijasialuk!

I am also thankful to the late Markoosie Innualuk for teaching me how to speak Inuktitut properly. I must have spoken like a little boy, just learning how to put words together. I had always thought I knew my culture and language until Markoosie pointed out otherwise. He was the first Inuk who patiently taught me how to use Inuktitut grammar the right way, without laughing at me like my uncle.

Young Husband, Young Hunter

Like my skills as a hunter, my education about my people really started only after I was married. When I was in school, history books were limited when it came to details about the contact era. For example, the textbooks told us that Louis Riel was a rebellious Métis who deserved to be executed for defying Canadian law. Over the course of time, however, history started to paint Louis Riel as a hero who helped the Métis people. Historical records state the "wild savages" stole from the English, provoking anger towards the Inuit. It is probable the English perceived the Inuit's curiosity as an intention to steal their things. What I have learned from my Elders is very different from what the textbooks said—very different from the missionaries' and historians' "official" versions!

When I first learned how far-reaching the missionaries' message was and how far it went in forbidding Inuit culture and other Indigenous cultures around the world, it was unbelievable! The Spaniards used missionaries and force of arms to conquer the Inca. In certain parts of the Arctic, drum dancing was banned and forbidden until the 1980s. The Indigenous peoples of the Northwest Coast had been told outright to stop their practice of potlatch dancing. Dancing is one of the main methods of expressing one's pleasure in life, of celebrating life, and marking special events.

Early contact between "primitive" cultures and Europeans around the globe was less than cordial. Many examples exist of how cruel the invading people were, sometimes killing the Indigenous populations who objected to their demands. What happened to the Indigenous peoples of South America is a prime example of violent confrontation. If Sir Martin Frobisher had heard about the Spaniards' experience with the Inca, it is no wonder he was suspicious of Inuit when he saw them in South Baffin. Five of Sir Martin's best crew went on an excursion and never came back. No trace of the missing crew was ever found. The English quickly concluded that the "savage Esquimaux" had kidnapped them. What really happened to them will remain a mystery, although many different theories have been written. I have my own thoughts on what may have occurred.

Frobisher Bay is full of islands, straits, and narrow passages that make navigation precarious if you don't know it well. My father-in-law spent much time hunting in the area in the summers. As a little girl, my wife remembers some passageways they had to negotiate carefully, some of which were very narrow and fast, the currents flowing like waterfalls during tidal movements. The English sailors could have lost control of their small craft and drowned going through such passageways between islands. It was also noted by one historian how deplorable the conditions were on Sir Martin's ship, which could have induced the sailors to go AWOL. When explorer Charles Francis Hall went to Frobisher Bay in 1860, he met Inuit who knew about Frobisher's voyages, the story having been passed down from Elders through oral tradition over the course of generations. They told him about five men who got left behind, who ended up making a small boat and leaving Frobisher Bay. Inuit could have shown them how to travel to the Labrador area, where their chances of survival would've been greater. But we can only speculate as to the details of their disappearance; we will never know what really happened.

Frobisher described the Inuit they encountered as savage, and his descriptions made them sound so wild, it was like they were cavemen. When they kidnapped an Inuk man and an Inuk woman from different places, they actually waited for the two of them to mate like wild animals. The English attitude towards our ancestors is so disgusting, it's beyond words.

Our culture is no less sophisticated than any other in the world. The Inuktitut language is very descriptive. We have names for the constellations (like *tukturjuk* for the Big Dipper), fables and legends that have lessons meant to teach our children, and very poetic drum songs.

Roots

The Commissioner of the Northwest Territories, Stuart Hodgson, came to Grise Fiord on his annual tour in 1973. His visit included a message from the federal government that Grise Fiord was a challenge to keep up and running. We were told the health centre might close due to the cost, and that the airport would be closed because of how dangerous it was to land due to the mountains above it. Hearing this news and seeing an opportunity, during the Commissioner's stay, my mom, my uncle, and Elijah requested to be taken to Inujjuak. It was a spur-of-the moment decision. I did not want to uproot my own young family, nor did I want my relatives to leave. But after so many years of trying and failing to go home, they took their chance. They were flown to Inujjuak on the commissioner's aircraft. Also as a result of this news, Ningyou Killiktee, Markoosie Innualuk, and Ookookoo Quaraq and their families left for Pond Inlet a few years later.

Being separated from them so abruptly was very hard. Most of my family stayed with me in Grise Fiord, which was lucky for me, but difficult for those that left. When I would hear from Elijah once they were back in Inujjuak, he would say that they were not coping well without us. After years of feeling the pull back to Inujjuak, they were now feeling a pull to Grise, to us. They felt a strong attachment to their roots in Nunavik, but the relocation had created a permanent division within them, and they were being pulled in two different directions. Eventually, they became so homesick for us that we scraped together the cost for a charter flight to bring them back after a year.

When they returned in April of 1974, Paul Kasudluak was with them. I first met Pauloosie Kasudluak from Inujjuak in Fort Churchill during my CVC days. My impression of him at the time was that he was just a kid with red cheeks. We did not get along right from the day we met; in fact, the few times we saw each other in Fort Churchill, we clashed. I don't remember ever seeing him smile the entire time we were at CVC. He was often in the company of Peter Kasudluak, who I later learned was his cousin. Unless Paul hadn't finished growing, he was a very short person, and Peter was much taller. The pair reminded me of circus trapeze members.

When he arrived in Grise Fiord in 1974, I did not recognize him at first. Instead of a little kid, I saw a street-smart guy from a much bigger community who had come to a tiny village somewhere in a forsaken land. I quickly dropped my old attitude when I saw he was serious about staying in Grise Fiord and especially when I saw how good he was as a hunter. Sometime around 1976, he married my niece Sarah. It was a triple wedding with Jimmy Nowra and my niece Alicee, and Looty Pijamini and Peepeelee Nutaraqjuk. My impression of him when he came to be my in-law overtook the old image I had of him.

Just a few days after arriving in Grise Fiord, Paul came over to the co-op, where I was working. He took out eight hundred dollars in twenty-dollar bills! Cash was still hard to come by in 1974. He told me he wanted to buy a 440 TNT Bombardier snowmobile. At that time, there were only model 400s available, so he settled for that. He paid for practically the entire snowmobile with the money he had earned playing pool in Inujjuak. It turned out he was what was known as a "pool shark." He owned that 400 Bombardier for a long time, until he finally replaced it with a brand-new 440 TNT.

Paul quickly got involved with the recreation committee as a projectionist. Until 1980, we watched movies in the community hall with Jopee Kiguktak and Paul running the projector in turns. The same movies would be shown four times a month. As a result, I enjoy watching the movies I like over and over.

From the day Paul arrived, he started hunting. I enjoyed going out on the land with him. Not only was he good company, he was also a crack shot with any rifle. Not unlike my ningauk Pauloosie, Paul livened up our lives, especially the lives of the Nungaq family—he was their ningauk. "My first hunting trips were with Paul when I was just a young boy," Kuni Nungaq recalls.

* * *

In 1974, the Inughuit from Siorapaluk and Qaanaaq were still coming to visit the relocatees. When they came that year, Ilanguaq Kristiansen gave me two dogs, a male and a female called Lady. I had always wanted to own a dog team, and I had started in 1973 with a few dogs from Elijah's old team. When Lady gave birth to six puppies, I started a whole new team. It was the first time I had my own dog team, one that I had trained myself, and there was tremendous pride attached to them. When I was on the trail with them, I saw and appreciated my surroundings that much more. Having a dog team is a full-time occupation. You must hunt for them to keep them fed. In order to have a good working team, you have to pay attention to them every day, in all seasons. Each dog has its own personality, just like people—no two dogs are the same. I have seen and heard of dogs that were lost for a time, and when found again out on the land, they had become wild, as if they had reverted back to their natural way of being. Although I used my dogs for recreational purposes for the first nine years, they became a very important part of my identity and culture. I felt much closer to my roots, which I had lost so much of because of my time away at school in the south.

Having a dog team gave me a glimpse into what life was like before snow-mobiles were used and how Inuit travelled in the winter using the most primitive mode of transportation to hunt and migrate. The archaeologists' and anthropologists' theory that Inuit could have migrated across the circumpolar regions from west to east is plausible given how efficient our ancestors were when it came to travel. Inuit's possession of dog teams would easily have enabled them to have migrated from Russia to Greenland in just a few winter seasons.

For Canadian Inuit, daily dog-team travel is limited to eight hours in order to prevent the dogs from becoming too tired for the next day's travel. In special situations, when hunters are in danger of getting caught in a sudden thaw that could trap them on land, or with ice in danger of breaking up, they drove their dogs as much as twice that amount.

It is best to travel long distances after February each year. Although winter travel starts in late October, the days get shorter and colder until December 21. After the initial snowfall, it will keep getting deeper every time it snows. In the High Arctic, it's best to leave after mid-March, when the snow cover on the land and ice is equal, to take advantage of the warming days and the light and to maximize the distance covered. The turning point of winter is April. Inuit planned their journeys using April as the point of no return, always making sure they made their return no later than the twenty-first. After that, the snow will start to melt. It depends on the amount of distance you are planning to cover, but you want to leave not so early that it is still very dark and very cold, but not so late that you have to turn back before you want to in order to beat the thaw.

In late summer, Inuit would go inland when the caribou were starting to get fat and they had finished moulting and grown new hair. Families would walk carrying their tents, sleeping gear, pots, tent poles, and *kakivat*. The children and dogs would do their share in carrying the family belongings. Inuit would cache the harvested caribou for later pickup, marking each cache with antlers. The caches of Arctic char were just as important. When fall came and there was sufficient snow on the ground, Inuit wrapped frozen fish in caribou or sealskin hides to make sleds. The qamutiik crosspieces would be made out of caribou antlers and scrap wood. When the sled was finished, the family would start the journey back to the coast.

* * *

The Inughuit continued to visit the relocatees until 1993. It is no longer possible for them to come for two reasons: the first is that the ice bridge between Ellesmere Island and Greenland no longer freezes enough for them to safely travel over. The second reason, of course, is politics. It was embarrassing to us when our territorial government announced that if the Greenlandic hunters were caught hunting polar bear in Canada, the hides would be confiscated. This threat has been carried out at least once. A Vancouver-based tour company hired some Inughuit hunters to take them to Grise Fiord from Siorapaluk in 1997. The trip to Grise Fiord went without incident, except for lack of dog food, but the return trip to Siorapaluk resulted in the confiscating of the Inughuit's polar bear skins.

A biologist happened to be doing some polar bear tagging nearby in a helicopter with a renewable resource officer. International pressures have forced many countries to legislate polar bears, narwhal, and walrus without a proper working relationship with Inuit communities in Nunavut, Greenland, Alaska, and Russia. None of the species are in danger of becoming extinct, yet Greenpeace, the World Wildlife Fund, the Committee on the Status of Endangered Wildlife in Canada, and many other influential organizations persist. In 1973, biologists across the circumpolar regions of the world met and agreed that female polar bears with cubs should no longer be hunted. The governments in the region all agreed with the recommendation. Inuit, Iñupiat, Inughuit, and Yupik complied with the ban without question. Fifty years later, there are way too many polar bears, and Inuit no longer feel safe enough to go camping without watch dogs.

* * *

Instead of closing the airport at Grise Fiord, the territorial government decided to upgrade the airports in the Northwest Territories after many years of neglect starting in the fall of 1975. Private airlines and the DPW had first started building the dirt strips in most of the Eastern Arctic region. In the Eastern Arctic, runways were made on the ice when the sea froze until the spring thaw came in most of the communities. Proper airports with runways equipped with lights, snow-clearing equipment, and trained staff did not exist. Private airlines hired local agents to operate the company radios, report weather conditions, issue plane tickets, and receive and send mail and freight. The settlement council would be responsible for hiring weather observers and runway maintenance staff; the training and the equipment was to be supplied by the government.

Seeglook had left the co-op to work elsewhere, and the atmosphere was not the same without him, so I started looking for another job after three years of being there. I applied to be an observer/communicator trainee, but I was not accepted by the settlement council at first. Small-town politics get in the way of common sense a lot of times. But on the second round of qualification checks, I was chosen. The six-week training course was in Coral Harbour. People from all over the Eastern Arctic were there. After we graduated, Alice Panipakutchoo was the first Inuk woman to hold an HF (high-frequency) radio license in Canada.

I enjoyed taking the course, but I could not get used to the frequent blizzards. Listening to the wind howl at night, it sounded as if the whole world was in the middle of a storm. It was on a rare visit to the Coral Harbour settlement that I first met Jenny Gilbertson, a Scottish documentary filmmaker from the Shetland Islands. She was a very interesting person to talk to about filmmaking, and I was fascinated by what she did. I had my own interest in learning more about how to make movies, so I invited her to come to Grise Fiord to make a documentary about daily life in our settlement. She arrived in the summer of 1977 to do exactly that.

I thoroughly enjoyed working with and learning from her. She taught me about basic filmmaking. She had started her filmmaking career learning from none other than John Grierson, the founder of the National Film Board of Canada. She loved telling me she had been one of his pupils. She was seventy-four when she arrived, and she celebrated her seventy-fifth birthday in Grise Fiord. She was one tough lady. She endured not only the dark season, but also the cold winter. Yet that never stopped her from going on location to film. There is a scene in the documentary, called *Jenny's Arctic Diary*, of a muskox hunt Elijah, Samwillie, Paulassie, and Jimmy took her on in March across Jones Sound to Devon Island. It was during the coldest time of winter when temperatures could hover around -42°C even with the sun shining at noon. The muskoxen were taken at Cape Sparbo, seventy kilometres from Grise Fiord. That may not seem far, but when it's -40, it can feel like seven hundred kilometres. She once told me that the only thing she dreaded about working in sub-zero temperatures was the bother of having to remove all of her outer garments to go to the loo! I was privileged to have worked with her. She was a strong lady and had that twinkle in her eye!

Old Memories,
New Adventures

*I*n January 1978, my mother died. Fortunately, unlike with Pauloosie, we were able to have a proper burial service for her. The loss was hard, but I still carry with me the stories she told. I still remember her telling me about her life back in Nunavik, before I was born.

One of her stories that stands out to me today is about a time when she was a young mother. It was just before or after my sister Minnie was born in 1940, during the Second World War. My family lived on the Ungava coast at the time, and there were sometimes German U-boats in the area. She told of the time when blonde-looking *arnaqsiuqtit*, "women-seekers," would come to their traditional homes as if from out of nowhere in the summer when the men were out hunting. The arnaqsiuqtit would chase the women, who had begun to dread it when their husbands left, knowing what could happen. In the early 2000s, I saw former U-boat crew members on television speaking of going to the northern Quebec area during the war, which confirmed for me what my mother had experienced firsthand. She had seen the German U-boat crew going ashore to look for Inuit women.

One Sunday, most of the villagers were attending a morning church service. A man was alone at home in his tent when he was attacked by an *arnaqsiuqti*. I do not know if the attacker mistakenly thought a woman was still inside or if the man was his intended target, but he jumped on top of the unsuspecting Inuk's tent. But the victim was quick to defend himself. He had a large Arctic char to use as a weapon against his attacker, who was peering through the vent hole on top of the tent. The Inuk quickly stuffed the char through the vent hole and into the gaping mouth of the arnaqsiuqti, successfully repelling him.

I know the stories my mother told are true. I have no doubt the German sailors watched the Inuit camps through their submarine periscopes to see when the Inuit hunters left for hunting trips. A few years after Elijah went back to Inujjuak, an elderly Inujjuak woman told him there was a Qallunaaq who was in Inujjuak for summer holidays. She said she was shopping at one of the local stores when he came up to her to say he recognized her from "a long time ago" outside the Inujjuak area.

My mother also told stories of the bombings in London, England. She said after my sister was born, she heard about how England was being frequently bombed by Germans. Inuit in Nunavik were told what to do if an attack from the air came: if an aircraft was seen trailing what looked like a long tail underneath it, they were told to run to the hills. I guess the "tail" indicated tracer bullets or bombs coming down towards them. One day, an aircraft was seen approaching. Everyone ran to the hills to hide, but the plane was friendly. My mother used to laugh about how funny it had been when it was all over, after everyone had been running scared.

I remember one time my stepbrother Josephie was visiting us while we were living on Lindstrom Peninsula. He was looking at an old *Life* magazine that Mom had saved to plaster on the walls of our hut, as Inuit used to do to brighten the inside of their homes. The magazine had an article about the Second World War, and Josephie told me all about it. When I went to school in Fort Churchill many years later, I saw a movie titled *Battle of Britain*. It was like watching a movie of my own stepbrother's stories. I realized later that Josephie must have heard the war stories as a young man as they were coming in through the radio at the HBC.

About a year before we moved to Grise Fiord, we noticed a strange orange-red glow in the direction of the North Pole, above the mountains. It was around 1960 or 1961, during the Cold War. I remember that it was before daylight came back, so it would have been sometime before January. I have since learned that Russia detonated the largest hydrogen bomb ever created on October 30, 1961.

What we saw could very well have been that. It seems too unlikely to have been a coincidence.

Sometime around late 1961, we got a scare one night when two jets appeared above Grise Fiord, east of Lindstrom Peninsula. The sky was beautifully clear, with a full moon, and we could them so clearly. It seemed that one of them was chasing the other. My mother's memory of the Second World War came back. She was really scared. Minnie thought another war had started. Elijah and Pauloosie went to the RCMP detachment to find out what was going on. The police told them not to worry about anything. The explanation given was the "military testing their jets," which was good enough to calm everyone's fears.

* * *

That year, Samwillie, Harry Flaherty, Paul Kasudluak, and I went on a hunting trip to Goose Fiord to hunt caribou and muskox. Goose Fiord was where our beloved brother-in-law Pauloosie had died under tragic circumstances some sixteen years earlier. We picked up Isa Naqtai's sled that he had left behind over a decade ago. What a desolate spot to die, so far from home! It takes a whole day to travel there by boat, even one with large motors; believe me, it's not close to Grise Fiord.

That year, 1978, was also the year I went back to Inujjuak for the first time since 1953. I had never seen it as an adult, but as my family had talked constantly about Inujjuak for all my living memory, I had a very strong idea of what to expect. I had seen photos of it, and I had also been to Churchill, which is almost directly across Hudson Bay from Inujjuak, so I knew the terrain would be similar. I saw how big the contrast in temperature was between Inujjuak and Grise Fiord. It was warm considering it was September. We were using snowmobiles at home when I left, and when I arrived, I found myself in a summer place.

Samwillie had been visiting Inujjuak since about 1971 or '72. He had gotten a job with the NWT territorial government as a mechanic, and the benefits allowed him to take these trips. One day in 1978, he told me that he and Louisa were going to Inujjuak for a holiday, but that this time, they were not coming back. Samwillie had helped build Grise Fiord, but he was born in Inujjuak, and he still had a strong impression of his first home. Besides that, his wife's family, the Nowras, were also Inujjuarmiut, and he felt obligated to Louisa. I was very affected by his departure. It was quite upsetting to lose him. Two months after he moved, I used my holiday pay to go visit him.

I stayed at the home of my uncle Johnny Inukpuk. When James Houston introduced carving to Inuit as an alternate source of income, a viable means of making a living, my uncles Johnny and Philipoosie took up the trade. Johnny's skill as a carver was noted right from the start. When I was staying with him, I would get up in the morning and he'd already be up, polishing a carving. By 1978, he knew how long it took to get a carving done from start to finish. He passed away in 2007 at the age of ninety-six, having outlived two wives.

Both my father and Annie's were also included as early masters in the Inuit carving world. In fact, one of Manomie's carvings was given to Queen Elizabeth ll when she first visited Canada in 1951. The carving is of a woman tending a *qulliq,* an oil lamp, with a child on her back. A photo of the carving was made into a stamp. My father had natural artistic skills, and the few carvings he made are much sought after by art collectors today. Whenever my father came to Inujjuak from Uugaqsiuvik, teachers and local organizations like the RCMP and Environment Canada would rush to the store to buy his carvings. I met Rueben Ploughman, who had been a Hudson's Bay Company manager in Inujjuak between 1952 and 1954, during the relocation hearings in Ottawa in the early '90s. Rueben said he would buy quite a few of them for himself, thus accumulating quite a good collection of my father's work. He sent me a photograph of his collection. A *Globe and Mail* article on Inuit carving and art cited my father's talent as having been undervalued until now. He is the only Inuk carver who ever made the obituary section of *Time* magazine.

* * *

In the summer of that year, before I went back to Inujjuak, I applied for the position of Arctic Airports Officer in Iqaluit, as well as the Nunavut Teacher Education Program (NTEP), which was just starting in the fall of that year. I got accepted for both applications. I had the highest score on the test for NTEP, but I took the position as an Arctic Airports Officer, thinking I would be able to support my growing family better that way. Annie and I had had our second child, Laisa, in 1974. Unfortunately, once we moved to Iqaluit, I got off on the wrong foot. The nightlife quickly took over my life. I could not cope with alcohol being too readily available, and I only lasted six months. In February of 1980, the same month that our third child, Patrick, was born, we went back to Grise Fiord, and I went back to my old observer/communicator job.

Sometime around 1981, when I was back at my old job, a biologist, Kerry Finlay, with Gamaliel Akeeagok as his assistant, was doing an aerial survey of the area between Ellesmere Island and northwest Greenland. The aircraft was a DHC-6 Twin Otter, CF-NAN. It was owned by Bradley Air Services based out of Resolute Bay and was operating under the Polar Continental Shelf Project. When they left on the first day of the week-long survey, the weather conditions were marginal with whiteout conditions, too dangerous for flying. Thinking back, the aircraft should not have taken off in the first place!

Thirty kilometres east of Grise Fiord, the pilot crashed on top of Jakeman Glacier, losing the front wheel and the contents of the nose compartment only a few feet above the cliff. The sleeping bags tucked inside the nose were blown away in the drifting snow. Gamaliel thought they were going to die when the wheels hit the ice cap in full flight. The pilot radioed for me to call Resolute Bay. He said everyone was okay and went through the crash procedures, telling me how many people were onboard, their position, and the damage to the aircraft. With the sleeping bags gone, engine blankets were used to keep warm, with an emergency Primus stove lit inside. I asked to speak to Gamaliel and he assured me all was well. The nearest rescue station was in Halifax, Nova Scotia, at the other end of the country! I knew it would take a whole day of flying before rescue arrived. The pilot and I set up a schedule in which I called him every two hours until that happened. It was the longest night of my life. When it arrived, the helicopter had picked up a Bradley Air repair crew from Resolute Bay on the way to the crash site. The CF-NAN was flown to Grise Fiord from Jakeman Glacier for a temporary nose wheel repair until they could get back to Resolute Bay. I didn't sleep until everyone was taken safely back to Grise Fiord.

When I was an observer, I met many pilots, some of whom became my friends. One pilot I enjoyed talking to was Doug McLeod, who flew for Bradley Air Services. Doug always used to have funny stories to tell whenever I saw him. He told me about a time his ears froze so badly, the tips hung down at a strange angle. He also told a story about the time the door of his apartment in Vancouver got stolen while he was on a tour up in Resolute Bay. When he stopped for fuel in Grise Fiord, he would come by our house unexpectedly, saying, "Haha, oh, hi, Larry, do I smell fresh bannock?" He had a knack for coming in just when Annie was making fresh-baked round bannock. Maybe he could smell the aroma as he was flying in!

I first met Doug in late August one year when he came in on a little Beaver single-engine aircraft to take us to the lake Inughuit call Pirlirarvirjuaq. Starting in 1962, we would journey there each spring to fish. This time, we were going there to build a hunters and trappers cabin. The building materials had been taken over with snowmobiles and sleds the previous spring. He was to fly us over with Elijah and Imooshee Nutaraqjuk.

He was so careful that he first took off alone as a test run. After he came back, we boarded and were off. The flight was uneventful until we reached the lake. While we were looking for a suitable landing spot, we made a perfect circle and hit our wake (the atmospheric turbulence formed behind the aircraft), although Doug didn't tell me and Imooshee until the following year that that's what had happened. The aircraft nosedived, but Doug knew how to recover from the sudden situation we found ourselves in. We were still shaking when Doug took off after he dropped us off at the lake.

We had no radio to communicate home when we were at Pirlirarvirjuaq. The game officer had told us an aircraft would be coming in a week to pick us up. We worked hard to finish the cabin before the week was up. A week passed…nothing. Early the following week, we awoke when a helicopter arrived. There was a Coast Guard ship that had come to drop off barrels of aircraft fuel across the lake, and some of the people from the ship had come to fish at the lake. We told them what we were doing and that we were running out of food and fuel for our camp stoves. They went back to the ship and returned with food, cartons of cigarettes, and stove fuel. We had Christmas in September that evening. Just a couple of days later, Captain Bob Platt and co-pilot Brian McKinley picked us up with a Twin Otter. The flight in the Beaver had taken an hour. The return trip home took twenty minutes. I didn't even have time to finish eating the packed food Annie sent.

* * *

The local political scene had changed since the first time I had worked as an observer/communicator for the settlement council. From May to July, I couldn't sleep at night and couldn't get up in the morning because of my childhood eye injury. My problem of not being able to get up in the morning had infuriated my superiors back when I was at the co-op. Not long after I returned to Grise, my inability to get up in the morning was no longer tolerated. I got fired. I went from having a good job with good pay to working as a fuel man for the co-op. I got paid on commission: the more fuel I pumped, the more I got paid. In spring and summer when the weather got warmer, the houses didn't burn as much fuel as in the winter, and the pay got really low.

In the early 1980s, Canada North Outfitting started to bring sport hunting to Grise Fiord. They took clients for muskox hunts only at first, but in 1982 when the first polar bear sport hunt was set, Looty and I were hired to guide the very first hunter. Looty's job was to carry our supplies. The client was a retired gentleman from France who did not understand any English. We had to speak to him in sign language.

After ten days of hunting, I went back to Grise Fiord. With a new contract to extend the hunt, Looty continued guiding the French gentleman with his own team. I had a prior commitment with High Arctic International Explorer Services Ltd. to be a dog handler for a movie crew in Resolute Bay. The company was owned by none other than my old friend Bezal Jesudason. He had been working for the territorial government's DPW, but had resigned and started his own outfitting/tourism company. He was a very successful tour operator. His clients were from all over the world. He attracted regular tourists, many of whom were adventure tour groups trying to get to the North Pole. He often led four-day tours to Grise Fiord using snowmobiles fitted with sleds that had built-in compartments, specially built for his customers. He generated a lot of seasonal guiding jobs and catered to speciality groups like Japanese feature film crews. I was privileged to work for him.

The movie I was involved in as a dog handler was based on a true story about a Japanese expedition to Antarctica during the 1957–58 International Polar Year. The expedition members were picked up after it was over, but the dogs were left behind. Incredibly, when the rescuers were finally able to go back to the abandoned research station the following year, two of the dogs were still alive! The movie, *Antarctica,* depicted how the animals may have survived their ordeal. The main star was Ken Takakura, who later starred in *Black Rain* with Michael Douglas. Most of the location shots were filmed in Resolute Bay and a few in Grise Fiord. It was a very well-made film with great cinematography.

Two years later, I was involved in another Japanese movie, *Lost in the Wilderness*, through Bezal's company. The story was about world-renowned Japanese solo adventurer Naomi Uemura. He had disappeared at Mount McKinley a year prior. My title was "dog handler" in the credits; however, I was more than just a dog handler. I doubled for the star in some scenes, and I also got a small part in a scene as "Alaskan Eskimo." My dogs exclusively were used in the movie. Fourteen years later, in 1998, I played the role of Ahnalkah in a TV movie called *Glory & Honor*, directed by Kevin Hooks and starring Delroy Lindo and Henry Czerny. The film was a true story about one of Robert Peary's employees who had played a big part in Peary's expedition to the North Pole.

After Bezal had been running his company for a few years, he had developed a pretty good idea of which groups were serious about their quest to the North Pole and which groups were most likely to give up quickly because of the cold. Many groups never made it. Bezal and I used to run a small wager on which groups were going to give up. Once, there were two Italian men making an attempt for the North Pole who did not seem likely to succeed. Bezal told me they were probably going to come up with an excuse to give up their trip. I went home a few days before they left and passed through Resolute Bay a week later on my way to Iqaluit. I asked him what had happened to the Italian expedition.

"Oh, after a few days out on the trail they radioed me for emergency pick-up," Bezal told me.

"What happened?" I asked.

"The 'official' reason for having to quit their attempt for the North Pole…the four dogs in their team got into a fight. While trying to stop the fight, one of the men froze his hands and needed medical attention right away," he replied, laughing.

"Were his hands really frozen?" I asked.

"Yes, they were, but we'll never know what really happened," Bezal answered.

* * *

After the first polar bear hunt in 1982, Looty and I continued to help with hunting expeditions. It often seemed that the bigger the bear sought by the hunter, the smaller the catch. When the hunter was not particular about the size of his catch, he would get a big one. Watching dogs corral and hold a polar bear at bay for the hunter is quite something to see. The sound they make when they are at a polar bear is not the same as any other. It's unlike the sound they make during feeding time or the one they make when they are excited to run. I can't describe it well enough in order for it to be understood; you simply have to hear it for yourself.

Elders have said the only reason polar bears came to be was by way of shamans' magic. They said the creature had been willed into existence. I have seen unexplainable things over the course of my time guiding sport hunters. An American hunter once arrived with plans to shoot only a polar bear that was ten feet or bigger. He was not going to settle for anything less. The first two days, we saw two smaller animals. While we were camped in front of a large, flat iceberg, Elijah spotted a small polar bear. The wind was blowing, the drifting snow limiting visibility to about eight kilometres. He went up to the top of the iceberg every ten to fifteen minutes to keep an eye on the polar bear. After he came back down from a second look with his binoculars, he said it was only a fox. Later, when the animal was much closer, walking along the edge of the rough ice, he said it was a small polar bear. We decided to investigate. The animal was a small polar bear with legs that looked like they belonged to a huge, ten-foot bear! Its snout and neck were red-brown, as if it were a snow goose. It could not gallop, like a young polar bear should, but only pace. It looked as if it were a combination of two polar bears! It reminded me of a child wearing his father's boots that are too big.

On another hunt, I was with another hunter who wanted a big polar bear but ended up with nothing. He was a much nicer person to hunt with than the first guy, but he was very impatient. The only set of fresh tracks we saw in the first three days were bears with cubs. After more than five days of hunting, we finally found the tracks of single polar bear without a cub. We followed the tracks most of the morning and the afternoon. It was a beautiful day to start with, but just as the tracks were getting fresh and we expected to see the animal any minute, a sudden blizzard started. The tracks led us to the shore of Truelove Inlet. Just before we hit land, we lost them. We looked for them a mile in each direction on the shore of the beach. All we could see were the fresh tracks of a lemming. Did the animal turn into a rodent? Some Inuit legends say that polar bears turn into human beings once inside their dens. It has been said that when you enter a polar bear's den, the upper part of the inside looks as if it has soot on it, as if a qulliq has been used to heat the inside. If the stories about their ability to shapeshift are true, maybe they can also turn into lemmings.

Healing

*I*n 1978, a Nunavik land claim organization called Makivik Corporation was formed, and the relocatees from both Inujjuak and Pond Inlet started a new journey. Makivik and Inuit Tapirisat of Canada (ITC), now Inuit Tapiriit Kanatami, began lobbying for the government to investigate the circumstances surrounding our relocation. I was involved with this lobbying effort for almost eighteen years with many of the other relocatees from Inujjuak and Pond Inlet.

In 1983, Simon Akpaliapik decided to move back to Pond Inlet. In the early 1970s, Jackoosie Iqaluk, Alex Patsauq, and Andrew Iqaluk, and Samwillie in 1978, had paid their own way or used their vacation travel assistance from their jobs to return to their home communities. Like others before him, Akpaliapik asked the Government of Canada to take him back, as was promised back in 1953, but also like others before him, he was refused. Undaunted, he did what no one else before him had done, and went to ITC. He asked them to write an article about his situation. They not only agreed, they decided to take up his cause. It was very costly, and ITC could not afford it on their own. Very luckily, Makivik was there to carry on the fight.

The government had always refused to acknowledge that we had been forced to move. Occasional newspaper articles on the subject would show up every now and then during the 1970s and '80s, but the government always denied them, neutralizing our claims. But we never gave up. Some years we would go to Ottawa to meet with the Department of Indian Affairs and Northern Development

(DIAND; formerly the Department of Resources and Development) and would be met with flat refusal, going home empty-handed and humiliated. The government used delay tactics. Time was crucial. The number of original relocatees was getting fewer and fewer with each passing year. If not for the good lawyers and supportive leadership at Makivik, our never-changing story would never have started to finally show results.

After the federal election in 1984, the minister of DIAND changed. Makivik continued to lobby for compensation, and in September 1987, DIAND finally approved and financed the return of the relocatees to their homes in Inujjuak and Pond Inlet. Those wishing to go back had a three-year window in which to do so. I decided not to take the offer. I did not want to uproot my children like I was uprooted back in 1953. In 1988, Elijah moved back with Elisapee and their three children. Adoption is very common among Inuit, and they had adopted Eva in 1968 from Mimi Pijamini, Caroline in 1970 from our brother Samwillie, and Billy in 1974 from my niece Sarah. Anna moved back as well. She was a widow by then. Sadly, Paulassie had fallen through the ice while hunting polar bear in the fall of 1987. He had been looking forward to moving back to Inujjuak.

I tried to tell them not to go right away, but of course when the opportunity was presented after thirty-four years of being refused, they jumped at the chance. Can you blame them? Who can? Even after Elijah's experience in 1973, the pull back to Nunavik was still strong. And by then, both my mother and Philipoosie were gone. I suffered for the first two years. I had helped uproot my family, the only shelter, love, care, and everything else I had ever known! Then within two years of being in Inujjuak, if not sooner, just like the Inujjuarmiut had in 1953 and 1954, Elijah's kids started asking to go back to Grise Fiord. They had been born and grew up there. It was the only home they knew. They started to use drugs, drink. There was pressure from the new kids they met, and it was a strange environment to them. The fact that it got dark in the evenings was an adjustment in itself; exactly the opposite of my parents' experience.

It is difficult for me to talk about this sometimes. It's very close to home. I feel guilty for having lobbied too successfully when I think about the fact that I helped cause my family to leave.

But the fight was not yet over. DIAND considered the issue closed, but there had still been no real acknowledgement of how badly the government had treated us. We went to Jack Anawak, Nunatsiaq MP from 1988–1997, about our cause. His help was unceasing, but even he could only do so much. In 1990, Makivik and ITC got a hearing in Ottawa in the House of Commons. Relocatees, including Martha Flaherty, Markoosie Patsauq, and John Amagoalik, who was president of ITC, told our story. The Committee on Aboriginal Affairs recommended that we be given recognition and consideration of compensation for "service to Canada and for the wrongdoings inflicted upon [us]." In response, the government hired the Hickling Corporation to go to the four communities of Grise Fiord, Pond Inlet, Inujjuak, and Resolute Bay. They did their own fact-finding work and interviewed only select individuals. The report they came up with is called the *Hickling Report*. It is filled with incomplete stories. They wrote only what they wanted others to hear. It says, for example, that "the first group of Inuit relocated were not as well equipped as they might have been." As you may recall, we were ill-equipped because we had been promised that we would be provided for. The purpose of the report was to discredit our story of what actually happened.

Despite setbacks, we never gave up. Makivik and ITC never gave up. The help of Makivik lawyer Sam Silverstone and vice president Zebedee Nungak was indispensable, as well as some of the staff assigned to our cause. In December 1991, the Canadian Human Rights Commission issued a report that stated that the Canadian government "failed to meet its fiduciary duties of care and diligence in planning and carrying out the relocation." Finally, in 1993, all the living members of the relocation project were flown to Ottawa for Royal Commission Hearings to testify and tell the story of what had happened. I went with the thought, *At last, now I can speak on behalf of my parents*. I was very driven, like a soldier going into battle. It was as if my parents were in the same room when I spoke, or when we spoke. I was never so focused! It was all for my parents. It took eighteen years of bombarding DIAND with our story over and over until finally they were convinced we were not lying. Our story never changed.

As hard as it was, it was a healing process for many of us. In 1996, we were offered a $10 million trust fund as a settlement. A formal government apology did not come until 2010, almost sixty years after the relocation.

Even though we finally received an apology, the relocation had long-lasting effects. There are certain things that cannot be compensated for. The psychological traumas endured by the relocatees would last a lifetime. I saw my childhood *piqatialuk,* best friend, and qatangutiapik Charlie Thamoosie, in Resolute Bay in the early 1990s. He told me parts of his life story after having moved to Toronto. He lived on the streets of Toronto near Yonge Street for a time. He was tricked into becoming dependent on speed. On one trip, he came close to jumping off a tall building because he thought he could fly like a bird. He went through withdrawal in a jail cell. It was so horrible, he was on the floor screaming in agony. His medical treatment in an insane asylum marred him for life. He was given electric shock treatments, which were horrible to endure. The result of having been given the wrong medication and treatment left him unable to walk straight for life, and he could not stop his arms from twitching. He had been in prison before he came home to Resolute Bay. When I saw him, I almost cried. Even though he was younger than me, he looked five years older. His time in prison had made him unable to stay still for long. He had developed the habit of pacing the floor, a sign he had been in isolation often. Even then, his sense of humour and his poetry skills could not be taken away.

I will reflect on his life and his brothers' lives and ask, "Why?" Why did this have to happen? Would they all have lived longer if we hadn't been relocated from Inujjuak in 1953? Would they have lived longer if Simeonie Amagoalik been successful in taking them with him to Resolute when we were being separated in Craig Harbour? Would Charlie have led a different life had Thamoosie Amagoalik not left Grise Fiord in 1964? I have many questions with no answers.

Since I can remember, my mother had always told me to say my prayers before going to bed. I have taken her teachings seriously most of my life. Parental teachings are important. Yet despite all of what she said, there was a time I ran from those teachings. Despite Al Lewis's advice not to drink, I did not listen. At eighteen, I first took a sip of Labatt's Blue. Although I noticed how bitter the taste was, the giddy feeling it gave me made it worth it. Eventually I became an alcoholic, unable to stop even when I tried for many years. From not long after I quit school in 1971 until 1994, I lived the life of someone who lives only for the "good times." I used to think when I saw sober people, *Poor sobs, they don't know what they're missing!* Some stuff makes you feel invincible, makes you feel sorry for those who are sober. I thought I had discovered the meaning of life.

One time when I was working as a fuel man, I had to fuel an aircraft in the morning. I swear, I thought I was going to drop dead while pumping fuel. Another time, Elijah came to wake me up at daybreak one morning in September because whales were passing by. I had a responsibility, so I got up. There I was, sick as a wet dog, sitting in the front of the canoe holding my hunting rifle, wishing desperately to be home gulping down cold water. Miserable! I lived this way for more than twenty years. The Royal Commission Hearings in 1993 was the very first time I had spoken openly about the relocation sober, without the assistance of substances like alcohol. When I first started to drink legally, I used alcohol to help me stir up emotions, emotions I could not express when I was sober. Alcohol helped me to loosen my tongue. I would cry and lament what had happened to my parents, relatives, and most of all, to me. Nothing would come of it. I would remain bitter, angry, prone to violence. It was a dangerous cycle I was stuck in. My family lived in fear when I drank. My wife was stuck with a man who was a ticking time bomb, who would react some days to the slightest provocation. The more I learned about the history of our forced move, the more I learned just how complex the whole issue was, the angrier I got. I learned that my parents were only told part of how of the government justified the move, which was by naming it the "Eskimo Rehabilitation Program." It angered me too to find out that they had no intention of honouring their promise to return us home.

When I went to the hearings, speaking on behalf of my father and mother, crying and showing emotion without alcohol, I began to realize the importance of going through the healing process sober. I found out the hard way that trying to use booze to do that does not help. After the hearings, we were able to start working towards the next steps. It was at this time I decided to look at my life in a deeper way. When I drank after that, even though I would drink a very little amount compared to my past binges, alcohol still controlled me. I started having blackouts, periods where I did not remember events from the night before. The next morning, I would have spells of anxiety where my heartbeat was alarmingly high. It was scary for me. It was at this time I realized I was faced with a situation that was beyond my ability to handle on my own.

Healing

One night, I was lying in a hotel room in Iqaluit, scared because my heart would not slow down. I remembered the time Elijah had prayed when he almost drowned back in the late '60s. I prayed, "God, if you exist as my mother told me, if you are real, I need help now." I was not even on my knees. In fact, I was lying on my bed looking at the ceiling. I prayed out loud, not shouting as Elijah had, but with a desperate, pleading voice, as if I were talking to a person.

The following Sunday morning, I took the next step on the start of my journey of self-discovery. I went to the morning service at St. Jude's Anglican Cathedral in Iqaluit. At the altar call, I went up to kneel to be prayed for, to dedicate my life to the power of a higher being. It was as if nobody existed except me and God. Some people call him by other names, but I was baptized Christian. I went forward to follow Jesus. I began to feel the presence of something wonderful that I cannot fully explain. It felt similar to the presence I felt at the time of my father's passing as a three-year-old. When I was eighteen, back in Winnipeg, I'd had the experience of being "born again" at the Salvation Army church. Of course, being young, I had soon forgotten all about it. To my surprise, in Iqaluit when the reverend prayed for me, I felt somewhere in me that I was being told that I was already born again. When I finally decided to take God seriously, I learned once you have been born again, Jesus never leaves your heart. That is the best way I can explain the start of my healing process.

The next step that was necessary for me to take was to go through a grieving process, dealing with the traumas that had occurred in my life with the guidance of a trained counsellor. In dealing with the traumatic periods in my life, I found that in some cases I had formed coping mechanisms to deal with pain.

Please don't think that I am now a perfect person who doesn't make mistakes or think about bad things. Far from it—I'm an ordinary person like any other. I'm just sharing what happened to me. I am also not trying to tell anybody that what I did is what you have to do. No; I'm just saying that no matter how low you spiral down, there is a way out. I had to make a commitment to myself to not live in bitterness and anger all my life. It almost killed me. I decided to share what happened through positive means. I thank my family's continual support.

* * *

Healing

A lot has changed since my family's relocation in 1953; some good, some bad. We have lost many family members over the years. Josephie suffered from poor health in his later years and is now gone. My mother's lament when Pauloosie died that our family was destined to be a family of widows echoed loudly in 1987 when Jimmy Nowra died, and again in 2001 when it was Elijah. Jimmy had gone on a fishing trip to a lake on Devon Island over one hundred kilometres from Grise. He had gone with a few other hunters by snowmobile to ferry food and supplies to the lake, with Paulassie's family and his wife, my niece Alicee, to follow by charter. A third of the way there, Jimmy stopped to remove some plastic that was stuck in the track of his snowmobile. One of the hunters who had accompanied him came back from hunting seal. He had forgotten to unload the bullet from the gun's chamber. It accidentally discharged, hitting Jimmy in his bent torso.

In March 2001, Elijah was siphoning kerosene from a container to a fuel tank and accidentally swallowed some. He did not want to go to the health centre for treatment. He had always been someone who disliked going to doctors, and he did not realize it was as serious as it was. He didn't know his body would not be able to digest it eventually. He began sleeping on the couch all the time, being slowly poisoned over the course of about a week until the kerosene finally took its toll.

But we have also gained family. Annie and I have six children, eleven grand-children, and three great-grandchildren. The Greenlanders from Qaanaaq became like family to us over the years; we still call regularly to get the latest news. I have seen much more of the "outside world" than I could have imagined the first time I stepped onto that airplane in 1958. I have travelled as far as Israel and Japan. But Grise Fiord is still home.

What I have learned in studying the history of Canada's Confederation has led me to conclude that our prime ministers did not finish what they started. They expanded west with the Canadian Pacific Railway, but did not continue north. I have seen what southern cities and towns in different provinces have. They have infrastructure like roads and seaports. They have theatres, art centres, hockey rinks, swimming pools, hospitals with doctors within driving distance instead of two hundred kilometres away. They have amenities to make life easier for Canadian citizens, a group that should include us. Inuit have officially been equal citizens since even before 1953. We are Canadians. Come and visit me, and you'll see the Canadian flag on my house that Prime Minister Stephen Harper sent me a few years ago. We were used to pioneer the "New Land," as Norwegian explorer Otto Sverdrup called Ellesmere Island, without being provided with shelter. We were expected to fight for our survival. My attitude today is that the Government of Canada gave us the High Arctic to live in, to pioneer, and to make part of Canada as ordinary Canadians. I have accepted that. When we moved to Grise Fiord from Lindstrom Peninsula, there was only an RCMP detachment, a co-op store, a school, and a power plant. Today, we have a new gymnasium, a nursing station, a privately owned corner store. We have the Housing Association, Arctic Fishery Alliance, and Hunters and Trappers Association. But there is still much to be done. I have accepted that my life as a Canadian is here in Grise Fiord. That is why, once in a while, I will say that it is still too inaccessible, too expensive. The government still has things it needs to fix.

Like any story that affects people's lives, some parts of the tragedy will remain unspoken. I tell the story because it has to be told. It has to be told so that it will not happen again. Canada wanted to show the world that the issue of sovereignty was no longer in question. Because of us, Ellesmere Island is no longer the "No Man's Land" Rasmussen described it to be. We are now truly Canadian flag bearers and Canadian citizens. But what a cost!

Nevertheless, we are proud of our accomplishments. We are up here to stay.

Acknowledgements

I am grateful to my family, who helped me fill in the details of certain events when they knew my emotions would be difficult to contain, and to the relocatees, both those who are now gone and those who are still with us, who told me of the history of our early years on Lindstrom Peninsula. I am grateful to my friends and acquaintances who share my memories and whose experiences, like mine, needed to be told. I would like to thank the Inughuit who helped me fill in some of the gaps in our story, as well as Constable Bob Pilot and Corporal Glenn Sargent, who did their best to help me when my eye was in indescribable pain as a child. I would also like to acknowledge those who helped the relocatees throughout our many years of lobbying efforts, and my editors, who helped make my story make sense.

Glossary

Notes on Inuktitut Pronunciation

There are some sounds in Inuktitut that may be unfamiliar to English speakers. The pronunciations below convey those sounds in the following ways:

- A double vowel (e.g., *aa*, *ee*) lengthens the vowel sound.
- Capitalized letters denote the emphasis for each word.
- ŋ is a sound similar to the "ng" in the word "sing."
- q is a "uvular" sound, a sound that comes from the very back of the throat. This is distinct from the sound for **k**, which is the same as a typical English "k" sound (known as a "velar" sound).
- **R** is a rolled "r" sound.
- **ll** is a rolled "l" sound.

For additional Inuktitut-language resources, please visit inhabitmedia.com/inuitnipingit.

Inuktitut	Pronunciation	Meaning
aglu	AG-loo	seal breathing hole
agluit	AG-loo-it	seal breathing holes
aiqqatik*	aiq-QA-tik	a pair of mitts
amauti	a-MOW-ti	woman's parka with a pouch for carrying a child
amautit	a-MOW-ti	women's parkas with a pouch for carrying a child
Angijuuliruma maliqattalaaramali.	A-ŋi-JOO-li-ru-ma ma-li-qat-ta-laa-ra-ma-li	I'm going to take part in a trip (hunt).
Anitsaarualuk qaigit!	a-NIT-sa-RUA-look, QAI-git	My cousin, come back!
appaqsuit*	ap-PAQ-suit	murres
arnaqsiuqti	ar-naq-SIUQ-ti	women-seeker
arnaqsiuqtit	ar-naq-SIUQ-tit	women-seekers

ataata	a-TAA-ta	father
Aukataalungani!	au-ka-TAA-loo-ŋa-ni	Oh my goodness!
iglu	IG-loo	snow house
igluit	IG-loo-it	snow houses
ijirat	e-YE-rat	shadow people
Iqalummiut	e-qa-LUM-me-oot	people from Iqaluit
inugagulliq**	e-NOO-ga-gul-liq	little person
inugagulliit	e-NOO-ga-gul-leet	little people
Inujjuarmiuq	e-nooj-joo-AR-me-ooq	person from Inujjuak
Inujjuarmiut	e-nooj-joo-AR-me-oot	people from Inujjuak
inuksuit	e-NOOK-su-it	rock cairns used to aid hunters and indicate direction
inuusikillisaisuut	e-NOO-se-kil-le-sai-SOOT	slowly drain away life
kakivat	ka-KI-vat	traditional fishing spears
kamiik	ka-MEEK	two skin boots
kamiit	ka-MEET	many skin boots
Kina?	KI-na	Who?
Kinauvit?	ke-NAU-vit	What is your name?
maktaaq	mak-TAAQ	narwhal or beluga skin and blubber
maktak	MUK-tuk	bowhead whale skin and blubber
Mamanngittuq	ma-MAŊ-ŋit-tooq	the smelly one
mannguat	MAŊ-ŋuat	over-boots
Mittimatalingmiut	mit-te-ma-ta-LIŊ-me-oot	people from Pond Inlet
nakurmiik	na-kur-MIIK	thank you
Nanimiugugavin?	na-me-MEU-ŋu-ga-vit	Where are you from?
Niaquvinikuluk langala langala	ni-a-qu-vi-NI-ku-luk la-nga-LAA la-nga-LAA	Little Skull ("langala langala" functions the same as "ooh" in English songs—there is no translation as it does not mean anything)
Nikujjaaqtuqtuq	ni-kooj-JAAQ-tuq-tuq	the one who walks with her heels raised

ningauk	ni-ŊAUK	brother-in-law
nunaup inungit	nu-NA-up E-noo-ŋit	very tall, hairy creatures that walk upright
piqatialuk	pi-qa-TIA-luk	best friend
Qallunaaq	qal-loo-NAAQ	a white person
Qallunaat	qal-loo-NAAT	white people
Qallunaat nunangat	qal-loo-NAAT NOO-na-ŋat	the land of white people (southern Canada)
qamutiik	qa-mu-TEEK	sled
qarmaq	QAR-MAQ	sod house
qatangutiapik	qa-TAŊ-ŋu-TIA-pik	little cousin
Quisukkama.	qui-SOOK-ka-ma	I want to pee.
qulliq	QUL-liq	seal oil lamp
qunguliq	QU-ŋu-liq	rhubarb
qurvik	QUR-vik	toilet
Supuuqtuutilik	su-pooq-TOO-te-lik	the one with a pipe
tarriaksuit	tar-RIAK-soo-it	shadow people
Tukturjuk	took-TUR-juk	Big Dipper
tuurngat	TOOR-ŋat	ghosts
Uakallaluaraaluulauqtuq!	ua-kal-LA-lua-RAA-luu-LAUQ-tuq	It was too much!
Ualinirmiut	ua-le-NER-me-oot	people of the Western Arctic
ujjuk	UJ-jook	bearded seal
ulu	OO-lu	crescent knife traditionally used by women
ummimmaaluk	OO-mim-MAA-look	big muskox
usuaq	oo-SOO-aq	walrus penis

*this term is in Inuktun, a language spoken by Inughuit in northwest Greenland
**the spelling of this word is specific to Nunavik dialect

Bibliography

Canada. Evidence given at a hearing before the House of Commons committee on aboriginal affairs. 19 March. Available from the House of Commons, Ottawa.

Cantley, James. *1952 Report of the Eastern Arctic Patrol*, from Minutes of the NWT Council, 16 October 1952. Library and Archives Canada, RG 22, vol. 176, file 40-2-20 pt. 3, 1952. Quoted in S. Grant, *"Errors Exposed": Inuit Relocations to the High Arctic, 1953–1960*. Calgary: Arctic Institute of North America, 2016, 7.

Fryer, A.C. "Eskimo rehabilitation program at Craig Harbour." *RCMP Quarterly*, vol. 20, no. 2 (1954): 139-142.

Grant, Shelagh D. *"Errors Exposed": Inuit Relocations to the High Arctic, 1953–1960*. Documents on Canadian Arctic Sovereignty and Security, vol. 8. Calgary: Arctic Institute of North America, 2016.

Hammond, Marc. "Report on findings on an alleged promise of government to finance the return of Inuit at Resolute and Grise Fiord to their original homes at Port Harrison (Inukjuak) and Pond Inlet." Claims and Historical Research Centre, vol. 12. Ottawa: Indian and Northern Affairs, 1984.

Harper, Kenn. "Blood on the Snow: Robert Janes's Last Journey." In *Arctic Crime and Punishment*, 89–98. In Those Days: Collected Writings on Arctic History, Book Two. Toronto: Inhabit Media, 2015.

———. "The Trial and Punishment of Nuqallaq." In *Arctic Crime and Punishment*, 99–107. In Those Days: Collected Writings on Arctic History, Book Two. Toronto: Inhabit Media, 2015.

Hickling Corporation. "Assessment of the factual basis of certain allegations made before the standing committee on aboriginal affairs concerning the relocation of Inukjuak families in the 1950s report." Department of Indian Affairs and Northern Development, 1990.

Library and Archives Canada. Royal Commission on Aboriginal Peoples, "High Arctic Relocation Special Consultations, Ottawa, ON 93-04-05." Ref 2077-5 item 99, 1993.

———. Royal Commission on Aboriginal Peoples, "High Arctic Relocation Special Consultations, Ottawa, ON 93-04-06." Ref 2077-5 item 100, 1993.

Marcus, Alan R. "Inuit relocation policies in Canada and other circumpolar countries, 1925–60: A report for the Royal Commission on Aboriginal Peoples," 1995.

———. "Out in the Cold: Canada's experimental Inuit relocation to Grise Fiord and Resolute Bay." *Polar Record*, vol. 27, no. 163 (October 1991): 285-96.

———. *Out in the Cold: The Legacy of Canada's Inuit Relocation Experiment in the High Arctic*. IWGIA Documents Series, Document 71. Copenhagen: International Work Group for Indigenous Affairs, 1992

Morrison, William R. *Showing the Flag: The Mounted Police and Canadian Sovereignty in the North, 1984-1925*. Vancouver: The University of British Columbia Press, 1985.

Obituary of Akeeaktashuk, *Time Magazine*, Fall 1954. Quoted in S. Wright, *Our Ice is Vanishing/Sikuvut Nunguliqtuq: A History of Inuit, Newcomers, and Climate Change*. Montreal and Kingston: McGill-Queen's University Press, 2014.

Pilot, R. S. *Conditions Amongst Eskimoes Generally – Annual Report – Grise Fiord Area, N.W.T., Year Ending December 31st, 1958*. Library and Archives Canada, "Craig Harbour Area – General File (and Grise Fiord, NWT)," RG 85, vol. 1446, file 1000-133 pt. 1.

Royal Commission on Aboriginal Peoples. *The High Arctic Relocation: A Report on the 1953-1955 Relocation*. Canada Communication Group Publishing, 1994.

———. *Summary of Supporting Information Volumes I and II*. Canada Communication Group Publishing, 1994.

Sargent, Glenn. *Eskimo Conditions, Craig Harbour Area, Period ending December 31st, 1955*. Library and Archives Canada, "Craig Harbour Area – General File (and Grise Fiord, NWT)," RG 85, vol. 1446, file 1000-133 pt. 1.

———. *Eskimo Conditions, Craig Harbour Area, Period ending December 31st, 1956*. Library and Archives Canada, "Craig Harbour Area – General File (and Grise Fiord, NWT)," RG 85, vol. 1446, file 1000-133 pt. 1.

———. *Conditions Amongst Eskimoes Generally – Annual Report – Grise Fiord Area, N.W.T., Year Ending December 31, 1959*. Library and Archives Canada, "Craig Harbour Area – General File (and Grise Fiord, NWT)," RG 85, vol. 1446, file 1000-133 pt. 1.

Larry Audlaluk was born in Uugaqsiuvik, a small settlement west of Inujjuak in northern Quebec. He was relocated to the High Arctic with his family when he was almost three years old. Larry was inducted into the Order of Canada for his years working as an ambassador for the people of Grise Fiord, Canada's northernmost civilian settlement, and is the community's longest living resident.

Iqaluit • Toronto